THE 7 SECRETS TO
PEACE OF MIND

THE 7 SECRETS TO PEACE OF MIND

Your PEACE *Is*
Your COMMAND!

TONY CHARLES

iUniverse, Inc.
Bloomington

The 7 Secrets to Peace of Mind
Your Peace Is Your Command!

iUniverse books may be ordered through booksellers or by contacting:

iUniverse
1663 Liberty Drive
Bloomington, IN 47403
www.iuniverse.com
1-800-Authors (1-800-288-4677)

ISBN: 978-1-4759-1693-5 (sc)
ISBN: 978-1-4759-1694-2 (hc)
ISBN: 978-1-4759-1854-0 (ebk)

Library of Congress Control Number: 2012909152

Printed in the United States of America

iUniverse rev. date: 06/05/2012

CONTENTS

Preface..xv
General Introduction...xix

THE 1ST SECRET

THE SECRET FORMULA FOR
TRANSFORMING YOUR WHOLE LIFE

Special Introduction to "The Secret Formula for Transforming
    Your Whole Life" 3
The Secret Formula for Revitalizing Your Mind, Body, and Spirit 7
The Secret Formula for Recovering Your Dynamism 7

FIRST SESSION

The Secret Breathing Formula... 9
The Secret Formula for Protecting Yourself from Evil and
    Harmful Attacks 11
The Secret Formula for Protection and Sleeping Peacefully 12
The Secret Formula for Requesting Divine Intervention.................... 14

SECOND SESSION

The Secret for Changing Yourself 16
The Secret Formula for Developing Your Personality......................... 17
The Secret to Awakening the Powerful Forces within You................... 21
The Secret Formula for Creating a Powerful Emotional Shield 22
The Secret Formula for Remaining Cool and Calm at All Times 23
The Secret Formula for Securing an Automatic Protection 24
The Secret Formula for Acquiring a Lovely Magnetic Gaze 26
The Secret for Making Your Smile Infallible 28
The Secret Formula for Charging Yourself with Divine Power 30

THIRD SESSION

The Secret Formula for Communicating with the Universe.................. 39
The Secret Formula for Commanding Your Subconscious................... 40
The Secret Formula for Shaping Your Destiny................................. 45

THE 2ND SECRET

THE SECRET FORMULA FOR OVERCOMING ANYTHING AND ACHIEVING ANYTHING

Special Introduction to "The Secret Formula for Overcoming
    Anything and Achieving Anything".. 57
The Secret Principles for Miracles... 59
Don't Stop Believing... 60
The Secret Steps to Achieving Anything....................................... 61
The Permission to Prosper... 62
The Secret Formula for Prosperous Living.................................... 64
The Secret Formula for Winning at Any Game of Chance 66
The Secret Formula for Priming Your Subconscious 67
The Secret to Rapidly Climbing Any Professional Ladder................. 69
The Secret to Cooperating with Your Subconscious........................ 72
The Secret Formula for Attracting Real Love................................. 73
God Is Helping Those Who Are Helping Themselves....................... 76
The Secret Way to Rekindle Your Romance................................... 78
The Secret Formula for Bringing Back Lost Love 81
Your Subconscious Is Your Intimate Friend 83

THE 3RD SECRET

THE SECRET TO THE POWER OF POSITIVE THINKING

Special Introduction to "The Secret to the Power of Positive
    Thinking".. 87
The Secret Power to Attract or Change Anything............................. 88
The Secret Power of Your Personal Magnetism 89
The Secret to Reforming Your Way of Thinking.............................. 90
The Secret Formula for Reshaping Your Subconscious..................... 92

The Secret for Overcoming Shyness 93
This Is Your Moment! 95
When to Let Go and Just Rest.. 96
The Secret Formula for Having a Good Night's Sleep........................ 97
The Secret Power to Project Your Thoughts....................................... 99
The Secret Formula for Making Anyone Fall in Love with You.......... 100
The Secret to Being in Harmony with Your Friends 101
The Secret Way to Succeed in Anything You Do 103

THE 4ᵀᴴ SECRET

THE SECRET FORMULA FOR
PROSPERITY AND INNER PEACE

Special Introduction to "The Secret Formula for Prosperity and
    Inner Peace" 107
The Secret Power of the Ancient Magi.. 108
The Dream of Humanity versus Reality 109
How Society Has Captured Your Attention 111
Why Do We Pretend to Be Something We Are Not? 113
Why Does Society Judge Everything? 115
The Illusion of False Beliefs.. 117
How False Belief Has Affected You.. 119
The New Dream to Reclaim Your Powers... 121
The Secret Principles to Transcending Your Current Life.................... 122
Words Have Power—Be Very Careful with Your Words 123
Honesty Is Still the Best Policy 127
The Ten Commandments of Communication..................................... 129
Do Not Take Everything Personally.. 130
The Secret Formula for Maintaining Maximum Concentration 134
The Secret for Avoiding Suppositions... 137
It Is Always Better to Ask the Right Questions 140
Do Not Always Assume.. 141
The Secret for Always Doing Your Best 142
The Secret Formula for Expressing Your Personal Dreams 145
The Secret Rules of Providence... 149
Rule # 1: Love Prosperity to Let Prosperity Love You 149
Rule # 2: Have an Open Mind for Prosperity 150

Rule # 3: Focus Your Attention on Prosperity................................ 151
The Secret Formula for Developing Your Creative Thoughts............. 152
The Secret Formula for Prosperity...................................... 155
The Secret Formula for Visualizing Positive Idea Seeds.................... 155
The Secret Formula for Wrapping Your Visualization in Light.......... 160
Rule # 4: Allow Money to Circulate Freely................................ 161
The Secret Formula for Developing Your Optimism 162

THE 5ᵀᴴ SECRET

THE SECRET TO THE RULE OF LIFE

Special Introduction to "The Secret to the Rule of Life".................. 167
The Secret Principles of Life.. 168
The Secret Principles of Life.. 169
The Principle of Causality 169
The Principle of Correspondence 172
The Principle of Resonance 174
The Principle of Reincarnation... 179
The Principle of Cause and Effect 182
The Power of the Golden Rule 187

THE 6ᵀᴴ SECRET

THE SECRETS TO LONGEVITY AND WELL-BEING

Special Introduction to "The Secret to Longevity and Well-Being".... 191
Concentration Is the First Secret to Longevity and Well-Being.......... 191
The Secret Power of Maximum Concentration............................ 192
The Secret Principle of Reciprocation................................... 193
The Appropriate Time for Maximum Concentration 194
The Ideal Venue for Maximum Concentration........................... 195
Powerful Postures for Maximum Concentration 195
The European Posture for Maximum Concentration...................... 196
The Asian Posture for Maximum Concentration 197
The African Posture for Maximum Concentration 198
The Secret to Successful Concentration................................. 199
Visual Concentration 199

Touching Concentration 201
Breathing Concentration 201
Valuable Tips for Successful Concentration 203
Balance Is the Second Secret to Longevity and Well-Being 204
The Secret Formula for Taming Your Emotions................................ 205
Secret Facts about Emotions... 208
The Secret Formula for Being a Very Important Person (a VIP)......... 209
Positive Attitude Is the Third Secret to Longevity and Well-Being..... 213
The Secret Formula for Influencing Your Subconscious.................... 216

THE 7TH SECRET

THE SECRET TO BELIEVING IN YOUR HUMANITY AND DIVINITY

Special Introduction to The Secret to Believing in Divinity and
    in Your Humanity 223
The Secret to Believing in the Fulfillment of Your Goals 228
The Secret to Carefully Plotting Your Course 230
The Secret to Devotedly Prioritizing Your Goals................................ 231
The Secret to Faithfully Dealing with Setbacks................................. 233
The Secret to Always Focusing on Possibilities.................................. 234
Never Do Anything Halfway 236
The Secret to Conquering the Fear of Failure 238
Your Lovely Smile Is the Master Key to Everything 241

Epilogue.. 245
A Message for All Humanity 255
A Message for the Top 1 Percent.. 257
Acknowledgments 259
The Author 265

THIS BOOK IS WRITTEN WITH VALUE, COMMENDATION, AND FATHERLY LOVE FOR MY WONDERFUL CHILDREN:

Miss Tonia Isata Charles

Mr. Anthony Brima Charles

Mr. Sylvester Foday Charles

Mr. Lawrence Amara Charles

This is my message to each and every one of you—my dear children and the children of all humanity:

Go forward and believe in yourself.
Never allow your yesterday to hold your tomorrow hostage.
Be mindful that the significance of time is to move forward, not backward. Do not tie yourself to your past; tie yourself to your inner peace, and never give up except when it is absolutely necessary and for honor.

Remember that your history does not always define who you become; it is the rest of your story and the choices you make.

Be careful with how you spend your time and money.
In life, it is not how much money or time you have that matters; it is how you choose to spend it.

Do not ever forget, even for a moment, that unity is strength.
Love someone—and only from your heart, not *for* anything.

Please pay serious attention to this message and pass it on.
This is the secret.

The blessing of God will always be with you.
Amen!

DEDICATED WITH LOVE, PRAISE, AND GRATITUDE TO MY DEAR WIFE:

Mrs. Isha Lauretta Charles

My lovely lady:

You and my mother are the most important women in my life.
You mean the world to me, and I truly love you, darling.
Your dedication to our family is a clear manifestation that
you are a wonderful and a diligent wife.
I am proud of you, honey.
You are really an extraordinary mother.

Be assured that the love of God is protecting us.
The power of love is guiding us.
Divine love is within us.
We are in love, honey, and
all is well.
Amen!

PREFACE

The most powerful new book of knowledge is now in your possession. Pursued by many, envied by all, *The 7 Secrets to Peace of Mind* offers nirvana and tremendous wisdom to whoever possesses it. This indispensable new inspirational volume is the *master key* that will finally let you into the amazing world of *secret knowledge, grand ability, and ultimate freedom*. When you diligently read this new book of knowledge and precisely adhere to the suggested exercises, it will surely bring peace of mind including guidance, abundance, protection, good luck, good health, prosperity, longevity, tranquility, inner joy, inner peace, wealth, great power, the fulfillment of wishes, and real love into your life.

Please be reminded that all human beings have a pivotal moment in their individual lives when they discover something new, and nothing is ever the same again. For you, this is that moment! You are about to learn insider secrets from *The 7 Secrets to Peace of Mind* that will empower you and awaken your comprehension, your motivation, and your inspiration. You will also discover that at the highest level of human understanding, there is the realization that ultimately we are all cells in the organism called humanity.

The 7 Secrets to Peace of Mind is full of expected expectations. It is the new book of knowledge and the game changer that will make you think. This is the indispensable volume that will give you an in-depth wisdom of the following inner secrets: the secret formula for transforming your whole life; the secret formula for overcoming anything and achieving anything; the secret to the power of positive thinking; the secret to prosperity and inner peace; the secret to the rule of life; the secret formula for longevity and well-being; and the secret formula for believing in your humanity and divinity.

The 7 Secrets to Peace of Mind is one of the profoundest books in modern philosophy. It comprises insider secrets that represent everything in life that is peaceful, hopeful, joyful, affectionate, optimistic, productive, and positive.

This is the new book of knowledge that is composed of great wisdom of the ages that will let you be in harmony with your true nature and allow you to obtain the new and higher consciousness of humanity. This enlightening volume will offer you tranquility that will lead you to nirvana, free you from worries, and place you in a calm and peaceful dominion even when facing major challenges in life.

The 7 Secrets to Peace of Mind will make you better in everything, including your public life, your private life, and your spiritual life. Thus, you will secure competent, cooperative, and comprehensive relationships with others to enhance a greater degree of respect in your social environment and to have the peace of mind you deserve.

The book's subtitle—*Your Peace Is Your Command!*—is intended to prepare you to liberate the dynamic and explosive forces that lie dormant within you that will eventually enhance your peace of mind and let you be, do, or have anything. This new book of knowledge will let you know that any kind of winning is by choice, not by chance. You will be reminded also that *the major difference between the winner and the loser is that the winner will always strive to win.* This is the volume that will give you the secret formula for that powerful philosophy.

Do not forget, however, that graciously accepting the order of things can effortlessly make the difference between distress and peace of mind. You will also discover insider secrets that will allow you to influence people; easily get what you want; win the esteem and support of influential people; immediately silence anyone who tries to criticize or belittle you; make people change their opinions about you; and make anyone fall deeply in love with you.

Although life sometimes teaches harsh lessons that can create fear for humanity, nevertheless, you should never forget that the opposite of fear is knowledge. Thus, with the help of this powerful new book of knowledge, you will surely learn without any doubt that nothing is impossible if you truly believe you deserve it. However, please be mindful that the right choices will come from your intuition and not from external sources. Remember also that your value of fairness and your willingness to take responsibility are giant steps to a sustainable peace of mind.

Your Peace Is Your Command!

General Introduction

The mission of *The 7 Secrets to Peace of Mind* is to serve all humanity and to awaken the power within. Thus, it shall be done unto you according to your belief system, your frame of mind, and your understanding.

This new book of knowledge has been designed to let you know that you can accomplish anything, even when you think you can't. Therefore, you will be guided accordingly, step by step, and level by level.

This is your moment!

The 7 Secrets to Peace of Mind is a power-packed, inspirational, and motivational collection of dynamic insider information. It is an enlightening volume that is composed of great wisdom of the ages. This powerful and mind-jogging book was born out of careful research and a diverse number of contemplations on private devotions and training as a psychologist and a health and human services, human resources, and social services professional.

No matter your age, gender, race, color, or creed, this volume will guide you to secure love, inner joy, good health, longevity, tranquility, and the peace of mind that will surely lead you to nirvana. This is the new book of knowledge that is more about you and the new era of higher consciousness of humanity.

The 7 Secrets to Peace of Mind is full of expected expectations. It is the new book of knowledge that comprises awakening wisdom, knowledge, understanding, formulas, and principles that have never been revealed to the masses in this way until now. This volume was consciously and diligently designed to offer you in-depth awareness and realization of very deep and carefully guarded inside secrets.

Please be reminded, however, that this new book of knowledge is not just for information and education; it is more for implementation and application. Therefore, it is my hope that this indispensable volume will be the source of the breakthrough secrets that will finally help you to take the command of your own peace of mind and to finally be free from the manipulation of the top 1 percent that is controlling all humanity.

The 7 Secrets to Peace of Mind will let you discover the following inner secrets: the secret formula for transforming your whole life; the secret formula for overcoming anything and achieving anything; the secret to the power of positive thinking; the secret to prosperity and inner peace; the secret to the rule of life; the secret formula for longevity and well-being; and the secret formula for believing in your humanity and divinity.

This new book of knowledge represents everything in life that is joyous, affectionate, productive, optimistic, positive, and peaceful. This enlightening volume reminds you that as human beings, anything we do, we should do for *peace, hope,* or *love.* This is the *PHL* philosophy to always remember.

The subtitle of this book—*Your Peace Is Your Command!*—is intended to prepare you to liberate the dynamic and explosive forces that lie dormant within you. This volume also gives you the secret to influence anyone and anything; and to have, be, or do anything.

With the knowledge of these secrets, you will easily get what you want; win the esteem and support of influential men and women; immediately silence anyone who tries to criticize you or belittle you; make people change their opinions about you; and make anyone fall deeply in love with you. Eventually, you will harness the commanding combined power of peace, hope, and love. As a result, your peace of mind will be unstoppable.

This is the book of the light that finally shines for you. It will give you clear comprehension of your paradigm. Then you will be free from the apprehensive manipulation, matriculation, and domestication that have been imposed on humanity by the dream of society and by the top 1 percent who have ruled the world for many years. This volume contains deep insider secrets that have hitherto been religiously and selfishly guarded by the top 1 percent and by some powerful members-only organizations.

These powerful secrets will let you perform exploits that until now, you never thought were possible. They will let you influence anyone without his or her knowledge; help you attract whatever you need in life; and let you develop and use the wonderful possibilities that lie dormant within you. In fact, these seven secrets will let you perform outstanding and amazing feats that will astonish you.

Hopefully you will use these marvelous and life-changing secrets for your own good and for the benefit of your loved ones. Eventually you will see your whole life literally transforming and becoming more fulfilled and enjoyable day after day. You will see your deepest wishes come true, even those you have had for so many years and never thought would be realized.

When you consciously do the suggested exercises, you will at last utilize the amazing possibilities that are dormant within you. As a result, you will never be the same again. This volume is the ultimate weapon you need to finally acquire the irresistible personality, respect, and peace of mind you deserve. Please do not let anything stop you now. Just do the exercises accordingly; and always remember that action is the essential ingredient for achievement.

From this new book of knowledge, you will learn the inner secrets to communicate effectively. Of course, it is common knowledge that effective communication is a powerful skill without which your message can turn into an error, frustration, misunderstanding, or disaster. Without effective communication, your message can even be misinterpreted or poorly delivered. With effective communication, however, you will not only connect well with people, but you will also achieve phenomenal personal and business success. *The 7 Secrets to Peace of Mind* is therefore a very powerful transformational tool that will let you explore new ways of looking at communication.

This dynamic book of empowerment is the apparatus that will let you be or do anything and have anything and everything you need. It offers you in-depth knowledge of how to have inspiration, hope, inner peace, and inner joy. When you precisely adhere to the practices outlined in this book, you will effortlessly secure competent, cooperative, and comprehensive relationships with your true nature and with the people around you. Subsequently, your command of respect in your social environment will be tremendously enhanced.

This motivational book offers a variety of opportunities to learn. Some of the opportunities may involve experiences through which you will achieve greater understanding of yourself, greater understanding of the people in your life, and greater understanding of society in general. As a result, you will finally end the insecurities in your life. You will learn more about wisdom, discipline, meditation, patience, diligence, and generosity.

You will also be astonished to learn about the many gifts you will receive from *The 7 Secrets to Peace of Mind*. These gifts are always the perfect fit to secure true love, good health, longevity, and peace of mind. These are gifts that keep on giving. They are gifts that are perfect to accumulate wealth and prosperity, avoid danger, and even eliminate enemies. Eventually, you will receive the "Seven Gifts of God," such as the gift of wisdom, the gift of knowledge, the gift of understanding, the gift of counsel, the gift of courage, the gift of piety, and the gift of the fear of God.

This is the book with mind-bending and thought-provoking insights on issues that are vital to the peace and harmony of all humanity. You will find never-before-told ideas that will let you move beyond the status quo of society and develop a vision for yourself to be more fulfilled and peaceful. *The 7 Secrets to Peace of Mind* will surely make you better in everything: it will make you better in your public life, it will make you better in your private life, and it will make you better in your spiritual life.

Please be informed also that this new book of knowledge is hugely vital for your existence. Just as the moon directly affects the tides and weather, the seven inner secrets this volume is revealing will impact your life in many more ways than you might ever expect. In fact, the influence of this knowledge will eventually alter the course of your fate. The knowledge of these deep insider secrets will swiftly illuminate and transform your life in countless positive fundamental ways. This secret information will free you from worries and bring you peace of mind, tranquility, and the ease of being that may have been your most precious wish. Thus, I encourage you to please do the exercises outlined in this life-changing book for your own good and for the benefit of your loved ones.

At this point, I think it is important to let you know that *The 7 Secrets to Peace of Mind* is not about me or about my family. No, no, this is not about Tony Charles. This book of wisdom and enlightenment is primarily focused on you and on the people in your life. In fact, my major motivation for writing this new book of knowledge is to pass on to you the life-changing wisdom, understanding, and knowledge I have procured over the years from erudition, implementation, and education, and also from a variety of other powerful sources, including remarkable training acquired through many years of schooling in academic programs of various disciplines and levels. This also includes but is not limited to my background as a psychologist.

This motivational and inspirational volume is also derived from the knowledge that I have acquired from various initiations, members-only organizations, powerful business thinkers, great philosophers, decades of professional and personal experiences, and counsel from powerful, revered, intelligent, and learned masters, spiritual leaders, political leaders, and gurus of all aspects of life. Above all, the deepest fraction of my knowledge that crafted this magnum opus is derived from my mother and my father. (Mama; Papa; I will pay you back; and may God bless you abundantly.)

In addition to my academic accumulation of knowledge that partially unveiled *The 7 Secrets to Peace of Mind,* this volume is also the brainchild of my thirty-seven months of arduous of reading, researching, experimenting, interviewing, thinking, analyzing, and writing. This inspirational document is also derived from diligent contemplation and application of information from many different sources, including the sacred books of the Holy Bible and the Holy Quran.

Therefore, this motivational book of knowledge is no doubt the ultimate discourse on humanity and the nature of existence. It is surely a valuable resource for achieving a way of life that guarantees peace of mind. This volume will even tell you how to overcome chronic and overwhelming problems including anxiety, depression, lack of love, low self-esteem, and addictive behaviors.

The 7 Secrets to Peace of Mind is also designed to remind you that we—human beings—are no doubt like the rest of the natural world. So always remember that sadness, fear, frustration, or any troubling feeling cannot last forever. This is true because nature does not create any storm that never ends. Always remember that, *in any misfortune, there is good fortune.* However, the lessons and truths outlined in this volume should be discovered and applied individually. These are the lessons that will show you to the enormous wonders of your own being. Yes, this book will let you discover that you are in fact the universe at work.

Remember also that *The 7 Secrets to Peace of Mind* is about the new era of higher consciousness. It is a unique volume that should be read at a steady and slow motion. Thus, you will learn about many significant aspects of life, such as the power of your personal magnetism; how to govern your thoughts; how to conquer shyness or timidity; how to triumph in love; how to find good friends; how to succeed in anything you put mind to; how to recover your energy and your dynamism; and how to improve your vitality—to mention just a few.

This is the unique volume that reveals secret formulas that have never been revealed to humanity in this way. So as you peruse further, you will be offered practical formulas that will empower you accordingly. You will have the insight to apply your power to prevent illness and to rejuvenate yourself. Subsequently, your undertakings and your relationships will be blessed abundantly. This new book of knowledge will let you set aside some personal desires in the true name of the higher course of love. In fact, each and every one of the seven secrets revealed in this noble book has universal and practical treasures for you.

It is also very interesting to learn that *The 7 Secrets to Peace of Mind* draws your attention to the gospel according to Saint Luke when he hints at our transition into a new era. Our attentive awareness of natural disasters such as extreme temperatures, earthquakes, tsunamis, floods, hurricanes, diseases, famine, hardship, drought, wars, political turmoil, rebellions, family conflicts, social problems, religious conflicts, ethnic wars, civil wars and other such upheavals, including the Occupy Wall Street, Occupy Land, Occupy Everywhere, etc. are apparent parts of our transition into a new era of higher consciousness of humanity.

So many people are currently suffering from perpetual depression, confusion, anxiety, fear, anger, worry, insufficiency, and poor spiritedness. This turmoil is sometimes due to escalating unemployment rates around the world and other difficult circumstances. Many people are also suffering from pains, chronic conditions, and life-threatening illnesses. This, therefore, is a clear manifestation of the fact that people all over the world are currently in need of peace of mind. Thus, humanity seriously needs help. Fortunately, *The 7 Secrets to Peace of Mind* is here to render that needed help. This volume reveals the secrets that will stop or eliminate your sufferings forever and ever.

This volume is reminding you that you are no doubt in the process of transitioning into a new era of higher consciousness. *The 7 Secrets to Peace of Mind* is, however, the panacea that will extricate you from any conundrum during this transition period. This volume also suggests secret formulas that will transform and improve every aspect of your life. In fact, the maximum enjoyment and benefits that will eventually come your way will make you fall joyously in love with this motivational and inspirational new book of knowledge.

With the help of *The 7 Secrets to Peace of Mind*, inclusive of the social media, you will be guided to be more focused on your power to command your own peace. Of course, you may have noticed that many changes are already occurring around the world, politically, physically, scientifically, spiritually, morally, economically, geographically, and socially. Just look around; the evidence is everywhere. However, since we are just at the genesis of this new era of higher consciousness, *The 7 Secrets to Peace of Mind* is encouraging you to use the *power within you* to command your own peace.

This is the new book of knowledge that will prepare you for this new era of higher consciousness. In fact, it is during this new era that you should actually use your authentic power. Always remember that your authentic power is the difference between your divinity and your humanity. It is the difference between love and hate, peace and war, etc. Thus, it can be said that your authentic power is your ability to choose the "PHL" philosophy of peace, hope, and love in any given situation.

The 7 Secrets to Peace of Mind is therefore designed to let you know through the social media that the old era of emasculation, intimidation, manipulation, and control is history. As my daughter, Tonia, and her brothers, Tony and Sylvester, would say: "It is old school." Fortunately, in this new era of higher consciousness, you have the power to look inside yourself and see if anything anybody says or does to you actually resonates with you. In fact, it is in this era that you should let everyone know that you are *a person of value*.

This new book of knowledge is also designed to develop humanity's individual paradigm shift. Such a shift is, however, important because we are currently exiting an era that was dominated by that which was *property*. As such, some people are still confused and conflicted. Some are still caught in great struggles because they were deeply invested in the old approach toward *property*. Some were invested financially, some professionally, some with attitudes, some with beliefs, and some with behaviors.

The investment in the old era was in the primacy of *property*. However, this is not to say that we should ignore that which is *property* and its great benefits. Even in this new era of higher consciousness, *property* is still important. Thus, we should respect that which is *property*. But, in this new era of higher consciousness, it is the *power within* that has priority. "What is the power within?" you may ask. *The power within* is your *intuition*.

This new book of knowledge gives you the awareness of how your intuition communicates with you and with any other intuition in the universe. It tells you that the *power within* is the most significant entity in determining your directions and choices. Thus, in this new era of higher consciousness, you will eventually realize that *it is not what you have that matters; it is who you become. And what you have done to your fellow man; good or bad.*

When you acknowledge this reality, you will always be in a calm and peaceful dominion, even while facing major challenges in life—challenges like losing your finances, your business, your home, your job, the people you love, your health, your fame, your youthfulness, your physical beauty, your car, etc.

This is the new book of knowledge that lets you know that living the reality of the *power within* simply means that life choices, activities, directions, and all that is important are in harmony with your intuition. Therefore, living in harmony with your intuition is your true nature and your authentic power.

Please be informed that this new era of higher consciousness is also led by the intuition. Thus, this is the time when your intuition should be acknowledged, appreciated, and allowed to be the aspect, the approach, and the leader that should be considered decisive whenever you are making important decisions or choices.

Here is a simple comparison that might be helpful to understand the power of your intuition: Think about the importance of the conductor to an orchestra. In this new era of higher consciousness, your intuition is the conductor. When you pay attention to your intuition's directions, everything will eventually be harmonious and peaceful.

On the other hand, when you resist following the directions of your intuition, it is similar to an orchestra playing without paying attention to the conductor. It is as though every member of the orchestra is playing his or her own melody with its own tempo and rhythm and with total disregard of not only the conductor but also of the other members of the orchestra. You can just imagine what the result would be. Please be informed that the importance of following the directions of your intuition is one of the secrets that have been guardedly kept from you for all these years. This is your moment!

Be informed also that *The 7 Secrets to Peace of Mind* is not just a book like any other. It is designed to reveal the hidden secrets that will finally set you free from stagnation and commotion. With the help of this volume, you now have the opportunity to know insider secretes that were kept in the top 1 percent's circles and in the most unique, private, and extremely exclusive *members-only organizations*. These organizations were designed for only the select few and for the most-powerful people in society. In fact, the evidence is clearly manifested around the world that members of these clandestine groups have incredible advantages and opportunities for achievement.

The truth is that members of these organizations are wealthy because they know the secrets and they have been preventing you from knowing them. Fortunately, you will also now take advantage of the secrets they have been hiding from you. With the help of *The 7 Secrets to Peace of Mind*, you will learn the closely guarded secrets the select few and the top 1 percent have selfishly kept to themselves for centuries. Those powerful individuals can be compared to some of the people President Obama may have referred to as millionaires and billionaires. Some of those individuals are the people who know the secrets that have been beyond the knowledge of the 99 percent who have suffered until now through no fault of their own. Fortunately, this volume reveals the secrets that have been beyond your knowledge. This is your moment!

Spiritually also, *The 7 Secrets to Peace of Mind* contains valuable information that lets you find acceptance and inner peace. Thus, you will be able to build a stronger connection with the divine in a welcoming community. This volume offers life-saving information and contemplation that will help you to align your heart's deepest desires with the direction of peace and harmony.

Eventually you will become a peace-maker yourself. By so doing, you will raise global consciousness and create the best experience of life for yourself and for the people in your locality. Subsequently you will experience a genuine, ever-deepening experience of God's presence and power. When that happens, your peace of mind will be ensured for good.

Now let me reveal this to you: if you have attentively read thus far, then you are one of the lucky few who will hear about these incredible sources of power. This also clearly indicates your readiness to know the deep secrets that were closely guarded by the powerful insiders. These are the secrets one guru in Sierra Leone referred to as the *Kukujumuku* (for the sole knowledge of the insiders).

Please think about this very carefully: Have you ever wondered why some people are blessed with endless good fortune? More than just lots of money and good looks, these people overcome every obstacle. It often seems like nothing can touch them and that they navigate through life's waters with ease and always bounce back from every knockdown.

The 7 Secrets to Peace of Mind includes information that will give you the knowledge and ability to bounce back quickly from any setback life hurls at you, be it a hardship, failed relationship, or even just one of life's little annoyances. With the secrets that you will learn from this volume, your inner forces will always lead you to get exactly what you need at any time.

As you continue to read, your awareness of the secrets to your peace of mind continues to grow and blossom. Please be mindful that until recently, these secrets were only known to the top 1 percent and members only. These select few members would then share among themselves their rare and spectacular finds that they personally used to help themselves in their quests to reach their personal goals. *The 7 Secrets to Peace of Mind* is therefore open-mindedly written so that you, too, will have your own share of the same good fortune the top 1 percent and members only have been enjoying.

Not only is this volume unique in revealing these life-changing secrets, but it also taps into the world's most potent secrets to peace of mind and tranquility. Honestly, some of these secrets are just too powerful to be taken lightly. That is in fact why they have been kept to some members-only organizations and to a select few members of the top 1 percent.

Fortunately, you will now be one of the people who know these secrets. Please take advantage of this once in a life time golden opportunity. No matter what happens or how bad things get, you will quickly rise from the ashes. This volume contains the secret methods that will always help you to easily rise up.

That is why *The 7 Secrets to Peace of Mind* is one of mankind's most enduring panaceas for any conundrum. This powerful book is the ultimate tool and force to be reckoned with. This volume will help you break through every obstacle and rise to any occasion with grace, poise, and unstoppable personal power.

You now have the opportunity to know the secret to instantly bouncing back from any difficulty. You will be able to smoothly navigate life's bumps on the road and quickly bounce back from any awkward situation.

For example:

You will master the curves of life: With the help of *The 7 Secrets to Peace of Mind,* you will recover quickly from any setback.

You will always gain control: Sometimes it feels like life is an uphill battle. *The 7 Secrets to Peace of Mind* will help you to tackle even the most difficult problems and easily emerge victorious.

You will overcome life's little annoyances: Let's face it—life is full of little things that zap your energy. However, they are no match for the powers of your *inner force.* With the help of *The 7 Secrets to Peace of Mind,* you will always have some of your reserve energy in readiness so that you can overcome the little annoyances altogether.

You will be protected from negative influences: It is undeniable that you have noticed that in life, there is always at least one person against you or who simply just does not like you. *The 7 Secrets to Peace of Mind* will keep you protected from the troublemakers that stand between you and progress.

You will regain your personal power: We all need extra energy to cope when struggles arise in matters of the heart. Use the knowledge of *The 7 Secrets to Peace of Mind* to learn how to gracefully let go and move on.

You will procure a surge of strength and resilience whenever you need it: In the past, you may have struggled to recover from terrible events. It is frustrating when the people you trust turn against you. Believe me, I have also been there; but it does not have to be that way for you anymore. It is obvious that you do not always feel strong; after all, what human being does? But the truth is you have the power inside you.

As you continue to do the exercises outlined in this volume, you will feel your power starting to rapidly surge. You will feel stronger and surer of yourself. You will be ready to take on the world. And you will always have the knowledge of *The 7 Secrets to Peace of Mind* to draw on whenever you need it.

You will be refreshed and rejuvenated: Sometimes the worst part of dealing with life's problems is the physical stress and strains. When your personal power is drained, you might wonder how you will ever bounce back. You may have felt that way many times before. *The 7 Secrets to Peace of Mind* will show you how to use the forces of regeneration to instantly recover from any distress.

Finally, please remember that most of the powerful and influential people in the world have one thing in common: *this secret*. Now you have the opportunity to enter their secret world and uncover their best-kept secrets. This new book of knowledge has been designed to let you know just how many powerful secrets have been kept from you.

This is the new book of knowledge that will help you achieve your goals in a step-by-step manner, and you will be guided accordingly. Please be reminded also that in this new era of higher consciousness, you will finally have the opportunity and the power to command your own peace of mind. Therefore, you should take this volume to be a very special treasure that will show you the way to freedom step by step and level by level.

Let me now congratulate you and thank you for taking this unique opportunity to read *The 7 Secrets to Peace of Mind*. Not only will you never be the same again, but you will also from now on have the peace of mind you need. I am hopeful that you will be proud of yourself for doing the exercises outlined in this volume to obtain the maximum benefits. I devoted many diligent years to perfecting these exercises and can say that they have been tested and proven. They work! I also hope you will love the results accordingly.

When you read this new book of knowledge and do the exercises, you will never have to worry about anything again. It is like having your own *genie* with you telling you exactly what to do in any given situation. In a nutshell, this is a crash course on making your place in this *new era*. You now know the secrets to the peace of mind you have always wanted.

Congratulations!

Your Peace Is Your Command!

You should never worry about the unknown, because there is nothing you can do about it until it arrives. Remember also that your fear of what is coming next is always more disturbing than the actual challenges you may face.

Thus, please do not be disturbed; just be happy. You will be blessed and tranquil at all times, and you will always have the peace of mind you need.

Your Peace Is Your Command!

THE 1ST SECRET

THE SECRET FORMULA FOR TRANSFORMING YOUR WHOLE LIFE

You have the power to renew your mind and enrich your life. You will have peace of mind when you believe . . .

Your Peace Is Your Command!

Special Introduction to
"The Secret Formula for Transforming
Your Whole Life"

With joy, hope, and glad tidings, *The 7 Secrets to Peace of Mind* has been designed to inform you about the secret power. This is the power that will miraculously transform your whole life for good. The content of this new book of knowledge will give you peace of mind and let you become a person of virtue, power, and might. The information that is now available to you will be of a great benefit for your transformation into a more powerful person in society. This volume contains the much-needed knowledge that will lead you to the power that will transform your whole life in a very remarkable way and eventually let you be a person of value forever. Subsequently you will effortlessly have peace of mind, including tranquility, love, and the inner joy you surely deserve.

The 7 Secrets to Peace of Mind has been composed out of a conviction that it will be the release switch that will transform your whole life for good! You may also be surprised to know that there are natural talents hidden inside of you whose existence you may not have known. This is actually true because research has proven that each and every one of us has natural talents deep within us.

However, the reason why your power to transform your whole life has remained dormant does not really matter now. This volume will guide you step by step, level by level, until your power is finally awakened to free you from bondage and make you an admirable and personable person.

It is also very important for you to know that this volume will give you the instructions you need to take the actions that will let your power surge forth and eventually come to light in a very spectacular way. Perhaps right now you do not quite dare believe that all these are really true. You may be saying something like this to yourself:

> Yes, Tony Charles, I do hope that you are right, but to be honest with you, the news about my hidden powers is a surprise to me. I have known myself for so long . . . and up till now, I have never had the feeling that I possess qualities of any hidden power.

I know very well what you may be thinking, and I understand your concerns. However, please allow me to tell you an open secret: among the greatest people ever born on this planet, most of them have felt like you at some time in their lives. In other words, they were ordinary people just like you until the day they discovered their hidden qualities. On that memorable day, something, some event, or someone made them aware of their abilities that were dormant within them.

Perhaps you are also experiencing something like that. In fact, many of the successful people you admire today doubted their own abilities at first. Then they began to believe in their abilities that were small, and they began to use them little by little. Then they used them more and more until their lives were totally transformed to who they are today.

You may be astonished to know that in fact, it was even from very distant starts that some of the rich and famous people you admire today eventually became famous. They became famous because they exploited their qualities and abilities to such a high level in the fields of their choices. So rejoice and say, "Halleluiah, this is my moment!"

President Lincoln is one of the best-known cases of this. He was born poor and eventually encountered a variety of setbacks in his life. When he had knowledge of his power within, he exploited his qualities and abilities that made him the president of one of the most powerful nations on planet Earth. Think also about the first black president of the United States of America, Barak Obama, whose father was from a poor family in Africa. Or think about the modest beginnings of Earnest Bai Koroma and Julius Maada Bio, both of whom became powerful leaders of Sierra Leone, or think about an ordinary union steward with no college education, Siaka

Stephens, who eventually became the president of Sierra Leone and chairman of the Organization of Africa Unity (OAU).

Consider the amazing history of Arnold Schwarzenegger, who became the governor of California, which in my opinion is the most powerful state in the United States of America. Remember Oprah Winfrey, who became one of the richest women on planet Earth. A Sierra Leonean tycoon, Jemil Sahid Mohamed, was an ordinary driver who became an extraordinary international entrepreneur and a multimillionaire.

Of course, you will agree with me that history counts such men and women in the thousands. Many people have transformed their lives, whereas just a few years before, they would not have dared imagine such a transformation. Between what you are today and what you can become tomorrow, it is only you who will decide the road you want to follow. Whatever your present situation may be, and whatever you would like to become, the power is within you. Fortunately, this new book of knowledge will guide you to tap into that power accordingly.

Thus, I assure you to rest assured that the decision you have made to read this enlightening new book of knowledge marks the beginning of your new life and your transition into the new era of higher consciousness. When you make regular use of the secrets that are revealed in this inspirational volume, you will surely lead a life that is fuller and richer. You will lead a great life with regard to your potential for your love life and your peace of mind that will give you inner joy, good health, tranquility, and longevity:

- Day by day you will have greater confidence in yourself.
- You will feel able to cope with anything that happens to you in life.
- You will utilize the secret to greatness, peace of mind, and inner joy.

This volume reminds you that anyone who is peaceful makes use of his or her hidden qualities, abilities, and luck. Some people make use of them without even realizing it. Other people eventually discover the secret, just as you will soon discover yours.

"What should I do now?" you may ask. I think I should let you know that there is no quick fix. If you hasten to discover these secrets too quickly,

5

there is a risk of many things going wrong. Therefore, you have to start with the first step. This is the step that involves restoring your natural protective magnetism.

You are therefore encouraged to make good use of the secrets that will be revealed to you just by reading this powerful book. Eventually you will be brimming over with energy and full of vim and vigor. Subsequently, you will be shielded from evil and harmful waves forever. Some of these secret formulas may surprise you, but please rest assured that they work. This is your moment; let nothing stand in your way.

Be certain to always make good use of the
powerful secret formulas you know and
judge them by their results.

Your Peace Is Your Command!

THE SECRET FORMULA FOR REVITALIZING YOUR MIND, BODY, AND SPIRIT

This new book of knowledge is revealing a wonderful secret formula that will revitalize your mind, body, and spirit in a very profound and powerful way. You can then use this special scientific method to gain vital forces and energy that will enhance your peace of mind. To successfully accomplish this goal, you should perform the following secret formula if you can:

Sit down on a chair, bed, stool, or something similar. Dip your right foot into a bowl full of cold water and your left foot into a bowl full of warm water.

Do this exercise for a minimum of seven minutes or as long as you comfortably can. The science is that your body's contact with warm water and cold water simultaneously generates a special current of dynamic waves. This *special* current will recharge you with *special* energy, and it will reinvigorate you in a very *special* way. Do you see how simple this powerful secret formula is?

However, do not be misled by the seeming easiness of this formula. Trust me, it is very powerful. So until you achieve your specific goals, please continue to perform this formula at least once a day. You can also perform it any time you need to revitalize yourself for any particular reason.

THE SECRET FORMULA FOR RECOVERING YOUR DYNAMISM

The secret formula that will help you to recover your energy and dynamism, increase your vitality, and restore the protective radiance to your aura is very important for your peace of mind. This secret exercise is also vital for your love life and for your inner peace. In fact, this powerful formula is renowned for its euphoria-inducing virtues.

This is the secret exercise that helps to banish anger, sadness, and even depression. It helps to effectively and easily combat bouts of low morale, low self-esteem, anxiety, and stress. It gives you dynamism, strength, and vigor. This exercise also has many other qualities that are later discussed in this new book of knowledge.

The strengthening effect of this formula will tremendously increase your vitality and even your enjoyment of living. Thus, you will be more radiant and more dynamic in your activities of daily living. Great sages of the world and leaders from every period and nation have taught their followers this secret exercise, which is in fact a mainspring of strength and energy.

To be able to clearly make this explanation, let's use an image or an example you are familiar with: you can compare your energy level to that of a car battery. Every time you act or give utterance to a thought, you expend a given amount of energy. By so doing, there is a tendency for your strength to be lowered. Therefore, you should be mindful that every time you are worried, upset, or ill, you draw on your reserved energy to an extent that you cannot even conceive. It is as if you forgot to switch off your car headlights and later find out that they have seriously run your battery down.

Remember also that this notion is clearly expressed when you say things like, "I feel drained. I'm flat out." In fact, you should be mindful that when you are in that state, you can be more vulnerable to all kinds of negative events in life. As a result, you may feel like you no longer have the energy and the heart to enthusiastically move on. Eventually, everything may look depressing, confusing boring, dull, gloomy, fearful, and dark.

In other words, you are literally submerged in an environment of negative waves that are floating around you. It may seem like those negative waves are attracting other negative waves toward you and so on and so forth. Thus, as someone said, "When it rains, it pours."

Fortunately, this volume has been designed to give you the secret knowledge that will let you take the appropriate actions to easily recharge your batteries. You will be given the secrets to build walls of positive waves around you that will protect you and shield you from all kinds of harmful and negative waves.

One of the secret formulas this new book of knowledge is revealing to help you is the *deep-breathing* formula. This breathing exercise will quickly and totally recharge you, increase your dynamism, and restore your vitality in a very *special* way.

FIRST SESSION

- The secret breathing formula
- The secret formula for protecting yourself from evil and harmful attacks
- The secret formula for protection and sleeping peacefully
- The secret formula for requesting divine intervention

THE SECRET BREATHING FORMULA

The 7 Secrets to Peace of Mind has been designed to let you know the power of what we call *the secret breathing* formula. In fact, this breathing formula is one of the greatest secrets underlying occultists' powers. This is one of the secrets that the top 1 percent, which is comprised of the most powerful individuals in society, does not want you to know about.

You may be surprised to know that most of the powerful individuals in our society owe their powers and their apparent supernatural magnetism to the knowledge of this secret. These individuals are powerful because of their intelligent use of the energy that they literally store up by performing this *secret breathing* formula.

To have your own share of this power, you, too, should do this powerful *secret breathing* exercise every day. When you do that, it will then be left to you to judge its effectiveness. In your case, as a near fight, you should do this breathing exercise two times a day for at least seven minutes per session. You can also do this exercise whenever you want to feel good or come out of a difficult situation.

Please remember this: it will be more effective to do this *secret breathing* exercise for the first time in the morning, before beginning your daily activities. This means you will then have a feeling of enhanced strength and complete fitness that will help you to have a pleasant and lively day.

To begin the *secret breathing* exercise, you should completely empty your lungs. That means expelling all the air from your lungs. You should then inhale and exhale for about the same amount of time. For example, when you start the breathing exercise, you should breathe in for at least seven seconds or as long as you comfortably can, hold the air in your lungs for at least seven seconds, and then breathe out for at least seven seconds. Leave a gap of at most seven seconds between one breath and the next. After about seven days, as you continue with your daily exercises, you can increase or decrease the durations of breathing-in, holding the air in your lungs, and breathing-out according to your capability.

Please pay attention to the following stages:

Stage 1: Stand up straight or sit up straight. Breathe in through your nostrils in a steady and continuous way.

Stage 2: Hold the air in your lungs for at least seven seconds or as long as you comfortably can.

Stage 3: Breathe out slowly and empty your lungs completely.

Stage 4: Pause for at most seven seconds or as long as you comfortably can.

Then breathe in again, trying to avoid any gasps or lack of continuity in the movement. Hold the air in and breathe out slowly, as indicated above. Keep on doing this exercise for about seven minutes or as long as you comfortably can.

Please be reminded that *breathing* itself is energy. In fact, when you do these secret breathing exercises regularly, you will notice results that will be amazing, such as the following:

1. Your health and well-being will be improved considerably.
2. If you are on the edge, irritable, touchy, etc., a surprising calmness will take over from these depressing states of mind. Then you will eventually have peace of mind and tranquility.
3. Your ability to pay attention will increase amazingly. For instance, you will be able to read or perform other activities for hours on end without becoming perceptibly tired.
4. You will have enhanced intuitions, and you will discover ideas in which inspiration plays a large part.
5. Your memory will be improved miraculously.
6. Your willpower will become stronger day by day.

In short, you will make progress right across the board. To really achieve maximum benefits, you should do this breathing exercise for about seven weeks before starting the exercise in the *second session*.

THE SECRET FORMULA FOR PROTECTING YOURSELF FROM EVIL AND HARMFUL ATTACKS

There is a very powerful secret formula for the morning that will protect you from any evil or harmful attack. This formula was revealed by one of the greatest masters in beneficial occult breathing. It is a formula that calls on powerful forces in the universe to protect you whenever necessary.

What I also learned from that Great Magus is this: many people do not have the slightest idea that they have a hidden friend available to them: the power of the subconscious allied with the beneficent forces of the universe, always ready to protect them, to serve them, and to act in their defense.

Now that you know this secret, never undervalue yourself or your potential, because everyone has a purpose in life. Remember also that the universe is open to all those who are searching. Even the Bible said, "Seek, and you shall find." So please look for your potential. This is your moment!

Although some people may already have some knowledge of this notion, nevertheless, most people still believe that someone has to be endowed with some special gift to be able to take advantage of the benefits and the actions of the subconscious. Fortunately, *The 7 Secrets to Peace of Mind* has been designed to let you know that you do not need any special gift to take advantage of the powers of the subconscious.

When you need to resist any harmful attack, all you need to do is to counter the harmful influences coming from outside. You can do this with a protective bar of positive thoughts. You can also do this by calling on the *divine spirit* deep within you to work powerfully on your behalf. Therefore, each morning when you awake, say the following prayer aloud or silently to yourself:

> I reject any evil and harmful attack that may be done to me,
> whatever they are and however they are done. Divine Power
> that is within me, I charge you to always watch over me and
> defend me. Amen!

This is a short prayer addressed to the powerful forces that are watching over you and protecting you. Always remember that prayers are the supreme acts that can make anything happen at any time. Thus, with this powerful prayer, you are shielded from any evil.

The parapsychology here is that within yourself you are releasing an efficient self-protective mechanism. This is the mechanism of your unconscious spirit that you are linking with the powerful beneficent forces of the universe. These forces are to some extent what some clergy refer to as guardian angels.

Even if this idea may seem strange, you should do this for yourself. Repeat this prayer as often as you can. Every time you feel tense or distressed because of some difficulties, just say this prayer. Then notice how tranquil and protected you will suddenly feel.

When you say this prayer correctly, almost immediately, you will be able to sense calmness and peacefulness within you. Obviously you should be glad to learn that this is one of the most powerful prayers that reinforce the protection and actions of most of the powerful people in history and in modern society. Now that you know the secret, this is your time to be one of them. As a result, you will be as powerful as you choose to be.

THE SECRET FORMULA FOR PROTECTION AND SLEEPING PEACEFULLY

This powerful secret formula for the evening to help you sleep peacefully under the protection of beneficent forces has never been revealed to the masses in this way. For example, what would you say if you knew how to have the feeling every night as you went to sleep of drawing a mantle of peace, tranquility, love, and inner joy over yourself at the same time as you pull up your covers?

Well, from now on, every night before you go to sleep, imagine that as you pull up your covers, you are drawing a mantle of peace, tranquility, love, and inner joy over yourself. At that very moment, in the innermost depths of your heart, say the following powerful, secret prayer:

> I entrust my existence and my life to the source of my life, which protects me and blesses me throughout the night. In the morning I will wake up with a clear and untroubled mind. I will have spent a good, restful night, and my body will be ready to enjoy a good day. Amen.

When you continue to fervently say this prayer every night, you will be thankful for the effects it has. In a short moment, you will fall asleep with a feeling of profound peace. You will feel so well and sleep so deeply that you will be able to dispense with any sleeping pills that you may have been taking.

Hopefully by now you are beginning to be the person who will never again use his or her power and intelligence in a limited way. In a way, you will begin to use the infinite intelligence of the universe to which you are directly linked by the infinite intelligence residing deep within you.

Very soon, the forces of the source of your life will be awakened. They will then work day and night to serve, protect, light, and guide you. This intelligence—this force that is within you—is the power of your subconscious. That is what will transform your whole life as it has transformed the lives of those who know this secret. These are the people who know the secret to tame their subconscious and to command it accordingly.

Please relax and rejoice; there are more secret formulas that will soon be revealed to you as you continue to peruse this new book of knowledge. Thus, you are encouraged to please apply these powerful formulas to your life. Soon and very soon through your subconscious you will be able to attract peace of mind, including love, tranquility, and inner joy.

However, you should make the effort to be familiar with the first four stages you have just learned. Perhaps they seem a bit complicated, but you will soon see that they are very simple. Actually, all you have to regularly do is:

1. Do the foot-dipping formula to revitalize your mind, body, and spirit. This is the formula that will also reactivate your vital forces.
2. Do the secret breathing exercise to recharge yourself with energy and protective magnetism.
3. Repeat the protective formula for the morning to ward off harmful influences.
4. Repeat the protective formula for the evening to protect you throughout the night and to sleep peacefully.

THE SECRET FORMULA FOR REQUESTING DIVINE INTERVENTION

In parapsychology, the method of communicating with the universe is referred to as divine communication. This type of communication is intended to drive away harmful waves and accelerate the advent around you of a beneficent environment. It is through this action that you should faithfully ask for divine intervention.

Remember however that *silent prayer* is one of the most powerful ways to communicate with the divine. All you have to do is choose one day in the week to meditate or silently pray to the divine for at least seven minutes before you go to bed. During this time, make some excuses to be quietly alone. It does not matter where; just be in a place where you can quietly concentrate on the *power of the divine*. This is how a powerful divine communication is established between you and the universe.

During that meditation period, think of the *positive* help you need from the divine power at the very instant when you are personally subjected to the effect of divine intervention. This is the moment when the positive forces of God almighty are around you to help you. Through this meditation, you are placing the realization of your wish in the hands of the powerful force of the divine, who will eventually make it come true.

After your meditation period, there is nothing special you have to do to take full advantage of the divine's help. Carry on with your normal life. Just remember that God is with you and the universe is sending you the positive thoughts and waves you need to have peace of mind. These forces will be around you at all times and always protecting you.

From the very beginning, you should feel the benefits of these exercises when you do them accordingly. In fact, each and every one of them on its own is very effective. But together, their beneficial action seems to be multiplied in an incredible way so that it increases day by day. When you do these exercises, you will feel the effects on your well-being, vitality, morale, and optimism.

Please be informed that you will be very peaceful if you do this exercise for about seven weeks before doing the exercises in the *second session*. By adhering to this suggestion, you will quickly achieve your goals and finally have the peace of mind you need. This is the secret.

SECOND SESSION

- The secret for changing yourself
- The secret formula for developing your personality
- The secret to awakening the powerful forces within you
- The secret formula for creating a powerful emotional shield
- The secret formula for remaining cool and calm at all times
- The secret formula for securing an automatic protection
- The secret formula for acquiring a lovely magnetic gaze
- The secret for making your smile infallible
- The secret formula for charging yourself with divine power

However, you are reminded that for maximum benefits, you should do the exercises described in the first session for about seven weeks before doing the exercises in the second session. They are the exercises that will reestablish a beneficent environment around you. These exercises will also restore your vitality, and as a result, you will feel much better every time you do them. In fact, after doing the exercises in the first session, you will eventually forget the leaden feelings that previously weighed you down.

Remember also that during the *second session*, you should continue to do the special breathing exercise you learned in the first session for about seven minutes every morning. You are also encouraged to repeat the formulas that do you the most good whenever you feel the need. By doing this, everything will eventually work out better and better for you day by day. No more worries; you have got enough. Your time for peace of mind has finally arrived. This is your moment!

THE SECRET FOR CHANGING YOURSELF

The question here is how can you make use of the forces that are deep within you? You may also want to know how to make use of these forces to change your entire life. Fortunately, this volume reveals the secret formulas for the transformation of your life. As soon as you have prepared the ground to harness these powerful formulas, you will be assured of changing yourself and having a sustainable peace of mind in a very remarkable way.

The fact that you are already doing the suggested exercises is clear evidence that your transformation is already in progress. Soon the mechanism for peace of mind, including love and inner joy that will be released from your meditations or silent prayers, will work for you day and night virtually without any further effort on your part.

However, you still have to properly prepare your personality to use the forces within you. This new book of knowledge reveals the secret formulas that have been used for many years, but only by members of the top 1 percent. Fortunately, your time has arrived. This is the secret formula that will give you a fortified personality.

You will soon have the kind of personality that will be so magnetic that everyone around you will be changed effortlessly. This volume is designed to let you have more knowledge of how to have peace of mind, including love, tranquility, and inner joy. Trust me; this new book of knowledge is invaluable, and it offers positive steps to easily raise your self-esteem to a very high level.

The Secret Formula for Developing Your Personality

Improving yourself by investing time and money on yourself is the best investment you can ever make. Always remember that whatever you add to your personality is something nobody can ever take away from you. This is the truth and nothing but the truth. Those who personally know me know exactly what I am talking about.

Therefore, with the help of *The 7 Secrets to Peace of Mind,* you will have more self-confidence thanks to the secret formulas you are about to discover. However, do not be surprised at the simplicity of these formulas because the greatest secrets are mostly the simplest things imaginable.

Some of these secrets are so simple, in fact, that I am almost reluctant to reveal them. As you may know, there is an unfortunate tendency for people to think that only complicated formulas are effective. In many cases, that is wrong. But this is a habit that is so deeply ingrained in us by our influences and by our domestication into the dream of society.

For instance, here is a simple formula for developing your personality: to develop your personality, you first have to be able to make your muscles obey you. The psychology is this: you have to act on your body so you can act on your attitude. This statement may surprise you, but to make an impact on your personality, it is crucial to go through your mind and body.

However, even if you cannot control most of the muscles in your body yet, there are some muscles you can easily control. Examples of such muscles are the muscles that govern your breathing. In fact, the muscles that govern your breathing are in the group of the most important muscles in your body. Thus, it is vital to know that breathing properly is the basis of the control you exercise over yourself.

That is why it is vital that you do the breathing exercises in the morning. Why? The reason is simple: breathing properly is easier when you are in a good mood, when you are feeling optimistic, and when you are joyful. Fortunately, it works the other way round as well. That means if you breathe properly, you can automatically improve your mood and increase your vitality, optimism, cheerfulness, health, and dignity.

There are more advantages you will be able to observe as you continue with your breathing exercises. Moreover, your breathing can purify your organism, expel carbon dioxide, and directly stimulate the glands that contribute to ensuring your good health. You will surly agree with me that these are completely crucial for your peace of mind. Perhaps you are thinking, *Well, I knew all this.* Yes, you probably do, but the important thing is not just to know it. The most important thing is to do it and to put it into daily practice. Always remember that even though knowledge is power, nevertheless, *practiced knowledge is more powerful; it is what makes things happen.*

Therefore, *The 7 Secrets to Peace of Mind* encourages you to put this new knowledge into practice. Remember also that what you are inside can be clearly seen from the outside. What is more, you can check this out immediately. For example, look at yourself in the mirror. What feeling does the person you are looking at convey to you? Who do you see? Do you see a confident person? Do you see an optimistic person? Do you see a cheerful person? Do you see a charismatic person? Do you see an honorable person? Do you see someone who exudes self-confidence? Or do you instead see someone who is angry, who seems worried, or who looks depressed?

I am not picking on you, my dear. However, what this new book of knowledge is telling you may be just as true for you as it is for many people you meet. Your face and your external attitude are the mirror through which the world sees you. They are the reflection of who you are. Your entire inner world, your state of mind, your morale, etc. can be seen from your outer appearance. Without any doubt, they can clearly be seen on your face.

If you want to look annoyed, all you have to do is to adopt an aggressive attitude, clench your fists, clench your teeth, and set the muscles of your face. Then look at the result in the mirror. Do you feel drawn to that grim-looking person you see in front of you? Of course you do not.

The psychology is, when you appear angry, sad, depressed, or demoralized, it will be very hard for you to have the magnetic personality that influences other people. Therefore, to properly and positively make your place in society, you should work on your personality and your attitude. Remember, positive attitude will always attract opportunity. The magnetism that already exists deep within you should be seen at first glance every time you meet someone. Thus, do not wait for a next time, because you are going to be remembered by that first glance. As one person put it, "The first cut is the deepest."

Please allow me to ask you these questions: Do you want to look optimistic and actually become optimistic? Do you want to look cheerful and really become cheerful? Do you want to be more self-confident and eventually make it possible? Do you want to be at ease? Do you want to appear enthusiastic? If you answer yes to any of these questions, then this new book of knowledge is designed to help you accomplish your goal.

All you need to do now is to pay attention to these valuable suggestions: always put on big smiles; always stand up straight; always breathe properly; always look people straight in the eyes; always carry your head high; always remain cool and calm; always be unruffled; and always stay in your mojo.

Remember also that you are *the one and only*, you are the best, you are important, you are honorable, and there is nobody like you. This is actually your true nature; this is who you are. Therefore, this notion should not have anything to do with arrogance, boastful pride, or egotism. This is just a matter of letting others know your true nature. By acting on your exterior and on the muscles you can control, you are simultaneously acting on your inner state of mind.

First and foremost, do not wait until you are cheerful before you smile. Always smile no matter what. Your smile acts on your inner state of mind and on the people around you. An open, natural smile adds magnetism to your personality just as your gaze does—especially the type of magnetic gaze you will soon secure from the secret this volume will soon reveal to you. Just keep on smiling, my dear friend; and the people of the world will smile back at you.

In addition to your smiles, when you look at people in a straight and frank manner, you give the impression that you are revealing your soul and thoughts unreservedly. You show that you have nothing to hide. Eventually you will observe that this frank, open attitude is a very important element that helps people to feel drawn to you much more easily.

A truly magnetic gaze like the one you are about to acquire, will indicate to the people you meet that you have an attractive, generous personality. It shows that you are sincere in your approach to others. Of course, it is common knowledge that personal influence plays an important role in human relations, whether in friendship or in business. You should therefore exert your influence for your own benefit at all times. In fact, to influence people in your favor means being pleasant to others.

Always remember that *even though it can be nice to be important, nonetheless, it can be more important to be nice to others.* Therefore, you will very quickly observe that knowing how to be nice to everyone will also be an advantage to you. Being nice and pleasant to people is an excellent way to ensure your achievement without harming anyone.

When you continue to do the suggested exercises, you will eventually see that your personal influence will be evident immediately when you make contact with anyone. You will notice that your handshake, your direct gaze, and the frank expression on your face and in your eyes will immediately strike the person you are talking with. As a result, these things will favorably influence the person toward you.

All these things will have important positive results on the progress of your relationships with others. You will have far more trumps up your sleeve to influence people. Thus, your peace of mind will be assured wherever you may be. Therefore, contrary to what some people believe, fate is not specially directed against anyone. Nobody is condemned to an inexorable destiny. In fact, at birth every human being receives within himself or herself *powerful forces* for protection that he or she does not always realize exist.

These innate forces give us the opportunity to use our own free will to break away from a kind of fate we sometimes believe we are in thrall to. In many cases, it requires very little to enable our personal influence received at birth to be released and transform our destiny in a positive way. If this is the case for you, then this new book of knowledge has been designed to be your guide.

THE SECRET TO AWAKENING THE POWERFUL FORCES WITHIN YOU

It is important to let you know that this *second session* is the release mechanism that will awaken the powerful forces that are dormant within you. Then, as you feel the natural powerful forces with which nature has endowed you growing within, your self-assurance will become correspondingly greater.

As such, it will be possible for you to exert your influence discreetly, positively, and unflinchingly in the presence of anyone. This will be possible even if the person in question is a very high-ranking individual or has great authority and great knowledge.

This assurance and unshakeable confidence you will be able to feel welling up increasingly within you (and of course it has nothing to do with arrogance) will show through. It will be seen and felt in your whole attitude, as well as in your gaze. Your magnetism will become ever more perceptible and apparent. It will support your personal influence better and better, and it will make an ever-greater impression on others without their understanding why or how.

If you are doing the suggested exercises precisely, then let me be the first to congratulate you and to tell you that this is your time. Your moment has come to achieve the good results you need in life. To talk a bit more about this famous *personal magnetism* that enables some people to go through life having peace of mind almost everywhere they go, take a moment to think about the following questions.

Have you ever wondered why some people are always surrounded by good and loyal friends while others remain depressingly alone? Have you ever wondered why it is said of some people that they were born under a lucky star? Have you ever wondered why some people exert an irresistible fascination on those around them, with the hint of a smile from them being welcomed as a real blessing?

The answers to these questions are simple, and now you know them: their shared secret lies in their charisma, in their dignity, in their natural charms, and in their mojo. These are some of the secrets this new book of knowledge will share with you to improve your *magnetic personality*. Thanks to the natural charm of those who know this secret, they have no problem attracting the best things in life. Everything they do is joyful without their having to make any extra effort. It can be said that they are naturally magnetic and that they were born lucky.

The truth is that you, too, have these same qualities buried deep within you. So rejoice, clap your hands, and be happy. *The 7 Secrets to Peace of Mind* has been designed to help you bring those hidden qualities to light. One of the secrets of personal magnetism is to remain unperturbed whatever the circumstances. You should be inwardly untouchable so that your outer appearance, your attitude, and your face always remain cool, calm, and relaxed.

THE SECRET FORMULA FOR CREATING A POWERFUL EMOTIONAL SHIELD

Creating a powerful emotional shield to protect yourself from verbal onslaughts is much easier than you may think. *The 7 Secrets to Peace of Mind* guarantees that this shield will enable you to remain confident whatever the circumstances may be. Imagine meeting someone unpleasant who you do not like at all. Immediately your features tense up. Psychologically this encounter will give your face an angry look.

Here is how to prevent that kind of feeling and how to train yourself to overcome your feelings. The following is a simple formula that will help you:

Fix your gaze on a wall facing you at a point level with your eyes. You can pin up a black mark on a white background to help you if necessary. Keep sitting quietly without blinking your eyes and keep thinking of the word *point*. The psychology is that by doing this, you will distract your attention. You will stop thinking about your angry feelings, and your inner tension will soon disperse. Believe me—even though this is a very simple formula, it is so powerful and very fundamental. It works.

Keep doing this exercise without blinking for seven seconds, for at least seven minutes a day for about seven weeks. You can gradually increase the duration without blinking as the days and weeks progress. Your ultimate goal will be to go to about seventy seconds or more without blinking. If your eyes prick and water, it is normal for that to happen. Then, still without blinking, you can even walk around the room while becoming more and more aware of the muscles in your face. Practice relaxing your muscles immediately when you feel the slightest tension.

Repeat this exercise whenever you can. It will help you combat wrinkles and other signs of aging effectively. This formula will also help you acquire the lovely gaze that can be described as *magnetic.* Remember, there should be a total absence of tension on your face. Believe me, the cool, calm and relaxed look, along with your frank and direct gaze, will really increase your personal influence on people whenever you meet them.

THE SECRET FORMULA FOR REMAINING COOL AND CALM AT ALL TIMES

This new book of knowledge will let you know the secret to remaining in control of yourself even in the event of a very unpleasant verbal onslaught. For example, if you are a victim of a scathing, a reproach, an unpleasant verbal onslaught, a reprimand, or a public ticking off, all you have to do is to repeat this powerful positive phrase:

> *What so ever is done to me or what so ever is said to me or about me, I am a valuable person*

This is in fact one of the most powerful emotional shields this volume offers to help you through the challenges of life. Believe me, it works. Honestly, this was the formula I personally used as a shield when a group of disguised fiends organized a reproach for me during a speech I was giving at my niece's wedding in Stockton, California.

When you use this powerful secret formula, you will latch on to a positive feeling that is anchored deep within you at the time when you need it. As a result, you will be shielded from negative emotions or feelings such as fear, anger, or shame that could destabilize you and wound you deeply.

Do you want to know how this formula can produce such a powerful result whatever the circumstances might be? The answer is really very simple. The psychology is that two opposite emotions cannot occupy your mind at the same time. For example, you cannot be simultaneously joyful and be overcome by fear. It is thanks to this powerful secret that you can protect yourself from the negative emotions that might get in the way when you meet evil or negative people.

The secret is that when you firmly establish within yourself a positive feeling, you will easily resist the negative and disruptive feelings directed to you by evil or wicked people. You will then be a powerful person who is in control of himself whatever the circumstances may be. Therefore, whenever you are confronted with a difficult situation, repeat this powerful positive phrase:

> *What so ever is done to me or what so ever is said to me or about me, I am a valuable person*

Repeat this phrase with a large amount of confidence because you are truly a person of value. Thus, with such a statement firmly anchored within you, you will remain impassive even when you are confronted with the unkind words of wicked and evil people. I give you my word; trust me, I have been there. Try it out and you will discover that this formula is infallible.

THE SECRET FORMULA FOR SECURING AN AUTOMATIC PROTECTION

The 7 Secrets to Peace of Mind will guide you and give you the knowledge of the *protective wall* that will protect you automatically whenever the need arises. All you have to do is to precisely follow the suggestions made. One of the ideal ways to do this is to keep on repeating the phrases for the emotional shield until they become automatic reflexes, exactly as you would draw your hand back without thinking if you were to touch a very hot object or fire.

To produce amazing results, you should repeat your positive phrase every morning when you wake up and every night before you go to sleep. Do you remember the phrase? It is this:

> *What so ever is done to me, or what so ever is said to me or about me, I am a valuable person.*

You will see that this untiring repetition is a powerful exercise that inscribes this message in your mind in virtually an indelible manner. You will then observe that the phrase automatically acts on its own. This powerful formula will be useful to you in most of the circumstances that may arise in your life.

Here is another undoubted secret weapon that will protect you from any evil or wicked person who might want to upset you, belittle you, or put you down: The secret is that the people who use thoroughly base stratagems to trap you expect you to respond at the same level. They expect to see you defending yourself forcefully, fighting back, or getting angry and losing control of your emotion.

This new book of knowledge is encouraging you to please do not respond with that kind of intensity. In fact, do not put yourself on that level. Just be honorable enough to avoid their trap, even though you might think you can take on any of them at that moment, especially if you are feeling self-righteous.

The 7 Secrets to Peace of Mind will show you the way to avoid that kind of embarrassment and to maintain your majesty. There is a powerful secret formula for parrying this. The secret is to form a sentence of benediction in your mind, such as:

God will bless you.

Even if you do not believe in a God, it does not matter. Even if you do not feel like blessing the evil or wicked person facing you, it will work automatically just the same anyway. This phrase has so much power that it will work on its own. Do you want to check it out? Okay, just try this and see. Repeat the phrase, *God will bless you* in your mind and try to hate someone at the same time. Did you notice that this is impossible?

The psychology is that you cannot experience two contrary feelings at the same time. Thus, you cannot bless someone and hate him or her simultaneously. You may have no desire to put a real feeling into it, and that is not even necessary.

In fact, for your own good it is necessary that you bless anyone you come in contact with at all times. This is because repressed or locked-in feelings can be the cause of some of the serious illnesses in society today, so it is primarily for your own good that you should bless your verbal assailant regardless of the situation.

You should therefore think very carefully about this and simply keep the phrase *God will bless you* present in your mind at all times. Eventually you will see that anybody's insults can no longer affect you. You will feel as if you are far above your verbal assailant and that you are untouchable. This powerful secret formula means that you will never again be a victim of evil or wicked people. In fact, you will always be out of the reach of verbal onslaughts.

As a result, you will be shielded from all kinds of negative waves and unworthy attacks forever. The psychology is that by remaining serene and unperturbed and looking at these assailants in a calm and relaxed manner, you will be able to unsettle your adversaries. They will then notice that their evil and wicked behaviors have no influence over you, and they will eventually be ashamed of themselves.

THE SECRET FORMULA FOR ACQUIRING A LOVELY MAGNETIC GAZE

Do you want to have a lovely gaze that is magnetic? Of course—we all do. *The 7 Secrets to Peace of Mind* has been designed to give you the secret formula to acquire a gaze that is full of magnetism. This volume will also guide you in a step-by-step manner to the method of deploying this powerful magnetic gaze virtually instantaneously.

This is the secret:

1. Sit down in front of a mirror and stare fixedly at a point just between the eyebrows of your image facing you in the mirror. This is an excellent device if you ever dare to look another person straight in the eyes. When you look between a person's eyes instead of into them, the person will in any case have the impression that it is actually his or her eyes you are staring into, and that is what counts.

   When you first start the exercise, you might feel a bit embarrassed about looking staring at your own image in this way, but you will soon get used to it. Eventually you will be more at ease when you are looking directly at another person in the eye. Take care *not* to adopt the hard expression of someone wanting to make an impression. That is not the aim here; quite the opposite. All you have to do is to keep your face very sincere and relaxed.

2. The next part is so important that I should emphasize it. During the exercise, when you are staring fixedly at a point on the wall or when you are looking into your mirror, do not blink your eyelids. Do your best not to blink, even when you feel your eyes pricking and starting to water. Remain like this for at least seven seconds, trying to increase the duration of each session. This is how you will obtain the famous and lovely gaze that is described as *magnetic*.

3. While your gaze is fixed straight in front of you, you may use your peripheral vision to see the objects on all sides of you. By doing this exercise, you will notice an improvement in your visual observation. In addition to that, you will develop your power of concentration and your ocular magnetism enormously. This new book of knowledge is encouraging you to concentrate in this way a little longer every day for about seven weeks.

4. With the expressiveness of your gaze, you will show the person you are talking with that your interest is sincere. Your eyes will be attentive and fixed on his or her eyes. Obviously your gaze should

not express any curiosity, disdain, or superiority. Always do your best to fill your gaze with honesty, love, kindness, and respect.

When you do these exercises correctly, your charisma and your dignity will increase faster than you may expect. Subsequently, you will feel within yourself an unsuspected power. Yes, it is very important to feel powerful and self-assured and to gain ascendancy. As a result, you will easily have the peace of mind you deserve.

Do the best you can to always look at people straight in their eyes without fear and without aggression. Do not twist your head around in every direction. Do your best to appear as a calm and cool person, who you will truly be a little more every day as you continue to do this powerful secret exercise to acquire your lovely magnetic gaze.

When you do that, you will literally captivate anyone you are talking with. Always make your gaze almost unbearable by gazing at the other person calmly just between his or her eyebrows without blinking your eyelids. This will give you an irresistible ascendancy and assurance that will impress whoever you may be talking with.

However, if after some time you feel the need to look somewhere else, do not lower your eyes, whatever you do. That could be taken as a sign of inferiority, which nobody misses. Look instead at the top of the head of the person you are talking with. That generally creates a slight sense of unease in the other person, which will be advantageous to you. Then move your gaze horizontally away from the level of the eyes of the person you are talking with and finally look elsewhere. This is the secret.

THE SECRET FOR MAKING YOUR SMILE INFALLIBLE

If you want to make your smile immune from fallacy, *The 7 Secrets to Peace of Mind* will help you all the way through. This new book of knowledge will let you have a clear understanding that your smile is an infallible device for your peace of mind. When done properly, your smile will be the master key that opens any door.

Always remember that your smile has an extraordinary magnetic power. Do not forget also that your smile is your free gift that lights up other people's gloomy days. So every time your eyes meet someone's eyes, especially if his or her eyes seem sad, please just smile at that person. Even if it is someone you do not know, just smile at him or her for your own good and you will be blessed abundantly.

The psychology is that if he or she happens to be in a state of profound sadness or difficulties, by just smiling to him or her, you will give him or her comfort and feelings that are very reassuring. Honestly, it is incredible how alone and forgotten some people can feel sometimes. If you have ever had a sad experience like that yourself, then you know what it means to feel lonely at times.

Fortunately, you will never encounter a sad moment again. However, since you will soon begin to use the beneficent influence of your magnetism, always show kindness and generosity toward others. Your smile will also be an infallible tool. For example, in the event of any conflict, your honest smile will surely disarm your opponent. Furthermore, you will always remain serene, cool, calm, and in control of your impulses.

Your natural magnetism will intensify day by day as you keep on reading *The 7 Secrets to Peace of Mind* and doing the outlined exercises accordingly. Your magnetism will also be further intensified by the effect of the breathing formula you are already familiar with as explained in the *first session*. That powerful breathing exercise can also contribute considerably to the improvement of your radiance.

After you have done the other exercises in the previous session, do the exercises in this session for about seven weeks. When you do this, you will no doubt have the peace of mind you deserve. Do you still remember the exercises? What you actually need to do is very simple. In fact, all you have to do are the following formulas:

1. Do the *secret breathing formula* in the morning. This is the exercise that will charge you with energy, protection, and magnetism.
2. Repeat the *protective formula for the morning* to counter evil and harmful influences.

3. Repeat the *protective formula for the evening* for protection and to sleep peacefully throughout the night.

4. Repeat the *protective shield* formulas for difficult situations or verbal onslaughts.

5. Continue to do the exercises that will help you acquire a *lovely magnetic gaze* that will eventually change your whole life for the better.

THE SECRET FORMULA FOR CHARGING YOURSELF WITH DIVINE POWER

One of the most powerful formulas for charging yourself with divine power is by doing the silent meditation also known as the positive divine magneto action. You are therefore encouraged to carry on with this action again, which this time will be aimed at helping you to easily charge yourself with power and magnetism.

You do not have to do anything special to benefit from this divine help. The divine power you will be charged with will be sufficiently intense and regular to support you. The universe already knows exactly what you need, so just carry on with your life as normal. Continue to believe that the divine power is in you and that the universe is sending you the positive thoughts and waves to help you through.

Your silent meditation time during this second session will still be at your bedtime once week for at least seven minutes. You already know what you have to do. Take a blank sheet of paper and write the wishes that are really important to you.

During the period of your meditation, do your best to be alone and free from any disturbance. At that moment, think only of what you are asking the divine to offer you. The psychology here is that *thinking is power* and *thoughts are things.* This is the moment when you are personally subjected to the effect of the divine's intense positive magneto action. So think positively of what you are wishing for, and believe you will surely get it.

After your meditation period, take the sheet of paper on which your wishes are written, cut it into pieces, and discard it completely by any means. Then think very hard about what you have just wished for and say, "I will get it" or "I will get them." When you do these exercises precisely, far sooner than you may imagine, you will notice astonishing results that will transform your whole life for the better.

These exercises will continue to transform your life as needed, and they will surely astound you tremendously. Without any doubt, you will soon have the opportunity to test these new formulas that are intended to protect your self-image and intensify the magnetism of your personality. As a result, you will finally have the peace of mind you were born to enjoy.

Please be reminded also that you have to do the exercises in the *second session* before doing the exercises in the *third session*. When you do these exercises correctly, you will really be proud of yourself. Kindly do this for yourself; then most of your problems will be solved. President John F. Kennedy once said, "Our problems are man-made; therefore, they can be solved by man." This is your moment to do these powerful exercises to solve your problems because, as President Ronald Reagan put it, "The bridges and highways we fail to repair today will have to be rebuilt tomorrow at many times the cost." Thus, I am encouraging you to please do your exercises today.

THIRD SESSION

- The secret formula for communicating with the divine
- The secret to commanding your subconscious
- The secret to shaping your destiny

You should now be proud of yourself for successfully making it to the *third session* of this extended plan of action. This is the plan of action that will change your whole life for good. Hopefully when you finish reading this life-changing book, you will make an effort to read the *first, second, and third sessions* again for further contemplation, comprehension and application.

Eventually you will be able to fully tap into the dynamic forces that are deep within you. All you will have to do next is to allow your dynamism to come forth into light for the world to see. "What are these dynamic forces?" you may ask. Of course, you may have had some inkling of these forces without your knowledge or without paying proper attention to them.

In my case, I once read a story that jogged my memory to what my mother said to me many years ago. Please read my story very carefully and pay a very good attention to it. Maybe mine will jog your memory to yours.

This is how I myself came to know about the *forces* deep within me: Many years ago, my mother, Hajah Isata Charles, a wonderful thinker and leader of a very powerful women's organization in Sierra Leone, told me about the *dynamic forces* deep within me. At that time, I did not understand what my mother was telling me. Fortunately but unknowingly, the *dynamic forces* remained within me untapped until the right moment arrived when I finally became aware of them in a very strange and indescribable way . . . That powerful and wonderful enlightenment has opened my imagination and realization to realities that exist beyond the realm of language.

When I deeply think about it today, I understand now why my mother did not force my hand. I know now that I was not ready then to comprehend the power of the *dynamic forces* deep within me. However, my mother believed in me, and she knew that one day the light would dawn at the right moment.

It took me many years to finally understand what my mother told me then—many years during which I was vainly roaming around the globe. These were the years during which I was blindly touring the world, from Africa, Europe, and Asia to the United States of America in search of my dynamism.

To my greatest astonishment, I finally woke up to the realization that my dynamism can easily be derived from deep within me. I am actually surprised that for the whole time and for all those years, my *dynamic forces* were dormant deep within me. Thus, I am so grateful to the author of the story I read that jogged my memory to my own dynamic forces within me.

Hopefully by reading my story you, too, will be reminded of something someone might have told you about the *dynamic forces* within you. Honestly, I still find it very difficult to understand why most of the people in our society who know this secret are reluctant to reveal it to all humanity—especially to good people like you.

Instead, they choose to regularly use these powerful *inner forces* clandestinely to their discrete advantages. They know that these forces will continue to transform their lives to the point of reaching greater heights. Therefore, in order to gain dominion over others, they selfishly keep these life-changing secrets to themselves. This is your moment to know this powerful secret. Let nothing stop you now.

Fortunately, this new book of knowledge is drawing your attention to the notion that you, too, have *dynamic forces* deep within you without even realizing it in the slightest. When you begin to use these forces yourself, a certain presence will emanate from you that will give you the calmness and the power to command your own peace of mind. This is actually your birthright.

When that happens, you will effortlessly have the dynamic personality that will eventually make you the focal point of attention in your social environment. People will gradually see the transformation in your physical appearance, in your behavior, in your way of speaking, and in your way of doing the activities of your daily living.

Of course, this does not mean that you will deliberately set out to attract attention. No, that will not even be necessary. Your transformation will be registered automatically without any effort of yours. It is a gift of the divine to you. In fact, you will simply begin to become your true self. Therefore, this new book of knowledge has been designed to show you how to re-establish your connection with your true nature.

Eventually you will benefit from the power of your true nature and from everything that the universe has offered you. You will easily begin to free yourself from whatever was an obstacle to your full potential. You will be able to do most of the things you could have done earlier if you had known how to set about working with your true nature and your *inner force*.

You may however want to know what actually this *inner force* is into which you should tap to bring forth your *dynamism*. Again, the answer is very simple: It is you. It is the power of your *subconscious*, which you should release little by little to cope with earthly events. That is the force that will let you overturn the obstacles on the road of life and confront life's setbacks, whether they are economic, physical, political, spiritual, emotional, etc. This is one of the secrets the top 1 percent and the powerful members-only organizations do not want you to know about.

And yet again, this secret may seem so simple that if you were sitting across from me, you might say, "Okay, Tony Charles, if I possess the *inner force* you are talking about, why has it not been of any help to me up to now?" And here is what I would say to you: "Wake up, my dear friend, and see that you have got it wrong. There is a very good chance that your *inner force* may have brought you what you asked it to bring. Unfortunately for you, without being aware, you may have unintentionally made negative requests."

Therefore, *The 7 Secrets to Peace of Mind* has been designed to refocus your awareness to the power of your *subconscious*. This is the powerful *force* within you that faithfully records whatever you dictate to it. Your subconscious records your positive ideas as well as your negative ideas. It takes all of your ideas for requests that you are making. Since your subconscious is a loyal servant, it fulfills all of your requests accordingly. It does not matter whether they are positive or negative. That is how most people bring about their own disappointments, bad luck, anger, distress, setbacks, etc. They do so without being aware of the negative requests they ignorantly continue to make.

The 7 Secrets to Peace of Mind has been designed for you to realize that distress, bad luck, etc. are also very often poisons that have their origin in the *subconscious*, which in fact behaves exactly like a magnetic tape. Its role is confined to recording what the conscious mind asks of it and orders it to do or to program. Your subconscious does not think, nor does it make decisions. It just obeys and faithfully carries out what it believes you are asking it to do. It accepts what is transmitted to it by way of suggestion or even more, by way of mental imagery.

For example, if you are frightened of something and you always have the image of that fear in your mind, your subconscious might understand it as an order you are conveying to it. As a result, it might say, "That is what you want? Fine, let's go for it." Your subconscious organizes its actions and its searches, based on the order it thinks it has understood. It does this by reading your conscious thoughts and watching the mental images you conjure up. The work of your subconscious is to receive information, accept it, and then achieve what your conscious thought has transmitted to it.

Do you now understand why it is so important for you to have positive images and positive thoughts at all times? Just keep reading. This new book of knowledge has been designed to give you more comprehension of the considerable significance of your thoughts. For example, reflect for a moment and ask yourself what images the following words conjure up in your mind:

> *Suffering, death, war, killing, terror, poverty, evil, illness, sickness, old age, unemployment, sadness, ugliness, hate, hatred, hunger, fear, deprived, tense, pain, angry, edgy,* and *rebel.*

Do you feel good? I don't think so; because those words can conjure up negative images that can make you feel ill at ease. They are words that can conjure images of fear.

Now think carefully about what the following words conjure up in your mind:

> How do you feel about words like *shameful, defeated, bored, conquered, depressed, desperate, discouraged, disgusted, humiliated, weak, unhappy, rejected, sad, afflicted,* and *tired?*

Again, do you feel good? Of course not, because these words can conjure up images of sadness.

At this point, before you read any further, just imagine for a moment the damage that people who talk incessantly about their worries and woes can cause to themselves and to the people around them. Unfortunately, most of those people do so without being aware of their negativities, so please be very careful whenever you are around those kinds of individuals.

Those are the people who put themselves in a vicious circle of misfortune, distress, and sadness. This is simply because the words they use virtually all day long set up negative vibrations and influences in their minds. As a result, their negative vibrations also influence the minds of the people around them. So please stay away from such negative people as much as you can, if you can.

Now let us talk about you. Please remember that it is time for you to refrain from saying things like:

> *Luck like that will never happen to me. I am the only person to whom things like this happen. There is no point in me trying; I know I will not be successful. It is just my bad luck. I am always unlucky. I am fed up. I do not know which way to turn. When things happen to me, they are never nice. Another problem; they always come in series.*

The psychology is, when you think of the images these negative sentences can create, you can release mental and chemical forces that can sap your energy. These kinds of forces can diminish your vitality and engender negative and destructive conditions in your spirit, mind, and body. One example is that they can prepare and generate illnesses in the circumstances of your external life.

Actually, without being aware of what they are doing, most people are the ones creating negative waves that can attract even more bad luck and distress to themselves. However, *The 7 Secrets to Peace of Mind* has been designed to enlighten you in the way you will give yourself a shake and stop wallowing in gloom. This is your time to shine; do not let anything stop you now.

Honestly, you will find it very difficult to improve your life and have peace of mind if you go on dwelling on your misfortunes of the past. In fact, if you pore incessantly over events that you can no longer do anything to change, you might be doing yourself more harm than good. Therefore, this new book of knowledge is encouraging you to always remember the following powerful words of wisdom:

> *Move forward and believe in yourself. Never let your yesterday hold your today and your tomorrow hostage. Do not tie yourself to your past; tie yourself to your potential, and never ever give up except for honor.*

Of course it is common knowledge that if ruminating about gloomy ideas could resolve problems, there would be plenty of joyful people around the globe. Unfortunately, ruminating about your worries only serves to make things worse day by day, disturbing your peace of mind.

Let me suggest that you please stop reading right now and take a moment to do this simple psychological exercise:

> *Picture yourself making a bundle of all your problems. Imagine throwing this bundle of problems from the top of a high bridge and letting the current carry them away, with no possibility that they will ever come back.*

Please do this exercise perpetually to be free at last from all your worries. In fact, to enjoy a sustainable peace of mind, I suggest that you keep on throwing away those bundles of problems as quickly as you can any time they come your way. It is also my hope that you are practicing the secret formulas that have been revealed to you so far. If you have been doing the exercises precisely, you should have observed how effective they are at inducing feelings of peace in your innermost being.

Now please carry out the following experiment by concentrating solely on the following positive words:

> *beautiful, affectionate, pleasant, comfortable, enthusiastic, lucky, free, friendly, fit, grateful, happy, in love, blithe, hopeful,*

delighted, joyful, loved, loving arms, marvelous, tender, likeable,
peaceful, cool, calm, optimistic, prosperity, passionate, friend,
relaxed, contented, nice, warm, smiles, life, peace, wealth, good
health, youth, inner joy, beauty, kindness, love, and *confidence*

How do you feel? You feel better, don't you? Of course you do. What does this mean? The psychology is that it is better for you to convey positive images to release the creative intelligence of your *inner force,* which is your *subconscious mind.* Yes, positive words, thoughts, and feelings release positive creative forces within you and around you.

On the other hand, negative thoughts, words, and emotions attract forces that tend to be negative and destructive within you and around you. Remember also that negative deeds bring negative results most of the time. Therefore, you are encouraged to reinforce the positive personal magneto divine help the universe is sending you. You can do this by using the positive formulas this new book of knowledge is revealing to you.

It is also common knowledge that most people are vaguely aware of wanting to be peaceful, joyful, healthy, prosperous, wealthy, etc. Unfortunately, they get the opposite of what they wish for without knowing why. Do you know why that happens? It is because most people are so imbued with their negative thoughts, words, and emotions that the negative forces they generate also block them accordingly. As a result, a majority of these people do not achieve the positive results that could bring them the peace of mind they really need.

For example, in the course of my profession in the areas of health and human services and social services, I noticed that most human beings by accident use just sufficient creative forces and positive emotions in their thoughts to survive. Some people use just enough to be able to stagger along their road in life. Fortunately, this volume reveals the secret that will let you concentrate on the positive creative forces of your mind.

When you do these exercises precisely, getting the results you need will be simpler than you imagine. Just as the sun's rays can be concentrated by a magnifying glass to set fire to a piece of paper, in the same way, this volume will let you concentrate your dynamic mental forces. The formula is so effective that you can make it capable of illuminating the creative flame within you to transform your whole life and easily light up your way toward peace of mind and tranquility that will eventually lead you to nirvana.

THE SECRET FORMULA FOR COMMUNICATING WITH THE UNIVERSE

This is the new book of knowledge that reveals the secret way of communicating with the universe so that you can ask for your dearest wish to be realized. Of course you communicate with other human beings through the use of words. In the same way, you can create divine communication between your conscious mind, your subconscious, and the higher subconscious forces. These are forces that govern the universe. They are the universal forces that will help you achieve your requests for the wishes dearest to your heart.

One of the most powerful secret laws that are used to act on your subconscious is *the law of rhythm*. You no doubt know that repetition is the secret of efficacy. The psychology is that the repetition of a mental image or a clearly formulated suggestion enables your subconscious to be stimulated and shown what you want to obtain. This is the secret.

Doing this exercise is far easier than you can imagine, and soon, you will have proof of the result. But first, please make a short recapitulation. Now you know that for years you may have at least to some extent been programming some of the distress and the problems you have experienced or are experiencing. Of course you may have been doing so unawares, without suspecting it for a moment. Fortunately and from now on, with the help of this enlightened book, you can take action to make this process work positively for your own good.

The law of things that are alike says *like attracts like* and therefore *positive thinking attracts positive reality*. Thus, to release the mechanism leading to your peace of mind, all you need to do now is to reprogram your subconscious by regularly conveying positive requests to it. Then, just as it was able to bring you misfortune, your subconscious will obey you and bring more good fortune and peace of mind into your life.

The Secret Formula for Commanding Your Subconscious

Yes, it is true that you can actually give your subconscious mind positive and creative commands for peace of mind. This is how:

Every morning when you wake up, give your subconscious mind a series of creative commands consisting of formulas full of positive vibrations and animations. *The 7 Secrets to Peace of Mind* is therefore designed to help you through.

For example, whenever you have the chance, you should say some positive statements out loud if possible. When you say them aloud, the effect will be much faster. However, if that is not possible, repeat them to yourself, even in a whisper. Say them several times to give your subconscious a greater sense of conviction. Say them as often as possible in the course of the day. Any time you feel the need to have peace of mind, or increase your energy, your power, or your advisory intuition, just repeat the positive statements.

However, please do not ever forget that in life, you have to persevere and keep persevering until you get whatever you need. First of all, you have to persevere to block the negative effects that have been in your mind for so many years. Next, you have to persevere to receive the positive effects you wish to obtain.

I encourage you now to please take a moment to think about the following analogy: With the negative type of thoughts that have been implanted in most people for years, they are a bit like a big ship crossing the ocean. It is a ship that would like to go into reverse and radically alter its direction. You may realize that a ship carried on by its weight cannot stop short and turn around quickly just like that.

This example is a bit like most people today: They are carried along in life by the weight of their pasts and the load of their worries. As a result, the changes in their lives might not necessarily be immediate. However, the most important thing is that by reading this life-changing book so far and by doing the suggested exercises, the changes you need in your life have already begun.

When you diligently read this new book of knowledge and precisely do the suggested exercises, from then on, the most important thing will be that you have already released the positive forces that will transform you day by day. Yes, with the power and the knowledge you have procured so far, you can easily improve your life and alter your current state of mind. The power of your subconscious begins to work for you from the very minute you become aware that it is a dynamic, living intelligence that exists at the heart of your spirit. It is the intelligence that psychologically links you to the powerful forces of the universe.

Please be advised, however, that the power of the subconscious does not work in the same way for everyone. The effect of the power of the subconscious may take a shorter or longer time to become apparent, depending on the size and the importance of what you ask it to do. But if you persevere and have faith in the *power*, it will eventually ensure that you get whatever you wish for. There is no doubt about this. It is 100 percent ensured. All you have to do is to just believe and you shall see it without fail. This is another secret that the top 1 percent knows, but they do not want you to know. This is your moment!

Research has shown, however, that some people can see their wishes realized within a short period of time depending on the request. These are the people who make the effort to do the appropriate exercises accordingly. They also make requests of their wishes during their silent meditations with the divine. In fact, one thing you should always remember is that *silence is God's powerful voice.* Therefore, meditation is a powerful way of communicating with the infinite source of power.

For instance, when I suggested these exercises to some people during my research in preparation to write this book and for my counseling psychology program, one person's brother-in-law at last found a job after a long period of unemployment agony. Another person saw his wife who wanted to leave him change her mind and stay by his side, support him, and care for him in many ways. A lonely woman finally saw her son, whom she had not seen for many stressful years.

41

An unemployed woman found a job and eventually bought her college son the Mitsubishi Eclipse Spyder convertible sport car he always wanted. Another person's husband who had left her for a new lover eventually pleaded for mercy and went back home for good. A lady who has been a single woman for a very long time bumped into a longtime ex-boyfriend; they renewed their relationship and eventually got married. A woman I know rekindled the romance with her ex-husband after so many years of divorce, and they joyfully remarried.

There are many other people who have seen their wishes realized within a short period after doing the appropriate exercises. So, the ball is now in your court. This is your moment! Your peace of mind is at hand. Remember also that everything depends on your individual wish, your perseverance, and your faith in the *power.* However, please do not be disturbed. *The 7 Secrets to Peace of Mind* is designed to guide you step by step and level by level.

Let me repeat, however, that the results depend on your perseverance, self-confidence, and faith. That means you should regularly repeat your formulas between your meditations with the infinite source of power. This is because you must believe in something and you alone know precisely what it is you wish to see come true in your life.

In fact, when you religiously do the appropriate exercises, you will easily raise the level of your energy and your positive vibrations. You will also raise the level of your vibration by using words that engender positive power. You may use words and phrases like the following:

> *tranquility, love, kisses, joy, peace of mind, hope, achievement, winning, friendly, peaceful, wealth, prosperity, good health, cooperation, promotion, life, abundance, kindness,* and *forgiveness*

Repeat these words several times without ever doubting their power, even when everything seems to be going badly and nothing seems to be working out. Remember, life often works like that, as if it wanted to play a kindly trick on you. Things often seem to be going worse just before they get better or before a big achievement etc. As someone said, "Within misfortune good fortune hides."

Please be reminded also that most of the powerful and famous people started from nothing and eventually became powerful and famous. Most of those individuals became powerful and famous because they made use of the secret to produce a kind of positive chemistry in their minds. The secret is that they made use of intense thoughts that were charged with positive magnetism. These thoughts enabled them to resolve their problems and eventually became powerful and famous. This is the secret.

Many of those individuals experienced enlightenments that suddenly brought them much-needed answers. Sometimes they experienced sudden enlightenments during their silent meditations, sometimes in their dreams, sometimes during meetings with their spiritual advisers, sometimes through connections with other people, etc. Remember also that life is about connections; if you have the right connections, you will easily have peace of mind.

However, be mindful that some of the answers most of the powerful and famous people received from their experiences of sudden enlightenment did not necessarily come from one day to the next, especially when some of the experiences were questions of finding the solution to things that had never before existed. For example, it is thanks to the positive chemistry of one man's brain and perseverance that you can today benefit from electric light and the telephone, listen to music, and go to the movies.

That one man is Thomas Edison, who did not even have much conventional schooling. He was a self-taught man, and it was he who invented a form of telegraph, the gramophone, and the incandescent electric light. His kinetic-scope was a forerunner of the cinematograph. All these inventions came into the brain of Thomas Edison sometime after he had silently meditated or reflected adequately on his meditations.

You may remember, for example, that he found the secret of the filament used in the electric light bulb after trying almost ten thousand times. Therefore, it could be said that Mr. Edison seemingly failed about 9,999 times before discovering a filament that lit up without being consumed.

This new book of knowledge is therefore drawing your attention to the psychological fact that after one hundred attempts, one thousand attempts, five thousand attempts, etc., Mr. Thomas Edison could have given up in despondency. Each time, right up to the penultimate attempt, he could have said, "I'm fed up with yet another failure. That's it; I'm giving up, etc." Instead he told himself, "I have got still a bit closer to my objective." As such, he tried about 9,999 times without ever doubting that his *subconscious* would eventually direct him to the right solution.

Surely, in fact, one day his subconscious did guide him toward a material he had never tried before. Then suddenly, Thomas Edison discovered the electric light bulb. That was the extraordinary invention that changed the face of the world forever. And without any doubt, *the believing Thomas* made his fortune. However, Mr. Edison's difficulties were not over. For, of course, at that time there was no electric grid. Mr. Edison had to find a solution for transporting the electric current, and he had to create electric grids. After all that, he had to persuade people who had hitherto used only paraffin lamps for lighting that his discovery would be of benefit to them.

Therefore, it is hardly astonishing that a man like Mr. Edison was able to build up such a great fortune. Of course it was largely thanks to the positive *inner forces* that Mr. Thomas Edison had developed more and more for many years. And because of his positive thinking allied to the force of his subconscious mind, Mr. Edison became a powerful and famous inventor whose name is known around the world. (Even my 5th Grade son Lawrence Charles likes to talk about Thomas Edison).

You may be wondering why I have talked at such length about this one man called Thomas Edison. I have deliberately done so simply to draw your attention to the fact that Thomas Edison had no superiority in particular to differentiate him from you. In fact, he had no grand formal education; he had no strong political influence; and he had no great fortune when he was born.

The secret to Mr. Edison's success is that he used the forces of his mind and his positive thinking, and he persevered. So taking into account the qualities and the power that slumber deep within you, imagine what your life would be like if you used only a microscopic fraction of your mind in a positive way. Of course we all need the kind of trust and perseverance that a man like Thomas Edison exhibited.

This new book of knowledge has been designed to help you come up with positive thinking and faith in your power to have, be, or do anything and everything you desire. Yes, you can. In fact, you should know that just stating something positively sets in motion a process helping it to come true. Thus, it is the power of your words that is emitted with conviction and force that creates a true field of positive vibrations that will benefit you. As a result, you will have the peace of mind you surely need. Please have the courage to apply what you have learned from this life-changing book and persevere; then you will be able to see—as if by magic—circumstances becoming increasingly favorable for you.

When that happens, you will easily and permanently have the peace of mind you need. To begin with, you will perhaps believe that it is a question of chance, but believe me; all the great parapsychologists will tell you that chance does not really play a major role in achieving and having peace of mind.

THE SECRET FORMULA FOR SHAPING YOUR DESTINY

Yes, there is actually a secret formula for programming the advent of certain favorable circumstances in your life. This is the secret power to use if you wish, for example, to create harmony and peace in any situation you find yourself. This new book of knowledge will let you realize that repeated mistakes in business and at work or a lack of peace of mind are not always due to chance.

It is therefore necessary to use the secret formula for rebalancing the disruptive influences that are paralyzing the arrival of tranquility in your life. Some of the most potent means stimulating the arrival of tranquility are the prayers formulated by the famous Father Julio, who is no longer with the traditional church.

The 7 Secrets to Peace of Mind was written to let you know that these prayers have worked wonders in the lives of the people who knew the secret. These special prayers will help you to create positive vibrations around yourself that are in harmony with peace of mind, including prosperity, tranquility, inner joy, love, good fortune, and the like.

Scholars and great initiates to members-only organizations claim that Father Julio's prayers are infinitely potent texts. Therefore, whenever necessary, and if it is okay with you, you should say the following prayer to Saint Joseph:

> Saint Joseph, in your goodness, you fed your family through your labor and protected the Blessed Virgin and the Baby Jesus; be gracious toward me and attend to my affairs. Without harming anyone, help me to do well every time the opportunity arises; and grant me peace of mind, good health, good fortune, and prosperity. Amen.

You can also add this formula if you think it is appropriate for you:

> Saints in heaven and good spirits from the world beyond, through your virtue and goodness, put all my enemies to flight and bring me peace of mind, good fortune, good health, and prosperity in all I am planning to do and in everything I am doing. Amen.

Or if it is okay with you, you may add:

> Glory is to the Father and to the Son and to the Holy Spirit Amen.

Even if you have no religious faith, it will help if you say these prayers of intercession every day or whenever you need divine intervention. These are prayers you should always say with faith and conviction. When you persevere, you will surely note positive changes that will bring you peace of mind. These changes will transform your entire life just as it has transformed the lives of those who know this secret.

One example you should remember is that to load all the dice in your favor, you should imitate an actor who is about to step on to the stage.

Why? Because in the universe, everything is vibrating, and as such, your requests should vibrate with emotion. So do not be ashamed to stand in front of the mirror in the morning and recite your dynamic formulas with a firm and confident voice. If Father Julio's prayers are not appropriate for you, you can adapt them, keeping only the words that suit you. You can enunciate positive formulas that you have composed for yourself, or you can use the following examples:

> I command the forces of life to give me peace of mind and
> to obey me.

> I ask the universe to give me peace of mind and all the best
> it has to offer.

> I ask the invisible forces for peace of mind and all the
> abundance necessary to meet my needs in life.

You can also say these life-changing prayers of intercession with faith and conviction for the people you care about. Whether they are with you or they are far away, your loved ones can surely benefit from these powerful prayers.

Each day, sit down or lie down for a few minutes to concentrate on the power of the higher divine spirit that is within you. Then say your prayers accordingly. Say them in the morning when you wake up and in the evening before you go to sleep.

You will fix the positive vibrations by repeating the formula you have chosen for at least seven minutes. At the same time, you should be impregnating yourself with the feeling. Under no circumstances should you repeat your desire in a casual way. The secret is you have to do it with great attention and emotion to actually experience its intensity.

To concentrate the power of your inner higher divine spirit, which is your subconscious, make yourself a list of positive and constructive wishes. They should be the wishes that you really need in your life. These are wishes that will bring you peace of mind, including inner joy and tranquility. This list should include your condition with your family, your condition at work, your home, your social life, your gifts and talents, your finances, the state of your health, and your love life.

Do not be afraid to ask your inner force for anything you wish for. Remember, it is just a small part of the higher force that created the infinite universe that is now 13.7 billion years old and still counting. Thus, rest assured that the same *higher force* will work for your benefit to bring you the peace of mind you need.

For example, you can make your requests in the following manner:

A. I am changing my job. Help me to find a better work in . . . (Indicate the kind of work you want to do).
B. I am depositing an extra $50,000 into my account to be able to buy what I need: a television set, a car, a pair of shoes, a house, etc. (Specify in detail the things you want and conjure up a clear mental image of them.)
C. I am finding love and meeting a partner with the following qualities . . . (Describe the person you wish to meet with his or her physical and moral attributes.)
D. I love to travel. Help me to find the opportunity to travel to . . . (Name the place you would like to visit.) For example, you can say, "I would like to travel to Sierra Leone to visit the beautiful Lumley beach and the other beautiful places of the spectacular West African nation of Sierra Leone."

You may be thinking that this seems too wonderful to come true, but just do it with all the faith you can summon. Above all, carry on without losing faith. When you do that, your wish will be granted accordingly. Please remember that if other people have seen their wishes come true, you, too, will see yours come true.

You never know what path the goodwill of the higher forces of the universe will come by. So be always ready to grab the opportunities that come your way. Please allow me to share with you the story of a young lady who made a request during the time I was doing the research for my counseling psychology program. The young lady made a request she truly believed in. She only asked the divine to help her travel, simply because she loves to travel.

Shortly after she did the silent meditation I suggested, she found a job as a flight attendant with a major international airline. During one of her flights to London, she met a wealthy businessman who fell in love with her and eventually asked her to marry him. In the end, that young lady achieved two of her objectives: she had the opportunity to travel, and she married a wealthy man.

Remember that you never know the path goodwill is going to come by. Therefore, whatever you do, avoid having set ideas about the way in which the result you are waiting for may happen. As soon as you have released the extraordinary power of your higher divine spirit, you will begin to see minor wonders cropping up on every side. Things will happen in your life that you never have thought possible.

This new book of knowledge will help you to have more trust in the power of the *divine*. Never doubt the reality of the divine for even one moment. In fact, it is undeniable that the very fact that you exist is a living proof that an infinite source of divine power and light exists in the universe.

The 7 Secrets to Peace of Mind is designed to remind you of the infinite source of power that is more intense than any other force. Therefore, whatever your material problems may be, you will easily overcome them through your subconscious. You will overcome them by calling upon that *supreme force* that is the infinite source of all life and all things.

Thus, it is very important that you learn how to listen to your intuitive feelings. It is through these intuitions that the infinite intelligence can give you the answers you need most of the time. Therefore, you should always trust your intuition. Your intuition is the inner power speaking to you and wishing to guide you on the right path. Here is a quote from a master in esoteric:

> "Nothing is impossible for the person who knows the vibratory power of his own spoken word, and follows the promptings of his own intuition. Through the spoken word

he activates invisible forces capable of transforming his affairs. Anyone who studies spiritual laws knows that divine abundance answers all requests, and that the spoken word makes it well up."

This new book of knowledge is reminding you that the key to reaching the subconscious is repetition. Please be informed that there are two favorable periods in the day for planting this *seed*. Yes, there are two ideal times of the day when your subconscious can be easily receptive. These two ideal periods are in the morning when you just wake up and at night just before you go to sleep. At these ideal times, your subconscious is in a totally receptive state.

Therefore, you should always let the last thought you have before you go to sleep be entirely serene and positive (even if the reality is different). This is not a matter of you hiding the truth from yourself or deceiving yourself. The psychology is that it is a matter of programming positive circumstances in your life. Many scholars, gurus, and great masters have said that your last thoughts at night recur as the first thoughts when you wake up.

Remember also that your subconscious is there to obey the orders conveyed by your conscious mind (your thoughts) and to carry out those orders accordingly. Always remember that your subconscious does not reason; it does not reflect. It carries out your orders as it receives them. That is why it can be said that some people are able to dictate to good fortune or that they can command certain circumstances in their lives. This may be true about the top 1 percent and most initiates of members-only organizations because they know this secret.

Therefore, because of the knowledge of these initiates, they convey only positive orders to their subconscious. Even when circumstances seem to be against them, they remain confident and wait for a positive outcome to their difficulties. Fortunately, you will now know the secret. This is your moment! Now you know that you, too, can dictate to good fortune and to the favorable circumstances of your life that will bring you peace of mind. However, whatever you do, praise the *almighty God* for the positive results you achieve in your life. Remember also that you can always count on this *divine force* to support you for anything that is truthful, faithful, peaceful, hopeful, joyful, loving, positive, and productive.

Please be reminded that, when you diligently read *The 7 Secrets to Peace of Mind* and do the appropriate exercises, you will surely be excited about the peace of mind and the positive results you will soon have in your life. When that happens, you can count on the *divine power* at all times to support you for anything. What you have to do to continue enjoying the maximum peace of mind, inner joy, and tranquility you need is still very simple. Again, all you have to do is to keep on doing the following exercises:

1. Keep on performing the secret breathing formulas. This will easily recharge you with energy and protective magnetism.
2. Keep on repeating the protective formula for the morning to counter harmful influences and the protective formula for the evening to protect you throughout the night.
3. Keep on repeating the protective shield formulas for difficult situations or verbal onslaughts. Eventually they will be reflexes anchored deep within you.
4. Keep on performing the formulas that will let you have a lovely magnetic gaze and personality.
5. Keep on saying Father Julio's prayers for peace of mind, good fortune, and inner joy at least once a day.
6. Keep on performing any other formula you may choose. Repeat it for as long as you consider necessary for your request.

Your silent meditation or prayer time with the divine should still be at your bedtime at least once a week. Hopefully, you already know what you should do at that time.

Spend at least seven minutes of your meditation time in a quiet place. Think of the help you are asking the divine to give you at that very instant. This is the moment when you are personally subject to the effect of the universal intense positive magneto action. This time the meditation is intended to speed up the realization of your wishes.

Think very hard about what you are wishing for and say, "I will surely get it." All you have to do after that is to believe you will get what you wished for. The psychology is that any reasonable positive desire will come true if you believe long enough. So always believe, persevere, and be patient.

Once again, beware of the seeming simplicity of these formulas. They seem so simple that a bewildering number of people have failed to enjoy the peace of mind they deserve just because they do not believe. The problem is they rushed into judgment and refused to take the time to reflect on these powerful formulas.

Most of those people would rather go on banging their heads against stone walls and obstinately sticking to their blindness. They would continue to create all sorts of distress and depression for themselves, putting their health at risk by failing to believe in the *inner power* that is dormant deep within them but always ready to help them.

Do you still remember my story when I told you that I myself marked time for many years, and yet my *subconscious force* was there, deep within me, ready to help me? All I had to do was call on it to come to my aid, but I stubbornly failed to do so. Had I known then what I know now, these secret formulas would have saved me many tears and much gnashing of teeth.

As for you, I have written this new book of knowledge to prevent you from reaching a point of despair as I did before realizing that within me, there is a powerful *force* that asks only to be used. I hope also that you are ready to make use of your new knowledge of higher consciousness.

Simply because you have read this new book of knowledge thus far and you are doing the appropriate exercises, you have already released the mechanism for your peace of mind. Your subconscious already knows what you need and therefore is working for you accordingly. Hopefully you are prepared to do the exercises regularly for your own good.

Remember also to always persevere in emitting positive vibrations because perseverance is a key to achievement. All you have to do is to perform the secret formulas you now know with confidence, attention, and emotion.

And in all circumstances, keep on doing the secret exercises that have been revealed to you. As a result, your peace of mind will be assured. Subsequently, you will be rewarded abundantly. Above all, *always believe, and never stop believing!*

Do your best not to get very discouraged by attempting to accomplish too much all at once. Therefore, instead of rushing ahead without a good plan, just take one determined baby step at a time. In fact, small incremental accomplishments, improvements, and modifications have a better chance of lasting into a peaceful future. So please take your time, relax, be cool, and be calm.

However, when you pay attention to the secret formulas and follow the suggestions, you will make one of the best investments in yourself. It is an investment that you will get back umpteen times over. This is the investment that will keep on giving until you get the peace of mind you need.

This is your moment to have the peace of mind you really deserve.

Your Peace Is Your Command!

THE 2ND SECRET

THE SECRET FORMULA FOR OVERCOMING ANYTHING AND ACHIEVING ANYTHING

You have the power to discover your divine potential. You will have peace of mind when you believe . . .

Your Peace Is Your Command!

Special Introduction to "The Secret Formula for Overcoming Anything and Achieving Anything"

This may seem surprising, but you actually have the power to overcome anything and to achieve anything. With this knowledge and awareness, the best part of your life now starts. You now have the knowledge to put the cosmic forces to work on your behalf. These are the forces that will quickly bring you the peace of mind you surely need. By putting into effect the easy steps outlined in this insider information book, you will be on your way to a life overflowing with almost all the good things you ever wish for.

"What exactly are these cosmic forces?" you may ask. And what are their secret powers? You may also want to know that the term cosmic stems from cosmosnomy (cosmos = universe and nomy = law). This is referred to as the universal law. This new book of knowledge is designed to let you know the connection between the universal cosmos and your human cosmos, which is your subconscious mind. When you put this powerful discovery to work in your life, you will be in awe, and you will have the peace of mind you need.

Remember that buried deep in your subconscious mind is a force beyond anything you have known before. By tapping into this power, you will quickly turn your life around easily and effortlessly. Everything your heart desires—peace of mind including, inner joy, prosperity, love, tranquility, etc.—will soon come to you.

Research in parapsychology involving many experiments has revealed the amazing and powerful steps outlined in this startling informational new book of knowledge. We also have to thank the work of international organizations, including the United States of America, for their study of the power of the mind. In fact, parapsychology is now a major official science in many Eastern and Western countries.

The 7 Secrets to Peace of Mind is designed to let you compare nature with the subconscious. For example, when you drop a pebble into a brook, circles develop outward. This is a fact of the law of nature. By the same token, when you command your subconscious to follow your instructions, circles of power and thought flow from your conscious being into your subconscious.

Without even realizing it, you may have actually done this exercise before. For example, if you have ever been very upset or worried, you probably closed your eyes to calm yourself. Right then you sent out circles of calm that your subconscious mind picked up, and it made you tranquil. Without you knowing it, these were cosmic forces at work for you.

Think also about the number of times you have thought of a friend you have not seen or heard from for a long time. Suddenly, the phone rings. That very friend is on the line. This, too, is an example of how the waves and circles of your conscious power draw the object of your attention to you, just like a magnet.

For example, one Sunday afternoon I was just thinking of my sister-in-law, Vicky, who I had not seen for a very long time. Then suddenly I bumped into her in a Save Mart grocery store far away from both of our neighborhoods.

"Tony, I have not seen you for a very long time. What are you doing here?" she screamed.

"I should be asking you the same question," I replied.

Most people consider such happenings to be coincidences. But actually, happenings like that are far from coincidences. My studies in psychology show that these examples and many more are telling us something more vital and deeper than we may think. They are telling us that the power of the subconscious mind knows no bounds.

The psychology is that you are at one with nature. You are made of the substances of nature. And as such, you are capable of creating conditions that cause your subconscious mind to obey. In fact, with such capabilities, you can even create miracles. However, to make miracles happen in your life, you should know and understand certain secret principles. Thus, *The 7 Secrets to Peace of Mind* has been designed to reveal those principles to you. This is your moment!

THE SECRET PRINCIPLES FOR MIRACLES

The 7 Secrets to Peace of Mind is designed to let you know about the secret principles to perform miracles in your life. In fact, you will get anything and everything you wish for if you precisely adhere to these principles:

First Principle: Your desire should be realistic. For instance, you cannot wish to be a teenager again when you are already over fifty years old, but you can bring peace of mind, including, romance, inner joy, prosperity, wealth, and true love, into your life no matter your age.

Second Principle: Never expect your wish to come true in five minutes. This can happen, but usually it takes time and perseverance to make good things happen. The most important point, however, is that you should not give up. By doing the suggested exercises outlined in the previous chapter and the ones that follow, you will no doubt see wonderful, exciting, and positive changes in your life.

Third Principle: As you formulate your wish, see it in your mind's eye very specifically. For instance, if you want a promotion, picture yourself being called into your boss's office and him or her telling you about your promotion to the new position you want.

Fourth Principle: There should be a good reason for your wish. For example, if you have worked hard and deserve a better position, your wish will come true.

Another example is if you have been lonely for a long time and deserve true love, you will surely find real love.

Fifth Principle: You should believe it; then you will see it. As Dr. Norman Vincent Peale nicely put it, "You'll see it when you believe it."

The psychology is that you cannot go into the life-revitalizing program without truly believing in it. Therefore, if you are halfhearted, your miracles can hardly come to pass. Thus, all you really have to do is *believe*.

Sixth Principle: Anything you wish for, you should desire it intensely, emotionally, strongly, and overwhelmingly. A slight wish half spoken has a slight chance of coming true. However, when you repeat the suggested steps outlined in this book over and over with intensity, your wishes will surely come into being. *Just believe and persist.*

Seventh Principle: Say and repeat the steps time and time again. Your subconscious needs talking to, so talk to it. It also needs prodding. For example, if you told an unruly child to mind his manners, he probably would not listen the first time. But if you told him repeatedly, he would eventually obey. The same is true with your subconscious.

Eighth Principle: Ask for what you need enthusiastically. Do not be shy. Ask for whatever it is that you need, and almost demand it. Truly believe you have the right to it. When you do that, you will no doubt have the peace of mind you need, including love, prosperity, wealth, and tranquility. The psychology is that the more enthusiastic you are, the more good people and good things come your way effortlessly.

Congratulations. You now have knowledge of the secret principles to let miracles happen in your life. Thus, from now onward, your dreams will come true and your peace is your command!

DON'T STOP BELIEVING

The phrase, "Don't stop believing" is a philosophy you should never underestimate. This is a philosophy that should always be taken into great consideration. Thus, it is advisable to always keep on believing and never stop believing even for a brief moment. In fact, psychology tells us that you can actually attract anything including even prosperity when you believe you are prosperous and when you act accordingly. Therefore, when you follow the suggested secret and powerful steps precisely, you will procure the power and the know-how to attract prosperity like a magnet. You have the right to live a prosperous life and to look good. Do not let anyone tell you otherwise.

Just look around. Every day you see people driving luxurious Mercedes Benz SUVs, Mercedes Benz cars, Mitsubishi Eclipse Spyder convertible sport cars, Chrysler 300 cars, Cadillac cars, BMWs, Hummers, and other luxurious vehicles. The truth is, most of those people are not smarter than you are. They just happen to know the *secret* to attract prosperity into their lives.

When you make use of your subconscious power, you, too, will find prosperity coming into your life almost effortlessly. This is as sure and certain as the fact that the sun will come up tomorrow morning. The most powerful key to prosperity is to mentally see yourself prosperous—not only being prosperous but also enthusiastically enjoying the pleasures of prosperity.

THE SECRET STEPS TO ACHIEVING ANYTHING

Step 1: Mentally see yourself getting the things you need. For example: promoting your lifestyle, taking advantage of money-making opportunities, seizing the moments of prosperity acquisitions, etc.

Step 2: In your mind's eye, picture yourself surrounded with the evidence of prosperity: luxurious cars for you and for your loved ones, beautifully furnished homes, beautiful clothes, expensive jewelry, etc. See yourself taking expensive vacations, enjoying life with your loved ones, running your own business, and buying the things you want. Do not limit in your mind as to how prosperous you can be. The more elaborate your visualizations are, the better it will be in reality.

Step 3: See yourself becoming more money-minded. For example, visualize talking with your friends and relatives about money and prosperity. Instead of you saying to them, "I guess I will never be rich," hear yourself saying, "I am prosperous." But remember, you have to believe what you are saying with all your being.

Step 4: Visualize making and receiving money from all sources, including unknown or even unexpected sources, from part-time businesses, etc. Or even imagine it coming from relatives who leave you huge sums of money. Again, do not limit your picture making. Just believe in your visualization; it works.

Step 5: Spend about twenty-one minutes a day with these dreams. Spend about seven minutes in the morning, about seven minutes in the afternoon, and about seven minutes in the evening just dreaming of your prosperity.

I encourage you to please take Nike's advice and "just do it." Then believe it will work. Why does it work? It works for several reasons. For example, no one in the history of wealth has ever become wealthy by not wanting to be wealthy. Just think about that.

It is much like wanting to make good grades in school. As I tell my children, to be able to acquire good grades in school, they have to want to have the good grades. This means they have to do what it takes to get them. The same thing goes for prosperity. By conditioning your subconscious in a prosperous-minded way, it will go to work for you to see that your wishes come true. This is your moment!

THE PERMISSION TO PROSPER

There are powerful secret habits that will easily permit prosperity to enter into your life. Therefore, to successfully obtain the permission to prosper, you should maintain the following effective habits of the highly proactive and prosperous people:

Habit 1: Always look as if you are already prosperous. For instance, instead of always wearing T-shirts, sneakers, and jeans, when you go out to important places, dress up. You do not have to buy very special expensive clothes for this. Just wear decent clothes and shoes. Always spruce yourself and be well groomed. The psychology is, the more prosperous you look the more people will assume you are prosperous. Remember psychology also tells us that, *that which you reflect comes to you.*

Habit 2: Go to where proactive and prosperous people mostly go. Therefore, instead of just going to the movies, dance parties, drinking bars, and night clubs, instead, go to symphony concerts or other live concerts, the opera, religious meetings, business meetings, business seminars and trainings, business conventions, classic cultural events, etc.

During the intermission, talk with people. Strike up conversations with the people you meet. By so doing, you can make valuable contacts. You never know who might take an interest in you and take you under his or her wing. Those kinds of things happen every day of the year. This is your moment for a good opportunity; let nothing stop you.

Habit 3: Continue to read powerful books like *The 7 Secrets to Peace of Mind* to procure more enlightenment and wisdom. You can go to your local library and check out good books on inspiration, motivation, and self-help. As you continue to read these powerful books, you will also start getting more and more ideas about how to start with a shoestring budget and acquire an empire. You may think this is ridiculous, but far from it. This is the serious truth. The psychology is that, the more you command your subconscious to achieve the things you need in your life, the more prosperity will effortlessly come your way.

Habit 4: If you are an employee, instead of going home immediately after you clock off work, spend some time with your boss in a professional manner. Make him or her feel comfortable working with you and have more professional interest in you. Make valuable suggestions on how to improve the workplace. You might even volunteer to do extra work, or take part in organizing events and activities at work if possible. Of course this may not take up much of your time. Eventually you will be perceived as a person on the way up and a progressive employee.

The psychology is, when you do these things, you will have a decided edge on other employees who always rush home after they clock out. When promotion time rolls around, who do you think your boss will think about? It is you! The secret is people primarily hire the people they like or feel comfortable working with, and they promote the people they like or feel comfortable working with. In fact, all those other things like qualifications, experiences, hard work, etc. are just secondary reasons why people hire or promote people.

Habit 5: If you are not already a student, you should enroll in evening classes or weekend classes if possible. When you do, take courses in self-help, personal development, community development, management, marketing, leadership, social studies, computers, etc. Make an effort to know your professors and talk with them after classes. Quite often you will end up with great leads you can follow up on. Most professors have contact with area leaders. Just think what it would mean if you could meet some of the powerful leaders in your city, county, or state through the connections of your professors.

When you successfully maintain these powerful habits, you will effortlessly obtain the permission to easily prosper and eventually enjoy the peace of mind you deserve.

THE SECRET FORMULA FOR PROSPEROUS LIVING

There are powerful secret formulas that will let you live a prosperous life. To realize the power of these formulas, you should precisely master some steps, such as:

Step 1: To live a prosperous life, you should visualize prosperity at least seven times a day.

Step 2: You should always be fully relaxed as you tap into your subconscious to craft your prosperous living.

Step 3: Picture yourself descending a flight of stairs.

Step 4: Go down each step gently and count down as you go, starting with seven, then six, then five, then four, then three, then two, then one, and then zero. When you get to zero, your breathing should be regular. At that time, you should start your visualization process according to what you need to see in your life.

Step 5: Never try to tap into your subconscious when your clothes are uncomfortable or tight. Loosen your belt or anything that is preventing you from feeling at ease. The science is that the wavelengths from your conscious to your subconscious should not be interrupted with outside influences during this exercise.

Step 6: Now relax, feel good, and then see yourself coming into wondrous and exciting prosperity according to your wish.

All you have to do next is to allow your subconscious to take over your very being and then watch what happens. When you practice these formulas precisely and persistently, you will unexpectedly welcome prosperity into your life. It may not be today or tomorrow, but just believe in the divine power; your prosperity will be manifested speedily and accordingly.

The Secret Formula for Winning at Any Game of Chance

If you ever want to win at any game of chance, this new book of knowledge contains powerful secrets that will help you to be a frequent winner at any game of chance. Do you really enjoy playing games of chance? Do you buy lottery tickets? Do you sometimes engage in harmless betting on the side? Do you sometimes go to casinos? If so, you will improve your chances of winning remarkably by putting your subconscious to work. This does not guarantee you will never lose money, but your chances of winning could soar dramatically. Remember also that winning is by choice; not by chance.

First let us talk about what games of chance are mostly about. We know that some people can become addicted to some games of chance, and we certainly do not recommend this to you. The truth is that real money actually comes through advancement, through other earnings, or through successful businesses but not necessarily from sudden windfalls. However, we also know that the subconscious can create an atmosphere in which winning has a greater possibility of coming about. With this in mind, you should think about the following secrets to winning at games of chance:

Secret 1: Find out how and where others are coming into big money. For example, if you take a trip to Las Vegas, Reno, Thunder Valley, Atlantic City, etc. in the United States or Casino Leone in Sierra Leone, find out from others in advance which casinos, machines, or tables to go to. Some have reputations for having more winners than others. The secret is that you should not go to where the house is known for winning most of the time.

Secret 2: Enter into any game of chance with a light heart. Think of it as something you really enjoy doing. Do not think of it as an ordeal or a difficult task. If you get overly distraught, then you should not play games of chance. The reason is that sometimes you can be so uptight that winnings can be nowhere in sight.

Secret 3: Always stay sober. Be mindful that drinking and games of chance should not mix. Unfortunately, you will find that many casinos generously promote drinking. Do you know why? It is because they know you will take unwarranted risks when you have had a few glasses of your alcoholic drink of choice. Therefore, when you are offered, ask for soft drinks instead. Soft drinks will keep you clear-headed so that you can concentrate on winning instead of drunkenly risking your money.

Secret 4: Try out the various games available and see which one or ones are the most exciting to you. Never mind the fact that your friends like poker best. If you also like it, fine, but if you do not like poker, pass it by. You may prefer blackjack, slot machines, etc. The psychology is, you can hardly win at a game you do not like. Your subconscious knows what you like best. If you go contrary to your basic being, there may be an inner conflict, resulting in you losing instead of winning.

Secret 5: Read everything you can get your hands on about the various games you like to play, whether lotteries, slot machines, black jack, poker, bingo, etc. The more information you possess, the easier it will be to prod your subconscious into bringing "Lady Luck" to be on your side.

Secret 6: Do not fall for the tall tales you hear about or the easy shortcuts to winning. There are none. Fortunately, however, what does happen is that, through some powerful exercises, you will prime your subconscious, which in turn creates a winning atmosphere for you. As a result, you will always win when you truly listen to your intuition.

THE SECRET FORMULA FOR PRIMING YOUR SUBCONSCIOUS

This new book of knowledge has been designed to let you know the powerful secret steps to prime your subconscious:

First Step: Relax. Go down those seven steps described earlier in the secret formula for prosperous living: Count down from seven to zero. When you reach zero, you should be able to breathe regularly and be quite tranquil.

Second Step: Picture yourself picking the right game at the right time. Note those last key words: *the right time*. Tell your subconscious to alert you to the right game at the right time. For instance, many people find their lucky streaks occurring over and over at certain times of the day or night, or on certain days of the week, etc.

Through your experience, you may find that you have more luck at a certain time of the day, such as early in the morning, in the afternoons, in the evening, or even in the wee hours of the night. You will be surprised how your subconscious will tell you when it is the right time for you. Sometimes when *the right time* comes, you will actually feel it. You will really sense it and the intensity can be indescribable.

For example, my sister-in-law told me about one of her friends who discovered that between 12:00 a.m. to 2:00 a.m. are always the best winning period for her. She had tried 4:00 p.m., 10:00 p.m., and even 11:00 p.m., but nothing worked like 12:00 a.m. to 2:00 a.m. for her. She lost some sleep, but her bank account—thanks to the gigantic winnings—got better and bigger.

Third Step: Always ask your subconscious to inform you of how much money to bet at any given time. Notice what happens after doing so. You can be at the game table thinking about betting, let us say $10. Suddenly, a small voice at the back of your mind says, "Make it $5 instead." Always follow your instincts. Sometimes your instincts will tell you to bet more, and sometimes to bet less. When that happens, it is your subconscious mind that is looking after your best interests. Most people who lose great sums of money while playing games of chance do so because they do not follow their hunches. Your hunch, after all, is no more than your inner-mind that is talking to you.

Fourth Step: Ask your subconscious to give you confidence. This is of utmost importance. Always remember that without confidence in yourself, you cannot expect to come out ahead in anything. With confidence, however, your chances improve tremendously. As the saying goes, "Cool-headedness creates winnings." Thus, by telling your subconscious to enhance your ego and to give you a shove in the right direction, you are far more likely to bet the right amount and at *the right time.*

However, one strategic word is needed here. That word is *conservative.* In addition, if you are interested in winning at any game of chance, your subconscious will come to your aid. There is no doubt about it. However, if you honestly do not care for any game of chance, no matter the reason, I truly encourage you to stay away from playing it. The psychology is that you cannot do your best at anything you do not like.

It is like the story of the little boy whose father insisted that he *must* learn how to play football. Although the poor boy does not like football, but to please his father, he attended the football practices anyway. Invariably, he ended up playing in a routine, mechanical manner. There was no inspiration. Why? There was no inspiration because that little boy's heart and soul were not in football. The same is true for games of chance. Every part of your being should be involved in it so that, win or lose, you always have fun.

Therefore, always be truthful to yourself. In fact, always remember that by being true to your own being, you will find peace of mind including inner joy, tranquility, and good health. This is a basic principle of harmony that you should always practice.

THE SECRET TO RAPIDLY CLIMBING ANY PROFESSIONAL LADDER

One of the grandest ways to quickly gain promotions and enjoy any profession is to honestly believe in yourself and make the effort to get ahead. You can do that by working smart as a good employee with a great sense of duty and determination to effectively get the job done in time and accordingly. As a result, you will feel good about yourself, people will also compliment you, and they will look up to you for a good reason.

However, many people who do not know this secret plod along day after day, never getting a promotion. Those are the people who will never enjoy the thrilling feeling of climbing any professional ladder. The question is what is the secret for climbing professional ladder?

Based on studies, research has discovered that hard work has only a limited effect on climbing any professional ladder. What really matters is the psychology of believing in your very self. You can do that by conditioning your subconscious. When you do that, you will be astounded by how your career can take a whole new dimension.

Whereas you may feel stuck right now, the time will come, sooner than you may think, when you will attain promotion after promotion. Or you may decide to leave your present job behind and go on to a brand-new job—the kind of job that encourages growth and enables you to seek that pot of gold at the end of the rainbow.

However, to rapidly climb any professional ladder, you should consider the following secret steps. By doing so, your subconscious will realize that you mean business when it comes to achieving anything. As a result, you will be on your way up faster than you ever thought possible:

1. Talk to your subconscious in a very direct and specific way. Research has discovered that when you say, "I want achievement," your inner-mind does not sometimes understand what you want exactly. Therefore, you have to paint a glowing word picture. For example, say, "I, Matthew, want to relocate to Sierra Leone to serve in the government of my country as a Member of Parliament." By being that specific, the powers within you will guide you through the steps on your way to achieving your goal.

2. Not only should you be specific, but you should also tell your subconscious of the time frame involved. For instance, let us say you know that there is a position in your company to which someone will be promoted in seven months. Say to your subconscious, "I am qualified for that position. I want to be the one to be promoted in seven months."

Of course, your subconscious may not always grant your every wish, but it will show you how to be among the top ones considered for the position. If you don't use your subconscious power, chances are you will be lost in the shuffle. After all, the competition may be great, but with faith in your subconscious, you will be promoted.

3. Because of the importance of this achievement to you, you should set aside three specific times during the day (morning, afternoon, and night) to silently meditate, pray, or visualize getting the promotion.

4. As you visualize, see yourself on the job. Picture your boss telling you about the promotion. Then picture yourself holding down this high-ranking position. Always remember that the more precise the mental picture you see, the more your subconscious will understand.

The psychology is that your subconscious is like a child. You have to guide it hand in hand. You have to be as dramatic and graphic as if you were describing to a child what a wonderful future lies ahead for him or her.

5. Describe in vivid terms to your subconscious why you actually want that position. Is it for more money? Is it for prestige? Is it for the fulfillment of a lifelong ambition? What is it? Again, your subconscious needs details. Make an effort to spend at least seven minutes per session talking with your subconscious. Remember, your subconscious is your friend, so talk to it as if you were talking with a trustworthy friend. Be expressive, friendly, specific, enthusiastic, joyful, and sincere with your subconscious.

6. Always do your best to help your subconscious to help you. For example, if in order to get ahead in your field of work, you need more schooling, tell your subconscious to help you. Find out which school to go to if possible and which courses to take. With the help of your subconscious, you will be surprised by how the right answer can come to you right out of the blue. That is how your subconscious communicates with you. Therefore, what we call hunches or intuition is really the subconscious mind in contact with the conscious mind.

7. Tell your subconscious to help you develop your self-esteem. The psychology is that by increasing the estimate of yourself, you will easily impress other people. As this happens, all kinds of new avenues to achievement will be opened to you. Thus when your self-esteem is fully developed, doors that were previously closed will easily swing open. This is the secret.

The Secret to Cooperating with Your Subconscious

In addition to being in constant contact with your subconscious, there is a need for you to actually cooperate with it and allow it to help you. You can easily achieve this goal by taking the following steps:

1. If you are in business for yourself, read books on the market concerning the line of business you are in. You will pick up valuable tips you did not even know existed. Make the effort to read every day for at least seven minutes. Always remember that *readers are leaders.*

2. Study your competitors and particularly successful people in your field of work or in your line of business. By watching what the successful people do, you will have a better grasp of what it takes to be successful. Never make a decision without first looking around and finding out what others are doing or have done to succeed in the same area.

3. Never quit learning. This noble philosophy may not require formal schooling. You can even learn by just subscribing to trade magazines and newsletters in your field of work or line of business. Remember, just one idea—only one—is all it takes to give you an edge. Let your subconscious guide you to the right subscriptions to take out. By enlisting the help of your subconscious, you will make better decisions. That small voice at the back of your mind will always lead you to victory.

However, it is very astonishing that most people do not make the effort to understand the power of their subconscious mind. In fact, my research and studies point to one thing: people who set aside a few minutes per day to read, communicate with their subconscious, meditate, or pray are mostly more loving, more joyful, more tranquil, and more peaceful than people who do not read, meditate, or pray at all.

I was actually very pleased when I talked with one very successful woman who joyfully said to me, "I used to try to get ahead by following the old saying about flying by the seat of one's pants. Then I found that I was making the wrong decisions. When I saw I needed help, I found it by communicating with my subconscious mind that is so full of force and vitality . . . That little voice that wants me to prosper. Suddenly, as if by magic, I started going up in my career. I owe it all to my constant contact with my subconscious and through readings, meditations, and prayers. Their powers are gigantic."

So always remember, by believing in yourself and in the power of your subconscious, you, too, will eventually gain the promotion you need or the new job you need or you will gain a remarkable increase in sales and profits if you are in a business for yourself. Or you will win the election for any position you run for if you are in politics.

The Secret Formula for Attracting Real Love

You may not be surprised to know that there are hidden secret formulas that can actually attract true love into anyone's life. Nonetheless, you may be astonished to know that one of the saddest commentaries of our way of life in modern society is the number of lonely people in the world.

This is true for both men and women of all ages and in all locations. The sad part is when you think about it very carefully, it is very ironic that there are cities with several thousands of people with literally hundreds of lonely people in that same city. My suggestion to all humanity is that *it is better to be in love than to wish you were in love.*

> *The 7 Secrets to Peace of Mind* is designed to remind you that love is the icing on the cake of life. Love is the main reason for hopping out of bed every day. In fact, it is abundantly clear that it is love that makes the world go round. Remember also that nothing makes anyone feel more alive than being in love. So do not think you are unusual for wanting to be in love. The truth is every human being wants to be in love and be loved.

When you actually want to attract true love, there is one sure answer. It is to enjoy the direction and the gentle guidance that your subconscious gives you. This new book of knowledge has been designed to help you with the secret formula as follows:

1. Picture in your mind the kind of person you need in your life. Now this does not only have to be a rendition of height, weight, color of eyes, etc, it should also be concerned with those qualities you are looking for in your soul mate. For example, maybe you need someone with great sense of humor, someone whose sincerity knows no bounds, someone who has as much love to give as you do, someone who will take care of you, etc.

2. Tell your subconscious everything about the man or the woman you want in your life, and do not be bashful. It is quite normal to want to find someone to be in love with. Otherwise life can sometimes be so lonely, dry, dull, and bland. Sonya Spence put it best in her song, "It Hurts to Be Alone." Believe me; some lonely nights can be so stressful, so resentful, so dreadful, and so poignant. Please do your best to avoid those lonely nights.

3. Ask your subconscious to give you good luck. Yes, I mean good luck. We need good luck because meeting the right person is so often a matter of good luck. For example, let us say you work in a hospital and always have lunch at a small restaurant across the street, but one day you decide to go to another restaurant. Standing in line right ahead of you is a person who smiles at you and you smile back pleasantly. You then strike up a conversation. Soon you find yourself sitting together eating lunch and talking. You then immediately learn that you are both single. Before you know it, you are swapping phone numbers . . . The rest is easy to imagine.

This was actually a true story of a beautiful nurse who works at the Kaiser Permanente hospital. I interviewed her during my research into counseling psychology. Do you think the connection of these lovely people would have happened if fate had not directed that lady to the other restaurant? Psychology however tells us that when fate is given credit, it is sometimes the subconscious mind that deserves it. By keeping in contact with your subconscious, you can make surprising decisions—decisions you would not have made otherwise. Those are the decisions that will lead you to be in the right place at the right time. Some may call it a miracle or chance. However, psychologists refer to it as the love that your subconscious has for you.

4. Ask your subconscious to give you two more powerful qualities: *confidence* and *patience*. During my research, I talked to a lady who has looked for true love for many years. She had almost given up. Then suddenly one day, she was walking in the park in the vicinity of her home when a gentleman of her age approached her and asked if she could tell him what time it was by her watch. She glanced at her watch and simply said, "6:30." At that point she looked into the gentleman's eyes and saw the most wonderful, warm glow she had ever encountered in her entire life. They had some conversation and then became friends . . . To make a long story short; they got married eleven months after that memorable day.

5. With the help of this new book of knowledge, please remember that by faithfully contacting your inner mind, you no longer have to wait for many years to find true love. Now that you know this secret, you can find a loving mate far sooner than you ever thought possible.

   However, it is also important to remember that sometimes *patience* is a necessity to make good things happen. Never give up. Always believe that life can change at any time. What seems like a hopeless, woeful situation today can turn into a hopeful and joyful life tomorrow. This has always been true; and powerful scholars have discovered this truth several times.

6. When your subconscious realizes you need confidence, you will gain that too. For instance, you may think of yourself as not having much to offer. Some people feel this way due to all kinds of reasons. Some feel they are too heavy. Others think they are too old. Others think they are too short. Others think they are too plain. Others think they are not good enough, not beautiful enough, not handsome enough, not educated enough, not rich enough, not strong enough, not good looking enough, etc. *The 7 Secrets to Peace of Mind* is therefore encouraging you to cast aside any negative thought concerning your self-image and just fall in love with yourself. When you fall in love with yourself, others will admire your courage and they will fall in love with you too. The psychology is: *people love those who love themselves.*

7. Tell your subconscious to show you, in an amazing fashion, how to look in the mirror and see a wonderful, desirable you. Before you know it, you will find yourself saying, "I am a nice and good looking person who has a lot to offer." Remember the psychology is that if you love yourself, others will admire you and love you too. Therefore, without self-love, there is a very limited chance that you can find true love. Thus, please take care of yourself and love yourself more than anything but God.

GOD IS HELPING THOSE WHO ARE HELPING THEMSELVES

The phrase, *"God helps those who help themselves"* is a powerful phenomenon that is based on the philosophy that you can actually help your subconscious mind to help you reach your goals. This is your time! Yes, your subconscious mind is eager to enable you to improve your relationship or to find that *just-right mate* you are looking for.

There are several ways you can help your subconscious mind find you a true mate as quickly as possible. Some of the most powerful ways to help your subconscious mind to help you find love are the following:

1. Circulate! Never turn down an invitation to be with others, no matter what, whether the invitations are to ball games, concerts, dance parties, movies, dinners, seminars, organizational functions, and so on. When you go there, even if you did not meet anyone there with whom you could fall in love, you should still make helpful connections. Always remember that people know other people. Even if you did not meet your kind of person in that event, you may meet someone there who knows your kind of person. You could also pick up valuable tips left and right, here and there.

2. Let it be known that you are looking for a true mate, romance, or even just a close friend. As it has been mentioned before, do not ever be bashful. The riches of life are waiting for those who are not afraid to let their wishes be known, so be up front about it. If possible, tell your friends, "I want a true mate. Please help me find one." For example, when my cousin Joshua wanted a soul mate, he told his friends and relatives that he needed one. As a result,

today he is with a very beautiful lady from Sierra Leone (the land of very beautiful ladies).

Another example is, at the 2011 Sierra Leone independence party in Stockton, California, I counseled a beautiful single lady during which I talked with her about the power of her subconscious mind. In response, she told me she finds it difficult to tell anyone that she is looking for a soul mate. Laconically, I said to her, "If you think you cannot do this now, just pray over it for seven days. After being in contact with your subconscious for seven days, you will have built up your confidence to the level where you can easily get the word out to others that you need a soul mate."

Seven months later, the young lady excitedly called to thank me for my counsel. She told me that when she did what I told her to do, in just seven weeks, she met with the exact kind of man she had always wanted in her life. She went on to let me know that everything had been going smoothly since they had met and that they were deeply in love with each other. "The guy is going to marry me!" she exclaimed. That lady is currently one of the happiest ladies in California. I have many more stories that are similar in content, but please let me move on to the next step.

3. Go to where the type of person you want in your life is likely to be. For instance, if you are interested in sports and want someone who shares that interest, you should go to sporting events—My sons Sylvester and Lawrence are the remarkable individuals who have actually drawn my attention to how very interesting and exciting sporting events are—Remember also that when you are looking for your kind of person in sporting events, you should not hesitate to strike up conversations when necessary. The psychology is that it is very easy to connect with people when you share the same interest.

4. If you are looking for someone who is interested in the same kind of entertainment as you, go to concerts, dance parties, night clubs, movies, etc. You can even join some social organizations in your community. For example, you can join Tegloma, the Sierra Leone Humanitarian Project, and the many others. You can make

friends with local deejays, musicians, singers, etc. who can invite you to their events where you may be lucky to meet with the kind of person you need in your life. Again, when you are at these events, talk to the people you meet. Do not stand by yourself during intermissions. Find people to talk with. Remember, people know other people. Someone who may not be your ideal person might gladly introduce you to the ideal person you need.

5. Above all, always smile. This may be a strange or funny piece of advice, but your subconscious wants that glowing, radiant part of you to stand out. And the most wondrous thing you can do is to show the world you love life. You can easily show that by smiling, laughing, having fun, having a light heart, and enjoying yourself. When you hear a joke, remember it and pass it on joyfully. When you see a good show, happily tell other people about it. If you have been to a good movie, excitedly describe it to others. People love people who are open-mined, happy, and excited about this wondrous adventure called life.

The psychology is that you should always put your inner mind—that subconscious of yours—to work. Ask it to help you build your confidence. Ask it also to give you the glow that will attract your true love and soul mate to you.

THE SECRET WAY TO REKINDLE YOUR ROMANCE

There are powerful secret methods that can help to rekindle the romance of your life. However, always remember that into your life, it is natural that people can come and go. Thus, sometimes a person who meant so much to you can suddenly drift away. This may be a wife, a husband, a child, a mother, a father, a brother, a sister, a cousin, a friend, a coworker, a partner, etc.

Why does this happen? Most often, you will later discover that it is because of a lack of heartfelt communications. For example, maybe you had a lover or mate who found another. Your feelings were hurt. As a result, a warm relationship disappeared, and coldness took over your heart. Thanks to your subconscious, you will surely rekindle that romance of your life.

However, to easily do that, *The Seven Secrets to Peace of Mind* has been designed to help you pay attention to the following secret formulas:

1. Ask your subconscious to reveal to you why that dear person in your life has lost romantic feelings for you. You may not know the reason at first, but through the help of your inner-mind, it will be made known to you. For example, suddenly one morning, while taking a shower or while going to work or to school, you may think or say to yourself, "I know why. I know why my lovely Dave or Rosie does not have feelings for me anymore. He or she got tired of my continuous nagging or being overly critical or protective of him or her, or I did not give him or her enough trust or chance to explain." That is your subconscious talking to you. The next thing you should do is to call him or her. Explain the realization that just came to you. You will be surprised how he or she might say, "I have been missing you too. Let us make it up again. Let us give peace a chance. We should rekindle the romance of our lives." This volume is encouraging you to please make that move. You have nothing to lose by making the first move. In fact, you have everything to gain my dear friend. So make that move!

2. Impress upon your subconscious mind that you need romance back into your life. But remember, your subconscious may not sometimes listen unless you are very specific. Let us say, for example, that you need the romantic love of that person back because it gives you joy and it makes you feel good; then tell your subconscious about it. The next thing you have to do is to ask your subconscious mind to give you the strength to contact that person without being ashamed to do so.

Remember now that much of your happiness tomorrow depends on the way you take control of your life today. As the saying goes, "He who hesitates is lost." If you waste time on other things, like watching TV, surfing the Internet, face book, following your ego, chatting on the phone with friends who may be destroying your love life, etc., or if you are ashamed to contact your loved one, or you are reluctant to have a heartfelt communication with him or her, you will find him or her drifting farther and farther away from you. Therefore, it is advisable to take immediate action.

Meet him or her, or pick up the phone and call him or her. Do not be ashamed; be brave. Your subconscious mind will direct you. All you have to do is to count on its power to help you and *believe* you will be together with your loved one again. Always remember that *your success is based on 99 percent of your belief and 1 percent of your interest.*

3. Pray or meditate. Picture yourself and your loved one; the two of you romantically together in love again having the time of your lives. Feel the love that flows from each of you, warming the heart and soul of each other. Do not think in general terms when you are in contact with your subconscious mind. The rosier the picture you paint in your mind, the more likely you will be to quickly rekindle your romance. Always remember that *nothing comes to pass in life if you did not prompt it to happen.*

4. After meditating or praying each time, pick up a sheet of paper. Write in glowing terms why you want to rekindle your romance with that person. Then put it back in your purse or wallet. After seven days, go over what you wrote. Underscore the key points you have written, and then right at that point contact your loved one. Send a text message or an e-mail, call, or meet him or her, and be totally honest.

What I think I should remind you is that so many people in our society today are waiting for the other person to make the first contact. Of course you do not want to be one of those people who may be waiting in vain. So why wait? Love is not a game. Who cares whether you or the other person made the first move? The result will be the same anyway. As soon as the first contact is made, you will romantically share your love together again. Within seven days, neither one of you will even remember who made the first contact. So please do not listen to the "voices of the market." Just do what your subconscious tells you.

5. The next time you are in contact with your inner mind in silent prayer or meditation, hold a photo of your loved one in your left hand. Rub the index finger of your right hand across the photo as you talk to your subconscious. The science is that from your

fingertip, there will be circles of power that go directly to your inner mind, conditioning it for helping you find that love of your life and rekindle the romance you once enjoyed with him or her.

6. When you are finally together again with your loved one, do something new that is exciting or do some of the things you always wanted to do but you were ashamed to do or even talk about. Share your fantasies that can really be hot to talk about. In fact, this is the moment when you should actually talk about the fantasies you would like to enact.

Do your best to develop a sense of intimacy by talking softly or whispering romantically to draw your loved one nearer. Play with each other in the ways that can elicit different romantic responses. While doing that, laugh, and do not stop laughing. Always smile and romantically look at him or her straight in the eyes during most of your conversations.

When you continue to pay attention to these secret methods, you will have the power to overcome any relationship concerns. As a result, your love will always blossom without the help of any psychic or *alpha-man*. This is the secret.

THE SECRET FORMULA FOR BRINGING BACK LOST LOVE

In addition to keeping in contact with your subconscious, *The 7 Secrets to Peace of Mind* is revealing the powerful secret actions you should take to bring back your lost love:

1. Find out as much as you can about the present life of your lost love, such as the following: Where does he or she live now? What is his or her current occupation? Who are his or her current friends? What kind of car is he or she driving? How well or poorly is he or she doing financially? Take some time to really collect lots of information about your lost love.

During my research as I prepared for my counseling psychology program, one woman I interviewed told me her story about a gentleman she had been truly in love with, and he was also in love with her. But something happened and they drifted apart . . .

In short, however, after the lady carefully paid attention to my counsel, she decided, thanks to the guidance of her subconscious, to wait outside the building where her lost love worked. As he got off work one day, she was "accidentally" strolling by. She acted astonished to see him at first, and they eventually exchanged greetings.

At first they were awkward with each other, and then finally the young man said: "Would you like to join me for dinner?" Thus, they went to a nearby restaurant to eat and suddenly, as if by magic, they were back in each other's arms. He later asked her, "How come you happened to be walking by when I got off work?" She replied, "I don't know. Just fate maybe, or it happened accidentally I guess," as she smiled . . . The rest is the part of her story she did not let me include in this book.

2. Vow to yourself that once you get back together with your lost love, things will be different for good. Determine in your mind how things will be better. For instance, if the two of you disagreed on certain issues before, decide that you simply will not bring up those issues abruptly and harshly anymore, whatever they may be. If the two of you were not on the same wavelength when it comes to spending money, sit down and talk it over calmly and amicably. In other words, try something new. Do not fall into the same old patterns of nagging, blaming, accusing, labeling, distrusting, gossiping, cheating, etc.

3. Spend very little time talking about the old bad days and the problems that caused you to drift apart. Instead, talk about your current and future plans for a better relationship. And always talk in glowing and affectionate terms. Describe how you want your lives to be, and amicably ask him or her for his or her ideas. Eventually, by getting him or her to open up to you, you will see why the two of you drifted apart, and then you will know how to make sure it does not happen again.

4. If there are bad memories associated with your separation, do not relive them. Just do your best to avoid them so that they do not open up old wounds. Decide to forget the past, and work to make the future brighter, more beautiful, and all you want it to be.

Again, it will be better if you keep on praying, meditating, and believing. With the confidence and the determination your subconscious will develop for you, there will be nothing to stop you anymore until you bring your lost love back fully into your life again.

However, you have to make your inner mind truly believe that you deserve the inner joy and the peace of mind that the renewal of the two of you will bring. Please know that even though your inner mind is always looking after you, nonetheless, you should talk to it very often and very precisely in prayers or in silent meditations.

YOUR SUBCONSCIOUS IS YOUR INTIMATE FRIEND

This new book of knowledge is designed to give you more tips about how you can let your subconscious be your best friend. Throughout this revealing book, you will continue to find step-by-step procedures to achieve *The 7 Secrets to Peace of Mind*. Please take your time and read everything very carefully. Do not rush; take your time to carefully read *especially* the topics dealing with your subconscious. The power of your subconscious depends on your acceptance of the beautiful, wonderful things your inner mind will bring you.

Honestly, when I started this arduous research on the cosmic forces' secret powers, I did not dream I would come up with such astounding findings. But when I later asked some of my colleagues and some of the people with whom I experimented to put these forces to work in their individual lives, I was even more astounded. Not only did the forces work for them, but they worked in magic-like ways for most of the people I experimented with. Thus, I am excited to remind you that this *force* that is the power of your inner mind is nothing short of sensational. It is really powerful.

However, I also want you to please remember that in a very real sense, your reliance on your inner mind depends on your faith and your belief system. Of course you will no doubt agree with me that the examples abound. Just look around and you will see so many instances of when people suddenly had insights that changed their whole lives for the better. Thanks to their communications with their inner mind, that is also the source of divine power.

During my research, there was a man I talked with who learned how to persuade his son to become an honest person, and he did so with his subconscious helping him. The woman I talked with who found her soul mate did so with the help of her subconscious. Everywhere you turn throughout life, you will find that life is so much richer when you enlist the aid of the power within, which is the divine power. In fact, it has been said that most powerful leaders of nations since the beginning of time used their inner power to make the right decisions. My grandfather—Sir Milton Augustus Margai, the first Prime Minister of Sierra Leone—was one of those powerful leaders in the world.

So it is all up to you now. This is your moment to use your inner power to make the right decisions. This is the time for you to live life to the fullest. You now know that you have the power to overcome anything and to achieve anything. Always remember that your subconscious is your intimate friend and it is always ready to do the very best for you.

As you believe, so shall it be unto you . . .

Your Peace Is Your Command!

THE 3RD SECRET

THE SECRET TO THE POWER OF POSITIVE THINKING

You have the power to change your thoughts and change your life. You will have peace of mind when you believe . . .

Your Peace Is Your Command!

SPECIAL INTRODUCTION TO
"THE SECRET TO THE POWER OF POSITIVE THINKING"

The secret to the power of positive thinking is not just a fancy or vague poetic phrase. This powerful phrase is based on the fundamental principle and the noble philosophy of the power to let go of your old and negative thoughts so that new and positive thoughts can find their rightful place in your new and higher consciousness. This is basically the fundamental concept of replacing your negative thoughts with positive thoughts.

In fact, let me quickly remind you that *thinking is power.* When one lacks the ability to think, he evidently lacks power. Therefore *thought,* being a very powerful phenomenon, is an essential part of you as a human being. Always remember that thoughts have power. Remember also that one of the most powerful methods of having peace of mind is to use the power of your thoughts in a positive way.

However, you may be astonished to learn that the most disturbing problem of our current society is that most people simply just don't think. You may also be surprised to know that out of those who do, only a few think positively. Therefore, *The 7 Secrets to Peace of Mind* has been designed to serve as a panacea to save humanity from such a contagious conundrum.

Please be reminded also that as human beings, we are nothing more than the way we think most of the time. Therefore, if you really want to change yourself and have the peace of mind you deserve, you surely need to change the way you think. Thus, to have a clear understanding of the power of positive thinking, please think for a moment about the powerful words of the great philosopher, Mahatma Gandhi, when he said:

> Keep your thoughts positive because your thoughts become
> your words. Keep your words positive because your words
> become your behaviors. Keep your behaviors positive

because your behaviors become your habits. Keep your habits positive because your habits become your character. Keep your character positive because your character becomes your destiny.

Of course you will no doubt agree with me that Mahatma Gandhi is one of the wisest peace-minded philosophers who ever walked on the planet of earth. You are therefore encouraged to take his words of wisdom into serious consideration while you are changing your way of thinking. When you diligently do that, your peace of mind will be surely assured.

Always remember also that the world can be changed for the better by ordinary people like you and me. When you change your thoughts and change your life, you can change anything; and together, we can change everything. When that happens, there will be a sustainable peace on earth and an everlasting joy to the world. You are the man in the mirror Michael Jackson was solemnly and emotionally singing about. So if you really intend to change the world, *please look in the mirror and let the change begin with you.*

THE SECRET POWER TO ATTRACT OR CHANGE ANYTHING

This new book of knowledge is designed to draw your attention to the following phrases: the power of attraction; the power of personal magnetism; and the power of the mind over body. This volume is also reminding you of the phenomenal energies of the subconscious, the creative forces, and the intellect. The question, however, is how you can mobilize these powerful forces to change your thoughts and to have the peace of mind you deserve.

However, even if you have an idea of what methods to use in pursuit of a sustainable peace of mind, you may not be sure of how to implement those methods accordingly. Laconically, however, the most effective way to achieve a sustainable peace of mind is by doggedly and constantly practicing the exercises suggested in this new book of knowledge.

Therefore, to properly use your power to attract anything, *The 7 Secrets to Peace of Mind* has been designed to take you by the hand through the powerful methods to use. These secrets methods will help you to climb the stairways to your peace of mind step by step and level by level. Remember also that as you overcome each obstacle, you will pass from one state of mind to another. As a result, you will be constantly ascending to a higher consciousness that will give you a sustainable peace of mind through the *magnetic force* that is the secret power of positive thinking.

The Secret Power of Your Personal Magnetism

The 7 Secrets to Peace of Mind is encouraging you to always treat your personal magnetism as if your life depends on it—because it does! You can use the power of your personal magnetism to change anything or make anything happen. Remember also that no one has power over your personal magnetism but you. In fact, no one can touch your personal magnetism, no one can see it, and no one can taste it. No one can even hear it. The power of your personal magnetism is imperceptible. It is like ultraviolet, infrared light, and ultrasound.

This invisible and powerful *force*, which exists in you, consists of radiations given off to different degrees by your body, your look, your voice, your thoughts, and even your mere presence. *The 7 Secrets to Peace of Mind* is designed to help you intensify these radiations, to focus them more, and even to channel them at your own command. Therefore, when you enhance your magnetic potential, your behavior will be effortlessly modified. Thus, your personality and your ideas will assert themselves naturally. When that happens, you will effortlessly shine wherever you are. You will adapt, you will achieve, and you will have luck at all times. Your peace is your command!

Therefore, it could be said that luck can be learned. Remember the words of Albert Camus when he said, "Luck is the ability to immediately adapt to things." However, in order to adapt swiftly and smoothly to situations and to people, you need to be aware of the problems posed by them. Thus, your energy should be gathered together and directed toward a single and precise aim and catalyzed by the ambition to have a sustainable peace of mind.

This new book of knowledge was designed to help you learn that when you combine the powerful elements of *awareness, energy,* and *ambition,* you will easily receive the power of projection that will eventually enhance your personal magnetism. This personal magnetism will then radiate over everything around you. This is the power that will have favorable influence on everything, and it can effortlessly open the doors to peace of mind, including love, inner joy, well-being, and tranquility.

THE SECRET TO REFORMING YOUR WAY OF THINKING

This new book of knowledge offers the opportunity to change your life by reforming your way of thinking. As Dr. Wayne Dyer put it, "Change your thoughts, change your life." Always remember that your brain is a mental mirror that registers and reflects ideas. Be mindful also that ideas have tremendous power. However, in the form of thoughts, your ideas are constantly coming and going, fluttering and whirling around, wheeling past each other, or frequently colliding, never knowing where to land.

Psychology tells us that the average human being has about sixty thousand to eighty thousand thoughts per day. Research has also found that power comes to those who learn how to channel their thoughts and govern them accordingly. When your mind takes command, it brings order to the chaotic and turbulent flock of ideas that are mostly thrown at you by external forces.

The 7 Secrets to Peace of Mind paves the way to the knowledge of how your mind recognizes its role and controls the unruly ideas that fly around your head. This new book of knowledge also helps you learn how to shift through the unruly ideas, select them, and sanction them accordingly. Once you finally have a valid set of ideas organized in your head, then and only then should you take a constructive action. One of the best ways of learning how to coordinate your ideas and how to take a constructive action is auto-suggestion. This is the method that will quickly set you on your way to peace of mind.

The psychology here is to revitalize your magnetic potential that may have been withered or waned. To achieve this goal, you should curb and control your emotions and imaginations that mostly dissipate and waste your magnetic power. You should also alter all your ingrained and automatic responses that make your actions purely habitual and worthless.

Always remember that your reasoning and your intellect should have the biggest influence on how you conduct yourself at all times. Therefore, it is not a matter of mobilizing your willpower to overcome your habits but simply a matter of using your imagination and emotions. Remember also that your personality has two sides to it.

There is your conscious personality, which depends on your intellect, reasoning, and thought. In principle it is this side of you that decides on the value and wisdom of certain actions. But all too often this decision clashes with the dictates of your unconscious personality, which is the seat of all the automatic behaviors that have been instilled in you since childhood and realm of the emotions, feelings, and imagination. Your unconscious personality may reject or modify the decision arrived at by your reasoning. When that happens, your *will* has no more hold on your reasoning, your intellect, or your unconscious personality.

Your unconscious side uses all sorts of means to modify or invalidate the decisions made by your conscious personality. Your emotions undermine your reasoning with over violent reactions. Your imagination exaggerates the difficulties and distorts and magnifies the obstacles. In the end, your intellect is no longer very sure of the true value of its intentions, and you are invaded by a lack of confidence, a certain hesitancy, vague misgivings, or even real fear and anxiety.

Just think for a moment about the kind of emotions that swamp you when you are watching a movie or reading a story. Do you remember feeling as though you yourself are the sheriff, the intrepid cop, or the hero? Have you ever wiped away tears or trembled with indignation? And yet it is only ink on paper or images on celluloid. The thought that makes you ill, the thought that makes you well, the emotions you experience when reading a book, the tears you wipe away at the cinema—these are all due to your imaginations or to suggestions. And as well as having the powers to do things, suggestions and imaginations have the power to undo and replace things.

If your imagination is subjugated to your conscious will, it can create images that, in certain circumstances, can lead your subconscious to abandon old patterns of behavior and form new habits. This is what is meant by discovering your power or higher consciousness. When you discover your power or higher consciousness, your suggestions will no longer be passive, submissive, and dictated by other people or by circumstances. Your suggestions will be active, deliberate, and oriented toward a precise aim. This is what will rid you of all the conditioning that weighs you down and paralyses you. Your suggestions will enable you to develop a new, profitable, and effective way of behaving.

THE SECRET FORMULA FOR RESHAPING YOUR SUBCONSCIOUS

The 7 Secrets to Peace of Mind provides the opportunity to have the knowledge of reshaping your subconscious. Therefore, instead of bowing to every pressure without exercising any discernment or control, and instead of allowing your imagination to run riot, you should ask your imagination to supply your subconscious with words and images that will eventually influence it or reshape it. This is the kind of formula that is also referred to as auto-suggestion.

The question therefore remains, how should you use auto-suggestion in practical terms? What steps should you take? The answer is, first and foremost, you should be calm and learn to control your thoughts as well as your actions. Without a calm and sober attitude, there can hardly be any mastery, inner tranquility, order, concentration, clear, and considered thoughts. As a result, there will be no single-minded or precise action. The psychology is, when you make the effort to reduce tension and agitation in your life, you will be able to control the impulses engendered by your senses and emotions. You will also govern your thoughts and enhance your magnetic potential.

Here is how:

Every day, practice a session of auto-suggestion before you go to sleep. Find a quiet and comfortable place that allows you to be completely relaxed. Sense the heaviness in each of your limbs, and keep perfectly still. Quietly close your eyes if possible. Do not think about anything. Instead, just concentrate on your breathing; feel yourself breathe. As you gradually train yourself, you will be able to attain this relaxed and mentally isolated state of mind more and more quickly. After winding down like this for about seven minutes, then you can begin the actual auto-suggestion formula by using positive phrases like these:

> I am relaxed, I am peaceful, I feel calm, I feel calmer every day, and I am in perfect control of myself. My movements are steady, my voice is firm, and I am in control of my behavior and emotions.

After a while, replace these phrases with images or better still a *film* that reruns the day that has just gone by. Relive that day, and replay in your mind the moments when you were dissatisfied with the way you reacted, or behaved, or when you were too agitated, hasty, or timid. Relive all those moments. Then, replace your actual behavior with the behavior you wish you had displayed and that you will display in the future.

This session does not have to last for a long time. Make it as brief as you comfortably can. Then allow yourself to drift into sleep. The psychology is that the impression made by the replaced images will remain in your subconscious, and the proof of this will be the gradual progress you will see in your life right from the first seven weeks.

However, there is one important point that should be emphasized: *Please stick to positive phrases.* So you are encouraged to always use positive phrases like, *I am . . . I can . . . I am becoming . . .*, etc. Do not use negative phrases like, *I am not . . . I am no longer . . .*, etc. Also, do not use formulae that express wishes, such as, *I want . . .* or worse, *I don't want . . .*

THE SECRET FOR OVERCOMING SHYNESS

The easiest way to overcome shyness is to use your mental power to conquer any feeling of timidity. When that is done, your life will be easily and effortlessly changed for the better. Therefore, you should never be shy at obstacles when you come across them. In fact, they may be the same obstacles that can develop your intelligence, your resistance, your spirit of initiative, and even your magnetism. Some obstacles can even help you to employ these powers and your other powers more productively and creatively.

Your peace of mind—like your whole environment and everything that happens in your life—depends solely on you. Be mindful also that life works with what you do. Always remember that fate is a myth and destiny is never against you. Therefore, it is purely the result of how you face obstacles and how you control your thoughts that you will discover the road to peace of mind and eventually realize your dreams.

Do not forget that every victory is an effort, and every effort is a victory. As one put it, "Certain inferiority complexes may oppress an intelligent and courageous person who is the victim of his or her own hyper-sensitivity. His or her major fear is that other people may judge him or her unfavorably. He or she is afraid of not matching up to others, he or she is afraid of seeming ridiculous."

When you think about that statement very carefully, it is easy to know that the performance of that kind of individual can be seriously handicapped by shyness or timidity and by the great malady called *self-doubt*. Unfortunately and very often, the sex life of that kind of individual is affected. Thus, if appropriate actions are not taken, such a shameful disturbance might lead to impotence or frigidity. Thus, a shy or timid individual, more than anyone, definitely needs to develop his or her personality and self-esteem. Fortunately, *The 7 Secrets to Peace of Mind* has been designed as the panacea for this shameful conundrum.

In the case of a timid person, the increase in his or her personal magnetism will be very spectacular. He or she will easily smash the world in which his or her upbringing and society have succeeded in mentally imprisoning him or her.

When you diligently adhere to the suggestions provided in this new book of knowledge, you will surely chalk up your first achievement, then the second, the third, and so on. Once you have achieved your first goal, this opens the door to further achievements, and these repeated victories will eventually free you from your prison of timidity.

By actively assuming responsibility, you will discover the joy of taking the reins and the glory of achievement, thereby gaining confidence in yourself. And by an imperceptible but infallible process, you will automatically find your new place in your social environment. When that happens, eventually you will no doubt have the peace of mind you deserve, including love, inner joy, good health, and tranquility.

THIS IS YOUR MOMENT!

This new book of knowledge has been designed to remind you that *the most powerful time of your life is right now!* Therefore, your time for action is *right now!* Thus, to properly use your power of the moment, you need to accept and make the most out of any situation in which you find yourself. Always remember that *wherever you are, there you are.* All you have to do is to make the best use of that moment. Therefore, this is your moment to exercise your power of now! This is your time for action. Thus, you should strive to make as great an achievement as possible of every immediate task, purely for the satisfaction of a job well done.

Always bear in mind that nothing happens until something is done *right now!* For instance, it may take you several days of *trying* to perform a task, but as long as you fail to do it *right now*, that task will remain undone. If you really want to change your life, you should always take charge of your moments. As a result, your scope will gradually increase, you will climb another rung, and then a series of rungs, developing your personality as you go, which will give you more power. As one person put it, "Your future is built on your present." So act now; this is your moment!

One thing you should always remember is that *power depends on how you use your mind to act when it is your moment.* When you do that, your ideas will only be based on your inner substance because what you are inside, governs your relationship with the world. That then determines your progress.

When you have grasped this powerful philosophy, you may feel inclined to enrich yourself and deepen your knowledge in some areas you may be particularly interested in, such as politics, business, social activities, spirituality, etc. You should also continue to read *The 7 Secrets to Peace of*

Mind, as your guide and the book that will always give you something to think about. This is the new book of knowledge that will improve your mind to enhance your every moment by doing what needs to be done. This idea reminds me of a poem I read in first grade that reads, *Tick says the clock, tick; tick. What you need to do, do it now!*

Always remember that "procrastination is attitude's natural assassin. There is nothing so fatiguing as an uncompleted task." William James, a founder of modern psychology, said those words, and I whole heartedly agree with the gentle man. I also strongly believe that *it is in your moment of action that your destiny is fulfilled.* This is because, no matter how hard you *try* to do something, it will never be done until you do it *now!* No matter how seriously you decide to do something, it will never be done until you do it *now!* This new book of knowledge is therefore encouraging you to avoid all the troubles of *trying* to do anything and follow Nike's advice to "just do it."

The 7 Secrets to Peace of Mind is also designed to reaffirm the philosophy to always "strike the iron while it is hot." Therefore, when you read this new book of knowledge, read it carefully instead of just rushing through the pages. Underline the main passages that stick out and explain the ideas therein. When you have finished reading, jot down those ideas in a few lines. Review your notes from time to time. By so doing, you will gradually build yourself a store of very useful reference materials to help you when the moment comes.

WHEN TO LET GO AND JUST REST

The phrase, "Let go" is based on the simple philosophy of *letting it be.* This philosophy is a very important aspect of our quest for peace of mind. However, in this competitive economy of today, most people easily forget about the important need to *let go and just rest.* After a period of intense labor, you actually need to rest and relax. But as you already know, this truth is often ignored. All too often you soldier on in spite of your fatigue without taking time out to recuperate.

This volume, however, is encouraging you to never push yourself too far beyond your capability. Try to realize that tiredness is an alarm signal that indicates you have used up all your reserves for the time being. In fact, as soon as you feel tired, you should stop whatever you are doing and just rest for a moment at least.

The stressful issues and strains of a permanently hectic life can eventually wear you out without you even realizing it. Such issues and strains can prevent most people from resting, and what starts as mere insomnia may develop into depression. If people are constantly on their toes and overworking, this might cause psychological problems as most of their energy becomes blocked. It is therefore in your best interest to always do your best to keep your nervous tension within acceptable limits.

Thus, this new book of knowledge is encouraging you to always live in a calm and relaxed manner. Contrary to what many people believe, you will not waste any time (the great phobia of our society) by interspersing your activities with periods of rests. Instead, you will even gain time because when you are refreshed and relaxed, you work better and faster. As a result, your output will be increased accordingly.

Henceforth, when you feel tiredness creeping over you, just do this simple exercise:

> *Close your eyes, and then, using your fingertips, gently massage your temples in a circular motion. Work across over your ears and down toward the nape of your neck, and then stop.*

> You should do this exercise seven times. Then breathe deeply seven times, and then yawn seven times.

When you do these exercises regularly, you will become something that is very rare to find these days: *a calm and relaxed person*. By virtue of this fact, you will be capable of working smoothly and efficiently. Eventually you will create peace of mind for yourself and for the people around you.

The Secret Formula for Having a Good Night's Sleep

Do you always want to have a good night sleep? Of course—we all do. This new book of knowledge reveals a secret formula that will help you to always have your much needed good night's sleep. When problems, nervous exhaustion, worries, or daily cares prevent you from easily dropping off to sleep at night, magnetism can help you to have a sound sleep. There is however, a secret to this. Here are just a few guidelines you should follow:

To relax yourself before dinner, you should have a hot shower or better still, a nice warm bath. The psychology here is to help you forget all the worries that have such a disastrous effect on your sleep. You are therefore encouraged not to spend all evening discussing your worries, mulling them over, and trying to find solutions. Do your best to also avoid any subjects that might cause arguments or disputes.

After dinner, to prevent your imagination from wandering and presenting you with all kinds of specters, listen to good music, watch an interesting show, or read a good book to enrich yourself and to become more cultured, nurtured, and relaxed. These little ploys will get you into the right frame of mind for bed. However, always remember that it is magnetism that will finally get you to sleep. So please do not force it; just relax.

Once you are in bed, stretch out on your back and yawn about seven times. Do not allow your mind to stray. If you do, your imagination will start to run wild. What you should do instead is to focus your thoughts on a peaceful and monotonous image. For example, the pendulum of a clock, waves breaking on the shore, a mountain, a waterfall, the sails of a windmill, etc.

If it is appropriate for you, you can also say the following powerful prayers by a reverend scholar that will help you to have a good night's sleep:

> As I surrender my cares to you, oh God, I enjoy a time of rest and renewal. Day-to-day worries, and the belief that I need to do everything by myself can interfere with my ability to rest and enjoy a good night's sleep. So instead of giving in to worries, I am giving in to you, oh God almighty. Amen.

> Or you may say:

I keep in mind that in order to give the best of myself, I must take care of myself. I am able to experience the peace of mind and body that leads to a good night's sleep and renewal. Thus, I will have a joyful and a more productive life. Amen.

Or if it is okay with you, you may say:

Oh God almighty, you created a world of order—one that requires time for rest as well as time for action. From now on, every time I am tempted to give in to worries, I choose instead to release it to you, oh God, and rest. Amen.

After that, all you have to do is to relax and put your hand (left or right) flat on your stomach (solar plexus). Now, just relax; do not move a muscle, not even a finger. Eventually you will sink into a deep sleep, and you will wake up with a clear and untroubled mind, feeling fully fit and alert in the morning.

THE SECRET POWER TO PROJECT YOUR THOUGHTS

Psychology scholars have referred to the concept of projecting your thoughts as "thoughts projection." This concept is a powerful method that can develop maximum power to attract anything. It is just as real and as evident as X-rays. This kind of method can even be used as a means of communication. Your thoughts produce vibrations that are propagated like electromagnetic waves, electricity, and light.

Each thought, voluntary or involuntary, creates thought vibrations that radiate through space. When the thoughts encounter a particular person, they influence that person's behavior. That is why when you come into contact with someone you might feel sympathetic, attracted, constrained, uneasy, or even hostile.

That is why a particular person can create a depressing or a stimulating atmosphere. For example, you can by a great effort of mind, send your thoughts in a specific direction. By focusing your thoughts, you can channel and project your thought vibrations and establish an unbroken link between yourself and other people, things and events. You can also establish an unbroken link between two people even if they are miles apart.

However, for you to project these focused thoughts effectively, you need to have a strong magnetism. For example, if you want to have progress in your professional life or in your love life and get what you want out of someone, you have to conjure up an image of the person you want to influence. Then imagine the person behaving in exactly the way you would like him or her to behave toward you.

Once you have properly focused your thoughts, the image should be perfectly clear. The vibrations will beam out and reach the mind of the person you want to influence. The more forcefully you transmit those vibrations, the faster and stronger their effect will be. Therefore, the power and cohesiveness of your thoughts and the intensity of your magnetism can determine your achievement.

THE SECRET FORMULA FOR MAKING ANYONE FALL IN LOVE WITH YOU

The 7 Secrets to Peace of Mind reveals the secret to make anyone fall deeply in love with you. This exercise is similar to the formula for projecting your thoughts. You can also triumph in love by learning the psychology of appealing to the people you like. You can apply the same method for irresistibly attracting the people you are fond of.

To be able to successfully achieve this goal, make yourself comfortable in a peaceful and quiet place. You should choose the time when you know the person you want to appeal to will be asleep or the most calm and relaxed and therefore receptive. Then proceed as follows:

Imagine this person in the way you would like him or her to be, whether it is leaning toward you, clasped in your arms, head resting on your shoulder, strolling romantically by your side, etc. Then think hard—really hard—until you see the person near you. Talk to the person very softly while thinking very hard about the words you wish to say to him or her and the replies you hear—replies you can invent as you wish. At this moment, a kind of telepathy will occur. When that happens, with a bit of belief, faith, patience, confidence, and perseverance, you will find that the person will gradually develop a warmer attitude toward you. Eventually your desires will be fulfilled just as you projected in your mind.

When you practice this secret formula accordingly, you will not have any need to consult anyone else on how to find a real love, how to make your love blossom, or how to even rekindle old flames. In fact, you should be reminded that there is no one in the world who is better placed to find you a real love than yourself. It is only you who knows the person you need in your life at any given time. This is perhaps what a Sierra Leonean singer meant by: "It is only you who knows why you love your banana."

THE SECRET TO BEING IN HARMONY WITH YOUR FRIENDS

The concept of being in harmony with your friends means having something in common with others. This is the idea of giving to others and hoping to receive something in return. Remember, however, that *honesty is an important component in any harmonious friendship*, and friendship is a give-and-take affair. So, because friendship is a give-and-take matter, a balance needs to be found or created. As my lovely wife, Mrs. Isha Charles, would say, "Friendship is a fifty/fifty business."

However, when you have a powerful magnetism, it will certainly help you to attract sympathy and influence opinions. Remember also that more mutual respect, ideas, and agreements are needed to create a harmonious friendship. To be successful in doing so, you should adopt certain attitudes.

Here are some of them:

First, you should banish any egocentricity that causes you to impose your own ways and views without respecting the ways and views of others. Always remember that true friendship requires an equal amount of *give and take* on both sides. Never forget that everyone has a sense of his or her own values that may be real or imagined and wants those ideas to be recognized. You should also be prepared to accept that other people can have different opinions from yours. Similarly, do not set yourself up as a critic and be automatically disapproving without first trying to put yourself in the other person's shoes.

When a friend does something, ask yourself the following questions and answer them honestly before you criticize him or her: Would I do it any better? Would I do it differently? Does it matter anyway? Always respect other people's opinions. If you really want to be a true friend, you should not impose, and you should not judge.

The best things you should do for your friends when they tell you their concerns are to listen and to truly pay attention. This new book of knowledge has been designed to let you learn that the fact that you are someone's friend does not authorize you to give advice when you have not been asked for it. Please be informed also that your friendship with someone does not qualify you to ask him or her awkward questions or to commit indiscretions.

If you really want to help, what you should do is to just listen to your friend and honestly pay attention. Perhaps the most important thing your friend actually needs is someone to talk to; or someone to listen to him or her. Therefore, you should just listen keenly and pay full attention until you truly understand what your friend is telling you. Thus, it is only after a full comprehension of the situation that you should ask for the permission to say anything concerning the issue.

This new book of knowledge is also reminding you to always think twice before sharing anything in confidence with your friends that you might regret later. If you do this, you will gain true, sincere, and devoted friends on whom you will rely and who you will be glad to meet during good times and bad times.

Do not ever forget that friendship is a balance. Therefore, you should make sure you or your friends do not tip the scales too far one way. Remember also that negative feelings can weaken your magnetic power and can eventually end up destroying it irrevocably. Thus, you should do your best not to be very negative with your friends without a good reason.

Please take the following tips into serious consideration when conversing with your friends: Do not try to hog the center stage all the time. Always make your words simple, clear, and precise. Do not drown your friends with superfluous or excessively personal details. Never, ever turn the conversation to a subject that could hurt or embarrass any of your friends. Finally, do not subject your friends to a recital of all your woes. In fact, you would do better to forget your woes rather than revive them anytime you are in conversation with your friends.

THE SECRET WAY TO SUCCEED IN ANYTHING YOU DO

Yes, you can actually succeed in anything you do if you change the way you think about it and honestly put your mind to it. In actual fact, succeeding in anything you do is much easier than you may think. Always remember that your magnetism shows through everything you do. It shows through your voice, your look, your thoughts, your attitude, etc.

All these factors should convey self-assurance, confidence, and a perfect resolution to the person you are communicating with. As such, the person will be impressed and will start to listen to you. Subsequently, he or she will have your respect and then your command.

You can also use this secret method to influence a superior, a friend, etc. It works in other situations too, such as convincing a seller or a buyer. All you have to do is empty your mind and then concentrate hard on the following phrases as you repeat them to yourself:

> I am the master of my thoughts. I will succeed in anything I do. I have huge possibilities. I can dominate all situations.

Then you can go ahead and talk to the person in question, as explained in the section entitled "The Secret Formula for Making Anyone Fall in Love with You." What you need to do now is to flood your subconscious with positive and constructive thoughts that will be beamed to your target, as though from a transmitter.

Your Peace Is Your Command!

THE 4TH SECRET

THE SECRET FORMULA FOR PROSPERITY AND INNER PEACE

You have the power to let your inner light shine through you. You will have peace of mind when you believe . . .

Your Peace Is Your Command!

Special Introduction to "The Secret Formula for Prosperity and Inner Peace"

The 7 Secrets to Peace of Mind is designed to be a precious tool in your quest for prosperity and inner peace. This is an invaluable source of help that will enable you to lead a serene and peaceful life. The secret formulas revealed in this volume are dated back in a straight line to ancient times, to a four-thousand-year-old tradition of initiates versed in parapsychology and gifted with sharp insights.

These powerful gurus devoted their existence to exploring and preserving spiritual knowledge, as well as the extraordinary power it confers. This esoteric tradition is therefore the guarantee of the ancestral wisdom of which it is the heir, protecting it from those who are not prepared to use it with respect or who might abuse it.

One of the main purposes of this new book of knowledge is to enlighten all humanity in the new era of higher consciousness about this powerful secret formula for prosperity and inner peace. This secret formula, although it has a scientific dimension, embodies an authentic lifestyle marked by the ease of access it provides to prosperity and inner peace.

Therefore, if you want to live a prosperous life filled with purpose and passion, *The 7 Secrets to Peace of Mind* is your book of guidance. This volume is full of practical apparatuses and secret formulas that will bring out the best in you. This new book of knowledge is also composed of fascinating exercises that will help you to escape the mistakes many people are currently making in modern society.

The Secret Power of the Ancient Magi

The ancient magi, also known as the first wise men, possessed a profound knowledge of the material and spiritual laws that govern the universe. They used their highly developed power of sharp insight to communicate with the universe.

This was the group of very intelligent people who understood that the great mysteries of life and human nature held no secrets for them. In fact, the three wise men—Gaspar, Melchior, and Balthazar, also known as the three wise kings—who visited Baby Jesus at his time of birth in Bethlehem were also from the group of the ancient magi.

The ancient magi saw very early that a greater fraction of human beings had very low consciousness. This large majority of human beings really did not know who they were and they did not even know what they were doing because a sort of fog cut them off from their divine nature. Thus they were prevented from achieving the prosperity and the inner peace that was their birthright.

These ancient magi on the other hand, were powerful sages who were masters of their own destiny. They knew from the beginning that everything that exists is a manifestation of the divine power called God. Those ancient magi were not separate from the rest of the creation. In fact, they saw themselves in everything. These gurus knew the secret that they were one with God. Thus, they see God in everyone and in everything.

It was Mother Theresa who said, "I saw God in each and every one of those hungry children in the streets of India." Similarly I say to you, that there is God in each and every one of those children, men, and women whose hands and feet were painfully amputated during the rebel war in Sierra Leone. Surely there is God in the people who are still suffering in Sierra Leone and Liberia because of the senseless rebel wars they lamentably went through for many years. (Please help Sierra Leone and Liberia however you can). *The 7 Secrets to Peace of Mind* is also encouraging you to acknowledge your oneness with God, wherever you may be.

As for the ancient magi, because they fully realized their oneness with the almighty God, they enjoyed immense powers, including the power to travel in their mind beyond the boundaries of time and space. In this way, they reached the understanding of what—regardless of time or place—prevented many other people in society from having peace of mind and living in nirvana.

Then, as a means of helping the rest of humanity to find their way back to the path of light and higher consciousness, and to achieve prosperity and inner peace, the ancient magi constructed a way of living based on four major principles. Each of those four major principles represents fundamental principles of living.

The 7 Secrets to Peace of Mind is therefore designed to discuss those principles that will let you discover the deep secrets of life. These secrets have power to open the doors to prosperity and inner peace. From this new book of knowledge, you will also learn about what generates all the problems, trials, and sorrows in the life of humanity. Those are the problems that have caused many people great unhappiness and distress in modern society.

THE DREAM OF HUMANITY VERSUS REALITY

To take full advantage of your dreams, you should make an effort to understand the secrets of the dream of humanity versus reality. Please be reminded that this new book of knowledge has been designed to also draw your attention to a concept that is hardly questioned: Here I am referring to the term reality. The truth is, what is usually referred to as reality is in fact a continuing dream. You may think it is quite disconcerting to learn this, but it is really the truth. The psychology is that anything you see, feel, or hear at any time is actually just a dream played by the waking brain.

Please be reminded that dreaming is your mind's principal function, and it does it twenty-four hours a day. It does it when you are awake and it does it when you are asleep. The difference is that in the waking state, your frame of reference of the material world makes you see things in continuum in a linear fashion. But when you are sleeping, it no longer has that frame of reference, so the dream tends to change constantly. But this is not a fundamental difference. It is common among human beings to dream constantly, believe it or not.

According to the ancient magi and modern philosophers, society is simply the product of a collective dream resulting from millions of smaller and individual dreams. Together these dreams form a family, a community, a town, a country, and a continent. This is what finally forms the dream of all humanity. This dream comprises all society's rules, laws, religions, cultures, lifestyles, governments, and social events.

The 7 Secrets to Peace of Mind is designed to let you know that everyone is born with the capacity to learn how to dream. Those who go before us teach us how to do it in the same way their society dreams. So when a new child is born, we also capture its attention and induct it, through the intermediary of the parents, schools, religion, etc. We place these principles in the child's mind that are in fact our own principles.

Be reminded however that attention is the ability to be selective and to focus exclusively on what you want to perceive, just as you are doing now while you are reading this book. Remember also that your brain is capable of perceiving thousands of things at the same time; but by paying attention, you can keep what you choose to keep at the front of your conscious mind. When you are a child, the adults around you capture your attention and introduce information into your mind through repetition. This is how we learn most of the things we know.

By using your capacity for attention, you have acquired an entire reality that may also be a whole dream. You have learned how to behave in society: what to think about, and what not to think about; what to talk about, and what not talk about; what is acceptable, and what is not acceptable; what is good, and what is bad; what is beautiful, and what is ugly; what is right, and what is wrong; who is black, and who is white; etc.

One very important notion this new book of knowledge has been designed to bring to your attention is that, before you came to this world, everything was already there. All the knowledge, all the rules, and all the ideas about how to behave in society, existed long before you were born. For example, at school, your attention is focused on what the teacher is telling you to do and what not do, and the same thing happens at home with your parents, your brothers, your sisters, etc. Everyone endeavors to gain your attention. For instance, my older children, Tonia, Tony, and Sylvester, are perpetually trying to gain the attention of their brother, Lawrence, through their numerous commands on how to do this or how to do that, how to behave this way or that way, etc.

As for you, you might not know this, but when you were very young, a whole group of people tried to gain your attention too. Likewise, you, too, have learned to capture the attention of others and you have also developed a need for attention that has become highly competitive.

I am sure you will have noticed how children always fight for the attention of their parents, brothers, sisters, teachers, friends, etc. Some of them may say things like, "Look at what I'm doing. Hello, here I am, over here." Children's need for attention becomes stronger and stronger, and it is most of the time perpetuated into adulthood. Fortunately, this new book of knowledge will enlighten and guide you to know how society has captured your attention and how you shall finally be free.

How Society Has Captured Your Attention

In a nutshell, your agreement to the dream of society is how society has captured your attention. Giving your agreement to the dream of society is the way the dream of society has captured your attention. Then it teaches you what you should believe, starting with the language you speak. As you may already know, language is the code of understanding and communication between human beings. Every word of your language represents a point with which you are in agreement.

For example, you say that an object is a chair; this means that the word chair is a term with which you are in agreement. The psychology is that every time you see that object, you recognize it and identify it as a chair. Once you understand the code, your attention is captured, and then during a conversation, there is a transfer of energy from you to the others who understand the same code.

The 7 Secrets to Peace of Mind is therefore reminding you that you did not even choose to speak your native language or dialect, whether it is English, French, German, Spanish, Arabic, Mende, Temne, Limba, Kono, Creole, Sherbroo, Fullah, Madingo, Vai, Soso, Loko, Koranko, Yarunka, Benin, Vietnamese, Chinese, Tagalong, Japanese, Korean, or any other language or dialect. Neither did you choose your religion when you were a baby. Unfortunately however, when you were still very young, society inducted you into all those things accordingly.

As you already know, all those things were already there before you were born. You did not choose even the tiniest thing to which you have given your agreement; you did not even choose your name. When you were still a child, you did not have the option of choosing your religious beliefs. Thus, without any knowledge and by no fault of yours, you gave your agreement to the information that was transmitted to you by the dream of the society into which you were born.

However, this new book of knowledge is designed to actually draw your attention to the fact that *the only way of retaining any information is to be in agreement with it.* The dream of society can capture your attention, but if you are not in agreement, you will not retain the information. In the same way, you may find what you are reading now interesting, but if you do not give your agreement to the secrets and the vital information this new book of knowledge is revealing to you, you will not retain them.

That is how we all learn when we are little children. In fact, from the moment we are in agreement, we believe in everything adults tell us. We are in agreement with them. The fact of believing unconditionally is so strong that this belief system controls the whole dream of our lives. What psychology is telling you is that you did not choose those beliefs, and therefore, in theory, you can rebel against them. But if you are not strong enough for such a rebellion, the result is a submission to predominant beliefs with your agreement.

Modern philosophers and even the ancient magi referred to that kind capture as, "The process of domestication of human beings." As a result of that domestication, you learn how to live, what to dream, and how to confront reality. Over the course of your domestication, the information about society's dream is transmitted to your personal dream and eventually forms your whole belief system. As children, we are taught the names of persons, places, and things like: Ada, Isha, papa, mommy, daddy, aunty, McDonalds, Bo, school, home, room, milk, toy, dog, pen, bed, car, book, uncle, car, etc.

Day after day, at home, at work, at school, on television, etc., we are told how to live and what constitutes acceptable behavior. Society teaches us how to be normal human beings. This is how we learn to judge. This is how we judge ourselves, others, the people we love, our neighbors, the government, etc. In fact, thinking about it very carefully, you could even say that as children we are domesticated almost in the same way as cats, dogs, or any lower animal. When you are training a dog, you tell it "off," punish it, or reward it according to its performance. Similarly, education trains us in almost the same way as we train a pet—through a system of punishments and rewards.

WHY DO WE PRETEND TO BE SOMETHING WE ARE NOT?

The concept of pretending to be something that we are not is one of our major roles in the drama of society. When we were children, our parents used to say to us, "What a good boy" or "what a good girl you are" when we did what Mama or Papa wanted us to do. When we did not do the things they wanted and instead did the things we wanted, we were punished. Every time we broke the rules, a punishment followed. When we followed the rules correctly, we were rewarded. Sometimes we were punished and rewarded several times in a day.

Soon we started to fear being punished or not getting our rewards, which often took the form of getting the attention of our parents, brothers, sisters, teachers, friends, etc. So we thought we needed to get the attention of others to obtain this reward; this is the gratification we get from feeling alive and loved. Thus, we carry on doing what others want us to do as long as we obtain this gratification that makes us feel good. Just because we are afraid of being punished or not being rewarded, we pretend to be something that we are not. We tend to do that to please others, to appear good in the eyes of others, etc.

Thus, by trying to please others, including our parents, friends, teachers, bosses, parish priests, pastors, and so on, we started to play roles. We tried to be someone we are not; out of fear of rejection. This fear then turns into the fear of not being like we should be, not being good enough, not being beautiful enough, not being smart enough, etc. Ultimately we become people other than ourselves. We become copies of the beliefs of others, including our mothers, fathers, spouses, friends, society, religious leaders, etc.

This new book of knowledge has therefore been designed to let you know how all your natural instincts from birth have been lost over the course of your domestication process. Then you reach an age at which you start to understand; you learn the word "no." This is mostly the first word we learn because it is constantly repeated by our domesticators any time we attempt to do anything we want to do as children.

And as you said "no" to defend your freedom, because you wanted to be yourself but you were too little, the grown-ups were too big and strong. Thus, their big "NO" always overrules your little "no" and you are punished if you disobey. The result is that after a while, you started to live in fear because you knew that every time you did something wrong, you would be punished.

So, with their immense understanding of human psychology, the ancient magi saw that this domestication process was so strong that there will eventually come a time in our lives when we will no longer need anybody to domesticate us—not a mother, father, school, religion, etc. When that time comes, you will be so well trained that you become your own trainers. Thus, you will no longer be aware that the fear of not being loved or good enough conditions most of your actions. At this point you can domesticate yourself according to the same belief system into which you have been indoctrinated, using the process of punishment and reward.

For example, you punish yourself when you do not abide by the rules of your belief systems, and you reward yourself when you adhere to them. This belief system is like the *book of the law* that guides your mind. Everything contained in this book of the law is your truth, without a shadow of a doubt. All your judgments are founded on the rules inscribed in this *book of the law*, even if they go against your own inner nature and your interests. One by one, all the agreements that you give are incorporated into this *book of the law* that eventually guides your life.

WHY DOES SOCIETY JUDGE EVERYTHING?

The idea of judging everything is a psychological concept of what some scholars have referred to as "The judge and the victim" in the dream of society. *The 7 Secrets to Peace of Mind* is designed to let you know that it is very important to understand how this concept of the judge and the victim in the dream of society works. This is how it works: one part of your mind judges each and every thing from the weather, to your neighbor, to the government, to your children, to your spouse, to your parents, to your teacher, to your boss, to your doctor, to the dog, etc.

The psychology is that the inner judge uses the contents of your own book of the law to judge everything you do or do not do; everything you think or do not think; everything you feel or do not feel; everything you say or do not say; etc.

Basically, everything is subject to the tyranny of this judge. Every time you do something that goes against your book of the law, your inner judge finds you guilty. This means you must be punished and feel ashamed. This happens several times in a day. It happens day after day, week after week, month after month, and year after year.

In parallel to this, another part of you, which we call the victim, is at the receiving end of these punishments. This is the part that suffers the rebuke, the guilt, the shame, etc. This is the part of you that says, "Poor me, I'm not good enough, not intelligent enough, and not good-looking enough; I don't deserve to be loved. I don't deserve to be joyful, etc." As such, you are preventing yourself from having the inner peace and prosperity you truly deserve.

The sad part is, all these come from a system of beliefs that you never even chose. These beliefs are often so strong that even years later, when you discover new ideas and try to make your own decisions, you realize just how much they influence your life. Anything that goes against these beliefs makes you feel fear. In fact, questioning these beliefs or contravening them, acts as an emotional poison, generating feelings of insecurity.

Even if your personal book of the law is wrong, it still gives you a feeling of security. Thus, our belief system, even if not of our own choice, is nevertheless something to which we have given our agreement. The influence of our belief system is so strong that even when we understand, in principle, that these beliefs are not true, we still feel guilt, shame, and criticism every time we break the so-called rule.

In the same way as a government has the law that controls the dream of its nation, your belief system is the book of law that guides your reality and your dream. All these laws exist in your head. You believe them, and your inner judge bases everything it says on them. The judge hands down a ruling, and the victim suffers the guilt and the punishment.

However, this new book of knowledge has been designed to let you know that true justice plays no part in this. The inner judge that is in every individual is wrong because the book of the law is false. You may be surprised to learn that 95 percent of the time, the beliefs etched on our minds are nothing but lies, and we continuously suffer from these lies.

After a long observation of humanity and its way of functioning, the ancient magi and some modern philosophers saw that the reason life is so difficult is because it is governed by fear. There is not a corner of our world today that is free of human suffering, anger, feeling of revenge, street violence, war, rebellion, etc. All of these are just reflections of a dream of injustice.

Religions often say that hell is a place of punishment, fear, pain, and suffering. Others say that hell is a place where evildoers are burned by fire. Fire burns from emotions born of fear. For example, every time we feel anger, jealousy, envy, or hate, we feel something burning within us. Therefore, we are perpetually living in an inferno. In fact, if you think of hell as a state of mind, then it is present all around you. No human being can condemn another to hell because humanity is already there. Fortunately however, *The 7 Secrets to Peace of Mind* has been designed to free you from this inferno and eventually take you to nirvana.

Every individual has his or her own personal dreams, and like society's dreams, your personal dreams are usually governed by fear. Of course, all of us experience the same fear in different ways, but we all feel anger, jealousy, hate, and other negative emotions one way or the other. However, this new book of knowledge has been designed to guide you all the way to nirvana. This is your moment!

THE ILLUSION OF FALSE BELIEFS

The truth is, all of humanity is seeking peace of mind, including love, respect, truth, tranquility, beauty, unity, freedom, and justice. We are on a continual quest for the truth because we only believe in the lies that are etched on our mind. We search for justice because it does not exist in our belief system. In fact, it honestly does not even exist in modern society.

Therefore, you never cease searching when in fact what you search for is already within you. All you need to do is to faithfully look deep inside yourselves to know your true nature. On page 353 of his book *Change Your Thoughts—Change Your Life: Living the Wisdom of the Tao* (Hay House, 2007), Dr. Wayne Dyer magnificently summed up Loa-Zu's legacy in the words of T. S. Elliot, from his poem "Little Gidding":

> *We shall not cease from exploration*
> *And the end of all our exploring*
> *Will be to arrive where wse started,*
> *And know the place for the first time.*

Thus, to really have a sustainable peace of mind, you should look inside yourself and focus on your true nature. This is the secret.

The ancient magi who were delivered from false beliefs knew this secret. In our current society, we do not find the truth because we cannot see it, obscured as it is by the agreements we have given and the false beliefs that clutter our minds. Human beings always have a need to be right and consider others wrong. We have confidence in our beliefs, and the fact is that it is these beliefs that sometimes condemn us to most of the sufferings we undergo.

In fact, for some people, life goes on as if they were moving through a sort of fog—a fog that is not even real. It is a fog that is nothing but a dream that is a personal-life dream made up of our beliefs, the ideas we have about what we are, the agreements we have made with others, ourselves, and even with society.

Do you now see what we really are? We do not even perceive that we are not free. Most people resist life, fearful of speaking the truth. As a result of that, peace of mind, inner joy, and true love are absent from their lives. Thus, such individuals are obliged to struggle constantly just to keep what they have or keep their suffering to a minimum. Simply being themselves is what most people fear most. They have learned to live by forcing themselves to meet the needs of others, to live according to the point of view of others out of a fear that they will not be accepted or that they will not be good enough in the eyes of others.

I am always proud of my son, Tony Charles. When he was leaving home for the first time to pursue his university education, my wife and I were very concerned about him going away from us. Our concern was based on how some college students would constantly strive to live according to the point of view of their colleagues so that they can "fit in."

When Tony knew that we were concerned about him, he clearly said to us, "Mom, Dad, you guys should not have such a concern. I am fine. I will never follow bad guys. I know who I am, and I will always be myself." That powerful statement made us happy, and to date, we are very proud of our son for focusing on his true nature.

This kind of frame of mind of focusing on who we are is what is recommended for all humanity in modern society. Fortunately, *The 7 Secrets to Peace of Mind* is designed to remind you that you not only have the power to change the way you see yourself, but also have the power to change the way the world sees you. Above all, do not ever lower your self-esteem.

HOW FALSE BELIEF HAS AFFECTED YOU

Without any doubt, false belief has a powerful effect on humanity, and it can definitely influence the way you live your life. The question is how has this false belief come to form part of your life? The answer is that it is part of your domestication process. You may not remember it, but you devised an image of what constitutes perfection so that you could always try to do the perfect thing to impress others.

You created an image of how you should behave so that you could be accepted by society. You also created an image of how you should specifically please your parents, spouses, brothers, sisters, friends, teachers, coaches, spiritual leaders, political leaders, bosses, etc. As such, and by trying to do the perfect things to impress others, you constructed images of perfection that are impossible to achieve. You created images that are not real, and therefore, you will never achieve perfection in this way. Believe me, there is nothing you can do to satisfy everybody, no matter how hard you try. So please just do your best and move on.

Remember also that by not being perfect, you have a tendency to reject yourself. As a child, your degree of rejection depends on how efficiently adults succeeded in destroying your integrity. Basically, once the domestication process is completed, it is no longer a case of doing the right thing in the eyes of others. From that time onward you are not doing the right thing because you cannot conform to your idea of perfection.

As a result, you are unable to forgive yourselves for not being as you would wish to be. You cannot forgive yourselves for not being perfect, so you feel wrong, frustrated, and dishonest. You try to hide it by pretending to be someone you are not. The result is that you lack authenticity and you wear social masks to ensure that other people do not see you for who you really are. You are so afraid that someone will discover that you are not who you pretend to be. Of course, you also judge others according to your own idea of perfection, and obviously, they also always fall short of your expectations.

The psychology is that *nobody can perfectly satisfy anybody.* The secret this new book of knowledge is revealing to you is that true justice actually consists in paying for each mistake once and once only. But because of your false beliefs, you punish yourself indefinitely for not being what you think you should be. You constantly treat yourself harshly and use other people to do the same. In fact, you mistreat no one as much as you mistreat yourself because the judge, the victim, and the belief system impel you to act in this way.

Think about this: Some people allow other people to behave appallingly toward them and will even put up with being physically and verbally abused, humiliated, and treated as if they were nonentities. Why? This is because, in their belief system, they say, "I deserve this insult. Joe or Mary is doing me a favor by being with me and sharing the nest. I do not deserve love and respect. I have not been good enough." Some might say, "Well, I am just hanging in there because, the way things are now, I don't think I can survive without him or her."

Therefore, it is very comical that you have the need to be accepted and be loved by others, but you are incapable of accepting and loving yourself. The more self-respect you have, the kinder you are to yourself. Being harsh with yourself is the result of a rejection of you. This in turn is the result of a failure to live up to an image of perfection that is honestly impossible to achieve. The fact is this whole infernal mechanism and this vicious circle, are sustained and governed by fear.

Here is the good news: With the help of *The 7 Secrets to Peace of Mind,* there is no need to live in this state of permanent fear. Don't worry; be happy. Just rejoice. You will soon know how to give the command to free yourself of all the negative conditioning that has been blocking your fulfillment. You are about to know the secret power to access a prosperous and peaceful life. Thanks to this new book of knowledge, you will have a beautiful dream, and you will create your own reality with hope, love, inner joy, and peace of mind.

With this foundational knowledge, I always remind my daughter, Tonia, and her brothers, Tony, Sylvester, and Lawrence, that in order to have a sustainable peace of mind, they should always strive to do their best in everything they do. However, I let them know very clearly that they should never strive for perfection with the sole intention to impress anybody.

Thus, I told my children the honest truth as it has always been said: "There is nothing one can do to perfectly satisfy anybody—no way."

The 7 Secrets to Peace of Mind is therefore encouraging you to always remember this phrase:

> *You can please most of the people in your life for some time and*
> *you can please some of the people in your life most of the time,*
> *but you can never please all the people in your life all the time.*

THE NEW DREAM TO RECLAIM YOUR POWERS

If you really want to reclaim your power, you need to have a new dream. It is obvious that you may have already signed thousands of agreements. These may be agreements with God, with the universe, with yourself, with your life dream, with society, with your parents, with your spouse, with your partners, with your children, with your friends, etc. However, the most important agreements are the agreements you have signed with God, with the universe, and with yourself. Through these agreements, you tell yourself what you are, what you feel, what you believe, and how to behave. The result is what psychologists refer to as your personality.

For an example, you say to yourself, "This is what I am, and this is what I believe. There are things I can do, and there are things I cannot do. This is reality. This is imaginable. This is possible, and this is impossible." Any of these agreements alone poses little problem, but in any number, they can make you suffer and miserably fail in life.

Some of these agreements can even prevent you from having the peace of mind and the inner joy you deserve. If you really want to have a sustainable peace of mind and inner joy, you should find the determination to break with these agreements that are only founded on fear. As a result, you will reclaim your authentic power, which is actually your true nature. This new book of knowledge has been designed to let you know that agreements that are founded on fear will eventually drain an enormous amount of your energy. On the contrary, agreements founded on love will help you to conserve your energy or even increase your energy level in a very remarkable way.

As any other human being, you were born with a certain amount of personal power that you can recharge every time you are resting. Unfortunately, you exhaust your personal power by making these agreements and then keeping them, making you feel powerless. You have just enough energy to get through each day because nearly all your power is used complying with the agreements that keep you in the dream of society.

The question now is how can you change the dream of your life when you do not even have the power to change the smallest of your agreements? If you are capable of seeing that your agreements are ruling your life, and if you do not want your life to be like that, then change these agreements. What you have to do is to sign up to a sort of new alliance or a new contract with yourself. This contract will be founded on four basic principles as devised by the ancient magi. These extremely powerful principles will help you to break the other agreements that are the product of the fear that literally drains your energy and confines you to a life that does not fulfill you.

You should therefore understand that every time you break an agreement, all the energy and power you put into creating it comes back to you. If you adopt these four powerful principles, you will accumulate sufficient personal power to be able to change the entire structure of your old agreements.

And when that happens, the transformation that will take place in your life will be amazing. Thus, instead of living in fear, misery, frustration, and want of all description, you will create a new dream. You will also create a new and fulfilling existence, love, inner joy, peace of mind, etc. As a result, you will create your own personal paradise wherever you are.

THE SECRET PRINCIPLES TO TRANSCENDING YOUR CURRENT LIFE

THE FIRST PRINCIPLE

- Words have power—be very careful with your words
- Honesty is still the best policy
- The ten commandments of communication

Words Have Power—Be Very Careful with Your Words

The first principle of this incredible contract for transcending your current life is the most important of the principles. This principle alone will allow you to transcend your current life and achieve peace of mind, including love and inner joy. It is a very powerful principle. It is formulated as follows:

Be very careful with your words.

Always remember that words have power. Thus, you should be very careful with what you say or write at any time. Do you know why you have to be very careful with your words? You should be very careful with your words because they are the magic keys that possess creative powers. These creative powers belong to you by right; they are gifts given to you directly by the divine. This truth is clearly stated in the Bible as it written:

> In the beginning there was the Word, and the Word was with God, and the Word was God.

Yes, your word truly does enable the expression of your creative power. It is through your word that you state things. Whatever is your manner of communication, your intention is manifested in your words. Your dreams, your feelings, and your real essence—everything is expressed through words.

Regretfully, most people are so accustomed to squandering their words that it comes as quite a surprise to them that their word is actually a source of power. Their thoughts, polluted by false system of beliefs saturated with subconscious fear, have in fact lost the energy and the natural power of their words.

It is also very vital to remember that your thought is energy. Every thought that crosses your mind is doubled by the emission of a quantity of energy that is recorded in the universal ether. This mental energy is colored by the various reflections, thoughts, emotions, and feelings that drive you to action.

Psychology tells us that the average human being receives a minimum of sixty thousand to eighty thousand thoughts per day. In fact, when a thought is expressed verbally, its energy is multiplied, and as a result, its power is significantly increased. Then the meaning of the word is increased by purely physical vibratory energy, even if it is uttered in nothing more than a whisper.

These vibrations are just as efficient, if not more, when expressed in a language that is unknown to us. Like thoughts, words act not only on human beings and animals but also on basic substances, objects, and even events in a very specific way. The secret is that this is not a special ability reserved for just the so-called gifted people or something that only happens at specific times. This ability is natural and systematic. In other words, when you speak, regardless of what you say, your words have an impact on your entire environment. Most importantly, your words have impact on yourself. When you speak, your words have impact on both your body and on your mind. Similarly, your words have impact on the body and the mind of the person you are talking to.

If in everyday life most people are not aware of this, it is because they talk a lot. And unfortunately, when most of them talk, they issue judgments, wishes, and contradictory feelings without distinction. This makes it impossible for them to identify the direct consequences of their words. Also, due to their false belief system, all they are often doing is repeating ideas they heard here and there.

Please be mindful that your words are not only sounds or written symbols. Your words are forces representing your capacity to express yourself, to communicate, to think, and therefore to create the events of your life. Your word is your most powerful tool as a human being. In fact, your words are magic instruments. Depending on how you use them, your words can free you or enslave you more than you could ever imagine.

Like a dual-edged sword, your words can create the most beautiful dreams: peace, prosperity, beauty, love, paradise, friendship, development, etc. Remember, however, that if your words are used wrongly, they can destroy everything and everybody around you. Depending on how they are used, your words have the power to create a nirvana or an inferno. For example, the words on the lips of a good lawyer fighting for a noble cause can preserve the rights of citizens and save people from iniquities. On the other hand, words on the lips of a manipulative tyrant have the ability to awaken the fears of a whole nation and lead everybody to hell.

To fully comprehend the point I am making, please take a moment and think about some of the peaceful words of Mahatma Gandhi. Then think about some of the diabolic words of Adolf Hitler. For instance, in Sierra Leone, it is easy to notice the vast contrast between the constructive and peaceful words of the first prime minister of the nation, Sir Milton Margai, and the destructive and hostile words of the rebel leader, Mr. Foday Sankoh.

Another example is to think of the words and the circumstances that led to the Second World War. Think of the words and circumstances that led to the Rebel Wars in Sierra Leone and in Liberia. Think of the words and the circumstances that led to the Gulf War in the Middle East. Think also of the words and the circumstances that led to the public demonstration against the governments of Tunisia, Egypt, Libya, and other parts of the world. (Such examples are also apparent *wake-up calls for Mama Africa to beware of a clever serpent that is aiming to swallow her again . . .*).

The 7 Secrets to Peace of Mind is designed to remind you that the human mind is similar to a fertile land where seeds are constantly sown. As human beings, our seeds are ideas, opinions, and concepts. We plant a seed or a thought, and it grows. Unfortunately, the ground often proves very fertile for the seeds of fear. That is in fact what it means when we say "Bad news travels faster than good news."

Do you now fully comprehend how much influence words have? Remember also that fear and doubts that are sown in your mind can create a dramatic succession of events. You just have to look around to see how someone can become blocked by a simple word or phrase and everything he or she might try to say after will be pointless and in fact will just make things worse.

Always be mindful that your words can have significant consequences for you. When your words are spoken at a sensitive point, they can make you do something or think something that conditions the rest of your life. Actually, you may be astonished to learn that every human being is a prestidigitator. Therefore, with your words you can cast spells on yourself and on others. Equally, with your words you also can release spells from yourself and from others.

For example, suppose you see a longtime friend and share an opinion with him or her in words like, "Oh you are not looking well at all. Your skin is like the color of someone who has a terrible disease. You really look very sick." If that person listens to these words, agrees with you, and continues to think of those words as true, eventually that person can contract a terrible disease. He or she will actually be sick. That is how powerful your words can be. So please be very careful with them.

Another example is, let us say you see a little girl and say, "Look how ugly that little girl is." The little girl in question will hear those words and then believe that she is ugly. She will grow up with the idea that she is not beautiful. It does not matter whether that little girl is beautiful or not. As long as she agrees with your opinion that she is ugly, she will grow up believing she is ugly. As such, she will be under the influence of a spell until one day another person catches her attention and with his or her words, makes her realize that she is beautiful. If she believes this second person, then she can sign a new agreement. As a result, she will no longer act as if she is ugly. The spell will be broken by the simple power of the words spoken by the other person who made her realize that she is beautiful.

A specific example of such individuals was Miss Magbidy Mosogboma of Imperie Chiefdom, who some people said was the ugliest woman in Sierra Leone. Miss Mosogboma later disagreed with the general opinion of those people and signed a new contract when a young man told her one day that she was beautiful and even married her. From that moment on, Magbidy believed she was a beautiful woman. As a result, she acted like one of the most beautiful women in the nation for the rest of her joyful life.

Please be very careful with the spells that others may cast on you or the spells that you may unconsciously cast on yourself and on others. Of course over the course of your domestication, your parents, brothers, sisters, friends, teachers, coaches, etc. might have cast spells on you by voicing their opinions about you without even thinking about what they were doing to you.

If you believed those opinions they had about you and grew up in the fear of what they conveyed—for example, not being good at sports, not being good at math, reading, or writing, or being lazy, slow, shy, stupid, ugly, etc.—then those opinions can come to pass. Therefore, you should be very careful with such poisonous spells. You should always disagree with the general negative opinion of others and sign new contracts.

The psychology is that 99 percent of who you are as a human being is invisible. So when others say words against you, they are basing their opinions on only 1 percent of who you are. Therefore, no one knows you better than you do. Please allow me to repeat the words of Eleanor Roosevelt when she said, "No one can make you feel inferior without your consent."

HONESTY IS STILL THE BEST POLICY

In anything you say or do, remember that honesty is always the best policy. Remember also that it is always very important to use honest words. Using honest words is what is commonly known as using true words. Thus, *The 7 Secrets to Peace of Mind* has been designed to remind you that the use of true words is one of the best ways to have a sustainable peace of mind.

For these very important reasons, it is always better to think before you say anything. The old French adage, "Turn your tongue seven times in your mouth before speaking," makes a lot of sense here, but the idea of true words most importantly means not rejecting, judging, or criticizing yourself through the language you use. In other words, do not use your own words against yourself.

It is also advisable not to use your words falsely against anybody. For example, if you meet someone you take a particular dislike to and treat him or her as if he or she is an idiot or a nonentity, even if you do not say anything out loud, you are using your words falsely against that person.

As a result, this person may also hate you, and his or her hatred will not do you any good at all.

So if you get angry and use your words to send others your emotional poison, you are in fact using your words against yourself. On the other hand, if you love yourself, you will inevitably and honestly express that love in your interactions with other people. Therefore, your words should always be honest. As a result, your actions will produce similar reactions.

The psychology is, if you honestly love others, others will honestly love you too. If you behave selfishly toward them, they will behave in the same way toward you. If you use your words to cast spells on others, you are also unconsciously casting spells on yourself and so on. That is what is meant by, "Whatever you do to others, you are doing it to yourself."

Honestly, true words also mean you should not use your words to insult, criticize, blame, destroy, or harm others emotionally through the expression of anger, jealousy, envy, hatred, etc. Rather, make good use of your words. This means you should use your words for truth and for self-respect. Always do your best not to create chaos with your words by using them in a disrespectful or dishonest way. Just remember that dishonestly using your words to create discord between people, families, tribes, nations, religious groups, political parties, races, etc. means generating and perpetuating a hellish nightmare. Therefore, never make speaking badly of others your principal form of using your words.

Now please take a moment and really be honest with yourself. Think very honestly of how many times you have nefariously used dishonest and negative words to describe someone you are close to with the sole aim of pulling him down. Or just think very honestly of how often you use dishonest and negative words to describe a close friend with the sole purpose of bringing others around to your own point of view. In the holy name of God almighty, please be very careful with what you say or do at all times. This is very important because if you are not very careful, your words and actions can come back to bite you when you least expect it.

THE TEN COMMANDMENTS OF COMMUNICATION

In the interest of peace and inner joy, please make the effort to always follow these ten commandments of communication during your interactions with others:

1. Do not use dishonest words against yourself or others.
2. Do not put yourself down for any reason.
3. Do not put others down at all.
4. Do not use words of criticism, blame, shame, or reproach.
5. Simplify your language as much as you can.
6. Be as concise and specific as possible.
7. Do not use words or expressions you do not know, as this can lessen the clarity of your thoughts.
8. Do not be judgmental. This is the worst form of emotional poison, and the negative energy it generates will inevitably come back to bite you. As such, you will be unconsciously casting spells on yourself.
9. Do not give your opinion about people you do not know very well.
10. Do not tell lies no matter what and always remember that honesty is still the best policy.

By obeying the ten commandments of communication, you will eventually sign new agreements based on truth. As a result, you will eventually free your mind and your personal relationships of all emotional poison. Your word will become purer and truer. Subsequently, your words will result in a sustainable peace of mind for you and for the people in your life. In addition, you will be immune to all bad spells others may attempt to cast on you.

When you obey the ten commandments of communication, you will then be able to evaluate how true your words are in the light of the love you have for yourself and for others. The depth of your self-respect and the feelings you foster toward yourself and others will be directly proportional to the quality and integrity of your words. When your words are true, you will surely have inner joy and peace of mind at all times.

Perhaps you would like to know what will happen on a practical level if you obey the ten commandments of communication. The psychology is that you will accumulate positive energy and increase the light of your aura, which will translate into greater harmony and respect in your social environment. Thus, little by little you will attract lucky opportunities, good people, positive circumstances, and peace of mind into your life. This is set down in the cosmic law that some psychology scholars refer to as the law of affinity. The meaning of this law is that negative attracts negative and positive attracts positive. In other words, a good attitude attracts a good attitude and a bad attitude attracts a bad attitude.

Therefore, when you obey these commandments, like a seed, the first principle of your contract will be sown. All you have to do is nurture the seed so that your words are always true. So please do your best to always use your words appropriately and honestly. Use them to share your love and to break all the little agreements that are causing you to suffer and preventing you from having the peace of mind you need.

Honest words or true words will lead you to a sustainable peace of mind, including personal freedom, achievement, inner joy, and love. True words will rid you of your fear by turning the fear it into joy and love. With honest words, you will truly live a peaceful life. When that happens, you will live in paradise amid thousands of others living in hell. Yes, this is your moment to live in nirvana. Congratulations!

THE SECOND PRINCIPLE

- Do not take everything personally
- The secret to maximum concentration

DO NOT TAKE EVERYTHING PERSONALLY

The classic idea of not taking everything personally is the second principle to transcend your current life and it actually flows from the first principle. Therefore, whatever happens to you in life, please do not take it personally. A wise philosopher once said, "To each man, his own view of the world."

Imagine, for example, the following scene. Someone sees you at school, at work, at a party, while you are out shopping, etc. Without even knowing who you are, that person starts to offload his or her negativity on you, not being aware that he or she has picked on the wrong person. Then he or she ignorantly projects his or her subconscious fears onto you in the form of criticism, reproach, or even insults.

If you are fully accustomed to using true words, you will not allow yourself to be destabilized by this person's diabolic and aggressive attitude toward you. You will not react by using the same tone and words as the tone and words this person has used. You will not do so because you know that those words can come straight back to you. You also know that this person's negativity has nothing to do with you and that, whatever it is, it is his or her problem, not yours.

If, on the other hand, you unfortunately take the matter personally, you might believe that such criticism is well-founded and then allow the victim in you to react. Even if the alleged pretext of your aggressor is absolutely wrong, you will definitely be tempted to react against it. As such, you will take the unfortunate opportunity to externalize your anger and frustration. Or you will suffer your annoyance and humiliation in silence. To put it another way, this situation will feed your doubts and validate your personal agreements founded on fear and guilt. You might even say to yourself, "How did this person guess that? Is it so obvious how hopeless I am? Does anybody else know this about me?" etc.

Of course you can find any number of examples of this type by just thinking of some past events in your personal life. But what always makes something personal in this way is when you give your agreement. Once you have done this, the emotional poison permeates you, and you are trapped. Therefore, please do not take everything personally. I am giving you this information out of a personal experience I had at a certain time when I was working for the county of Santa Clara in California. Those are bygone days, however, but I wish I knew then what I know now. So please take my advice: do not allow the victim in you to react. Always do your best not to take everything personally. The psychology is that taking everything seriously or personally can be a sign of egotism. Then the underlying factor can seem as if everything that happens is about you.

As with all human beings, this is a frame of mind that is rooted from your education and domestication, during which you learned to take everything personally. You do that because you think everything is your fault. As such, you keep on blaming yourself unnecessarily when things go wrong. As a result, you destroy your peace of mind by constantly pondering about what others might think or say about you and how the world sees you.

Please be reminded that in actual fact, you are absolutely not responsible for what other people think or say about you. For example, my daughter Tonia and I were discussing her educational strategies when I visited her in Maryland. During our interlocutions, she shared with me some of her concerns regarding what people might think or say about her educational plans. I paid keen attention to what Miss Tonia was saying to me. We then had a very long dialogue on the topic, and at the conclusion of all our discussions, I said to her, "Miss Tonia Isata Charles, whatsoever you plan to do, put it into prayers and do it well. Above all, always follow your bliss. What others think or say about you is not your business."

The 7 Secrets to Peace of Mind has therefore been designed to remind you that other people are responsible for their own words, thoughts, and actions. Everyone lives in his or her own dreams. Each individual lives in a world other than the one you inhabit. When you take things personally, you are assuming that others know what your world is like and that they are trying to set your world against their world. But that is not the case. Even when a situation seems very personal, for example when someone insults you, this has nothing to do with you. What people say, do, or think depends solely on the agreements they have signed in their own minds. Their point of view is the result of the programming they have undergone over the course of their domestication by the dream of life.

This is very important because you should not confuse what others do (the objective facts), what you think (the feelings and emotions that arouses in you), and what you subsequently do (your personal reactions and decisions). For example, if someone says to you, "You are really hopeless or worthless," do not take it personally because what that person is actually doing is confronting his or her own feelings, beliefs, and opinions about you. He or she is trying to make you feel guilty, and if you take it personally, then you will take his or her beliefs into your head and assimilate them.

132

Therefore, if you take everything that happens to you at face value, you will become an easy target for all those who want to draw on your energy. They can corner you with the mildest opinion and then administer all their emotional poison on you. They can weaken you and play on your emotions so they can feed on your energy.

When you take things personally, you feel offended and react by defending your beliefs, which often leads to conflict. You end up making a mountain out of a molehill because you need to be right and prove the other people wrong. I am therefore encouraging you to please remember that *it matters very little what other people think of you or say about you, whether it is good or bad. So do not take anything personally. What people feel, say, or think about you is their problem, not yours. Others' view about you is their own paradigm. That is their subjective way of seeing the world.* Some people will think you are lovely, and some will consider you to be annoying or selfish. Some will see you as skillful while others will see you as clumsy. Their opinions about you, however, will depend on their own belief system, not yours. Please do not worry about them; just do your best and be happy.

When you think of it very carefully, you might say that people who say negative words to you hurt you. This is not always the case. The psychology is that it is not what other people may say to you or about you that is actually hurtful. It is your own inner wounds that react when touched by the words people say about you. Therefore it is you who is actually hurting yourself. This is actually not a case of not having faith in others or not believing in people. It is rather of being aware of the fact that others see the world through their own eyes. Even you can only see the world through your own eyes. However, when you practice honest words, you will stop using the opinions of others as a pretext for getting annoyed, irritated, depressed, angry, or feeling hopeless.

If your emotions are negative or flattering, or if you are preening yourself, boasting, or convincing yourself that all is well, that should be your opinion. In fact, if you love yourself, if you live without fear, negative emotions will have no place in you. If you do not feel any of the negative emotions like anxiety, anger, hatred, jealousy, envy, confusion, sadness, guilt, shame, etc., you will feel good and those around you will see you for who you really are. Thus, you will feel at peace and fulfilled in your life. This is your true nature.

However, there will still be some people who will send you all the emotional poison they want. They will try to weaken you and play on your emotions so that they can feed on your energy, but they will fail every time they try. So do not worry about them; just be happy. *Your Peace Is Your Command!*

THE SECRET FORMULA FOR MAINTAINING MAXIMUM CONCENTRATION

The 7 Secrets to Peace of Mind is designed to reveal a secret formula that was used by the ancient magi in their attempt to save the rest of humanity. This method will enable you to defuse all kinds of negative emotions when they occur. This is one of the secret formulas that will prevent you from being contaminated by the harmful energy of negative emotions that can prevent you from maintaining maximum concentration.

Although this secret formula may seem very simple, nevertheless, it is very powerful and very efficient. This formula is based on concentration. It requires no effort on your part, and it will help you enormously in the application of the second phase of your contract for transcending your current life. This secret formula is so simple. In fact it consists of thinking only about what you say and what you do. You can do this without much effort for a short period of time that should only be about seventy seconds. Please be reminded that you already have within you the power you need to act. All you need to do is ask the power within for what you want and let it act for you. Never forget however that it is not you who is acting as a person, but rather your supra-conscious inner spirit that operates through you.

The purpose of this brief moment of concentration on a simple formula is to engage the participation of the mind and more importantly to prevent negative reactions. This formula is meant to specifically prevent unwanted negative emotions that feed the fears and the agreements of your belief system. However, the effectiveness of your mental concentration depends on two basic things, such as:

1. Your conscious mind can only deal with one idea at a time. When you bring your attention to an unimportant or meaningless task, it stops interfering with the positive influence of the supra-consciousness.

2. Your supra-conscious mind for its part, has the power to restore the entire subconscious mind's life in about seventy seconds. This period of about seventy seconds rests on a cosmic rhythm that is identified by the ancient magi through experience and through the science now known as parapsychology.

Here is a personal experience: When I was in Class 1 at Saint Columba's Primary School, Moyamba, our headmaster, Mr. Lebbie, often told us to recite the following phrases:

> One man went to mow, went to mow a meadow; one man
>   and his dog went to mow a meadow.
> Two men went to mow, went to mow a meadow; two men,
>   one man, and his dog went to mow a meadow.
> Three men went to mow, went to mow a meadow; three
>   men, two men, one man, and his dog went to mow a
>   meadow . . .

And so on; up to twenty men went to mow, went to mow a meadow . . . I had no idea what Teacher Lebbie was teaching us then until when I became a psychology scholar.

Therefore, even if you do not have any idea why I am suggesting that it is necessary for you to recite these words, it does not matter at this moment. What matters now is for you to please recite the words as written and as often as you can. Believe me, this exercise will suffice.

Similar to my Class 1 experience in reciting the "one man went to mow" phrases, my son Lawrence, told me that his first-grade teacher told them in their class to recite the following phrases:

> One ripe apricot, two ripe apricots, three ripe apricots, four
> ripe apricots, five ripe apricots, six ripe apricots, seven ripe

apricots, eight ripe apricots, nine ripe apricots, ten ripe apricots, eleven ripe apricots, and twelve ripe apricots.

Without any idea why his teacher told them to recite those words, young Lawrence was constantly reciting his words at home with great excitement.

Now it is your turn. Please relax and calmly recite these phrases, focusing solely on what you are saying without concerning yourself about the meaning:

> One man went to mow, went to mow a meadow; one man and his dog went to mow a meadow.
> Two men went to mow, went to mow a meadow; two men, one man, and his dog went to mow a meadow.
> Three men went to mow, went to mow a meadow; three men, two men, one man, and his dog went to mow a meadow, etc.

This new book of knowledge is encouraging you to please recite these phrases up to twenty men went to mow, went to mow a meadow. Or if that is hard for you to do, you can instead recite: "One ripe apricot, two ripe apricots," and so on up to twelve ripe apricots.

When you do these exercises precisely, let me be the first to congratulate you for completing a mental-magic exercise. The psychology is that if you attempt seven more times and manage to get up to twenty men went to mow, went to mow a meadow; or if you get up to twelve ripe apricots without becoming distracted, that means your supra-conscious mind is surely working to harmonize the tensions that aggravate your mental state.

You can also use any other phrase; for example, "One woman went to Bo . . ." Or you can use any fruit or any other thing, an apple, for example. You can also count from fifty to one, visualizing each number. There is no need to sit in any particular position or get into any special state; this formula will work at anytime and anywhere.

Please do these exercises every time you feel that negative emotions such as guilt, fear, anger, etc. are about to invade you. In about seventy seconds, you will be sufficiently focused, and you will not to make any situation personal. Of course, you can also do this exercise as a preventive measure to strengthen your mental abilities and your resistance to emotional stress.

You should also realize that most of the opinions you have about yourself are not necessarily true, so you are under no obligation to react personally to most of the things you say to yourself in your own head. When you finally get into the habit of not taking all of the things that happen to you personally, you will be able to avoid many problems in your life.

If you diligently maintain the habit of not taking things personally, emotions such as anger, jealousy, envy, sadness, etc. will disappear by themselves. In addition, you will break most of the little agreements that may be making you suffer pointlessly. And finally, you will have the peace of mind, including the true love and tranquility, you really need.

THE THIRD PRINCIPLE

- The secret for avoiding suppositions
- It is always better to ask the right questions
- Do not always assume

THE SECRET FOR AVOIDING SUPPOSITIONS

The third principle of the contract for transcending your current life also flows from the first principle. It is about avoiding suppositions. Therefore, regardless of what the circumstances may be, please do not make suppositions. When you avoid suppositions, you will surely enjoy a sustainable peace of mind.

However, due to the fact that we—human beings—are constantly seeking reassurance, you tend to make suppositions about everything. The problem is you then go on to believe that the suppositions you have made are true. My questions are: Do you habitually make suppositions about the intentions and reasoning of others?—And do you ever think about the consequences of your suppositions?

As a human being, it is common for you to misinterpret others, and poisoning them emotionally with your words. You take things personally and end up creating big dramas about very minor issues. That is how you unintentionally create problems in your life. *The 7 Secrets to Peace of Mind* is therefore encouraging you to please avoid suppositions as much as you can.

You may be surprised to know that the majority of the torments and difficulties humanity faces are rooted in unreasonable behaviors due to suppositions. Please be warned that speaking unkindly and making suppositions are the ways the dream of society wrongfully communicates. This is the way human beings exchange emotional poisons with each other. Since human beings are afraid to ask for explanations, we attribute intentions to others, making suppositions that we believe to be true. Worst of all, we are quick to defend our suppositions, declaring the other people to be in the wrong.

Please be advised, therefore, that it is better for you to ask questions than to make suppositions. After all, it is suppositions that program humanity to suffer most of the time. As I mentioned earlier, false beliefs create illusions in which the human mind bathes. This means you see or hear just what you want to see or hear. Most of the time, you do not see things as they really are. You mostly get into the habit of dreaming in a way that is disassociated from reality. Quite literally you are mostly dreaming things in your imagination, and when the truth finally emerges, you discover that things are really not as you thought they were.

Now please take a moment and think about this example: You are walking down the street, and you see someone you really like. She looks at you, smiles, and goes her way. This ordinary scene may give rise to a number of suppositions that can lead to an imaginary scenario. You are going to make yourself believe what you imagine and want to make it a reality.

Instead of restricting yourself to the objective reality—this person smiled at you and then continued on her way—you are going to give priority to one of several interpretations according to your own beliefs. Such as: that she was sending you an invitation to engage in a conversation with her. Or it was an attempt by her to seduce you. Or she was actually smiling at someone behind you. Or she was thinking about something funny and just happened to be looking at you. Or she thought you were someone she knows but then realized you were someone else, etc.

Basically, you carry on playing your inner film, and a whole dream is born out of the intentions you attribute to this person, such as, "Oh, she really likes me." On this supposition, you construct an entire relationship in your head. Perhaps you even imagine yourself marrying her. But this imaginary story exists only in your own dream.

As a human being, this is how you generally suppose that your spouse, business partners, or people in our life know what you need. As such, you think there is no need to tell them what you really need. You think they will do what you need because they know you well. If they did not do what you need, you feel hurt and treat them harshly, saying, "You should have known better." This kind of simple supposition can create a chain of problems in many relationships, so please avoid them as much as you can.

For example, a young lady decides to get married and assumes that she and her boy friend have the same idea about marriage. Then they start to live together and she finds out that her boy friend actually has a different idea about marriage. The result is a lot of conflicts, through which she continues to fail to clarify her feelings about marriage, etc.

A further example is that a husband comes home from work. His wife is angry, but he has no idea why she is angry. Perhaps his wife has attributed various intentions to him. Without telling him what she really needs, she imagines that he knows her well enough to know what she is expecting (as if he could read her mind), so she gets irritated because he has not come up to her expectations.

In other words, the assumptions you make about your relationships with others cause many misunderstandings, difficulties, and breakdowns in communications with those you are supposed to love. The fundamental questions therefore are: What is the psychological mechanism that drives people to behave in this way? How does the human mind work?

The psychology is that human beings have a need to justify everything, explain everything, and understand everything as a means of reassurance. As human beings, there are hundreds of questions we want answered because there are so many things the rational mind cannot explain. It hardly matters whether the answer is correct; just finding an answer is reassuring. That is in fact the main reason why we make assumptions.

IT IS ALWAYS BETTER TO ASK THE RIGHT QUESTIONS

As a human being you should never underestimate the significance of asking the right questions. When somebody tells you something, you quickly make assumptions about his or her motivation for doing so. But if he or she does not say anything to you, you make another set of assumptions to satisfy your need to know and to replace the actual communication.

In fact, even when you hear something you do not understand, you make assumptions about what it might mean, and then you go on to convince yourself that it is the truth. Most of the time, you make these assumptions very quickly and subconsciously. You do that because your agreements with the dream of society impel you to communicate in the following manner: it is dangerous to ask questions; if others love you, they should know what it is that you really want; etc.

Unfortunately, you sometimes assume that everyone sees the world as you see it, that others think as you think, that they feel things in the same way you do, and that they judge things as you judge. Those are some of the assumptions most people make. This is in fact one of the reasons why most people worry about being themselves: They think other people will judge them, treat them badly, and criticize them, as they do them. And even before someone can reject them, they reject themselves. That is how the average human mind works.

Think also of how we make assumptions about ourselves, which leads to much inner conflict: "I think I can do such or such a thing." You assume it, and then you discover that it is not the case. If this sort of thing happens to you, take the time to ask yourself the right questions and answer them honestly. Perhaps you need to reflect on what is it that you really need.

When you honestly do this, you will avoid the problem of overestimating or underestimating your potential.

The other thing is, as most human beings, when we are suffering, we often seek to justify the pain by blaming others. This is almost a natural behavior because it is common among humans to blame their fellow man. The area of relationships is a good illustration of this point. You either love somebody or you do not. Psychology proves that true love consists in loving people for who they are without trying to change them.

Therefore, if you want to change the person you are with, it is simply an indication that you do not truly love that person any more. Let us be honest here: you yourself naturally prefer others to accept you as you are and love you for who you are, don't you? Therefore, if your partner feels that you need to change things about yourself, it means that your partner does not truly love you anymore. So why stay with someone if you are not what he or she wants anymore?

If you decide to live with someone, you should live with someone who is exactly what you want rather than someone you want to change. It is therefore very important to be honest and to always be you. When you do that, you will not be forced to create a false image of yourself. When you are honest and you are yourself, the channels of communication will be clear, and the relationship will not suffer the types of conflicts that are most of the time generated by false assumptions. Therefore, it is always better to ask the right questions so that you can have a sustainable peace of mind.

Do Not Always Assume

The following principles will help you to avoid making unwarrantable assumptions:

1. Always ask the right questions.
2. Make sure you are communicating clearly.
3. If you do not understand, always ask again.
4. Have the courage to ask questions until everything is as clear as possible.

5. Never think you know everything about anything.
6. Do not be shy.

You always have the right to ask the right questions, and everyone is entitled to say either "yes" or "no." In the same way, everyone has the right to ask you questions, and you have the option of saying *yes* or *no*. When you ask the right questions and get the answers you need, you will no longer need to make assumptions.

If you communicate clearly, your relationship with others will be improved positively. For example, you can say to the people in your life: "This is what I want; tell me what you want." When you follow these simple instructions, you will eventually put an end to false assumptions. Then you will enjoy the peace of mind you need.

Most significantly, when you put this principle into practice, positive ways of doing things will become second nature for you. In addition to that concept, your determination and your concentration level will be improved enormously. Your words will almost become magic. Gradually all your problems will be resolved and your current life will be eventually transcended. What will then follow is the peace of mind you always needed, including love and tranquility.

THE FOURTH PRINCIPLE

- The secret for always doing your best
- The secret formula for expressing your personal dreams
- The secret rules of providence

THE SECRET FOR ALWAYS DOING YOUR BEST

The fourth principle of the contract for transcending your current life is to always do your best no matter what. This principle is actually about the application of the first three principles. But how do you put this fourth principle into action? The psychology is, *whatever the circumstances may be, just do the best you can—no more and no less.*

Be mindful however, that your best cannot always be the same from one time to the next. Remember also that everything is alive and everything is changing constantly, so your best can sometimes be very outstanding and at other times your best cannot be quite so great. For example, in the mornings when you wake up full of energy, your best can be better than when you get home tired at the end of a long working day. It may also vary according to how well you are feeling, whether you are happy or sad, angry, hungry, full of enthusiasm, etc. Your best can also vary according to environment and situation.

Therefore, depending on your mood, your best may differ from time to time or from one day to the next, and it can evolve over the course of time. But one thing is for sure: when you get into the habit of practicing the principles of the contract to transcend your current life, your best will become even better than it has ever been. So *The 7 Secrets to Peace of Mind* is encouraging you to *just do your best, no more, no less.* This is the secret. If you try to do more than your best, you will expend more energy than you need to, and ultimately, your best will feel like not enough. This is because when you do too much, you run down your energy levels in a way that is counterproductive, and it can take more time to achieve your goal.

On the other hand, if you do less than your best, you can risk feeling frustrated, guilty, and regretful. Therefore, always do the best that you can, whatever the circumstances may be. It does not matter if you are tired or not feeling well; just do your best. If you always do your best, you will not be susceptible to guilt, shame, or self-recrimination.

By always doing your best, you will be free of the negative agreements that can limit your potential. The psychology is that when you are doing your best, you will live your life with intensity. As a result, you will be productive, and you will be at peace with your true nature because you will always be giving the best of yourself. Thus, you will be giving the best to everything you do.

In fact, when you do your best, positive actions will follow. And in those actions, you will be doing something you love. However, most people do the exact opposite. They only do something when they think they will be rewarded for doing it, even when they take no pleasure in doing it. This is why those kinds of individuals do not always do their best.

Honestly, doing your best is not about going to work and waiting impatiently for payday or for the week end to have some fun. If you only work for reward, you fight against it, trying to avoid action. As a result, you will not do your best. On the other hand, if you act out of the pure pleasure of action without expecting any reward, you will discover that you enjoy everything you do.

You can be rewarded for what you do, but you will no longer be attached to the reward; you will get more than you would have gotten without expecting it. The psychology is that when you like what you do, you will always do your best almost effortlessly. Thus you will live a full life without boredom and without frustration. The psychology is this: *human beings work not just to earn but to become. What then follows is a sustainable peace of mind.*

When you do your best, you will not give your inner judge any opportunity to make you feel guilty. If you have done your best and your inner judge tries to criticize you, you will know what to say: "I did my best." And the good part is you will have no regret. That is why you should always do your best. And when you do your best, you will learn to accept yourself and you will learn from your mistakes. This will increase the awareness of your higher consciousness in a very remarkable way.

By always doing your best, you will not feel as if you are slaving away, because you will have fun doing what you do. Thus you will go about your business in a way that can never have any negative consequences. You will be trying your hardest because you want to, but not because you have to. You should not be afraid to express who you are, because it is in taking action that you can express your true nature. You may have many ideas, but what actually makes the difference is taking the step forward into doing your best. This is the secret to having a sustainable peace of mind.

THE SECRET FORMULA FOR EXPRESSING YOUR PERSONAL DREAMS

You surely have the power to express your personal dreams when you perform some simple secret formulas. However, in order to effectively express those dreams, you should understand the psychology that *taking action is a manifestation of being alive*. Therefore, always take action. Remember also that it is taking the action by coming out of your shell and expressing your dreams that can make things happen.

Be mindful however, that this is not the same as imposing your dreams on others, because everyone has the right to express his or her own dreams. So the idea of doing your best in everything you do is a very good habit. It is a habit that will let you procure the power to express your personal dreams without harming anyone else. It is also a belief like any other belief that you choose.

For example, when you are taking a shower, take the time to tell your body that you love it, feel the water on your body, and appreciate the sensation. Do your best to satisfy the needs of your body and receive what it has to offer you. I personally enjoy taking long showers. Whenever my lovely wife, Mrs. Isha Charles, reminds me of my long time in the shower, my reply has always been the same: "Thank you for reminding me, honey; I am just doing my best to satisfy the needs of my body."

The 7 Secrets to Peace of Mind is designed to let you think carefully about this fact: *The moment you came into this world, you were given a body; and whether you like it or not, it is the body that will house your soul for the whole of your life.* Your personality is part of your body. All your hopes, dreams, aspirations, and thoughts that make you a unique and irreplaceable being are contained in that body.

Your body is designed to serve as a buffer between your inner being and the outside world, and it is with you to carry you through life. Your body also teaches you some of the most basic things about the human condition. By listening to the teachings and the gifts your body offers, you will prepare yourself for wisdom and peace of mind, including beauty, true love, good health, etc.

The body that you have been given remains yours from your very first breath to your last one. It is up to you whether to love your body or hate it, but at the very least you should not consider your body to be a mere banal recipient. Your body is your partner and your best ally. Also, the relationship you built between yourself and your body is essential because it is the relationship on which your connection with the outside world is built.

Perhaps you think your body and your mind are a good match and that they are well aligned. If that is the case, then it is great. But perhaps you are unhappy with the way you are built; perhaps, you would like to be thinner, heavier, healthier, more attractive, less clumsy, etc. In fact, whatever you think about your body, it is yours forever. Thus, your mutual relationship has a significant impact on your whole life.

This new book of knowledge is therefore encouraging you to be at peace with your body, care for it, and love it. In return, your body will fulfill its role properly, and it will help you to assimilate the notions necessary for acceptance, high self-esteem, respect, dignity, and pleasure. Thus, focusing on doing everything well for your body is like purifying yourself every moment of your life. It is the best way of saying, "*I love myself and I love life.*" Then you will be loved by others. The psychology is this: people love those who love themselves.

Always take good care of your body and live in the present. The truth is, in order to make your personal dream come true, you should detach yourself from the past. Abandon your archaic belief system, abandon your negative agreements, and live in the moment. But if you unfortunately continue to live in the past, you will hardly appreciate what is currently happening. Thus, you will not use your power of now, and you will not fully comprehend this new era of higher consciousness.

When you live in the present, you do not have any time to waste with regrets about anything because you are alive. Always remember that as long as you are alive, you have the opportunity to move on. You have the opportunity to find something else or somebody else because you are alive. That is what is meant by, "Once there is life, there is hope."

Living in the past is like being just half alive, and this leads to self-pity, suffering, and tears. Consequently, you will forfeit the peace of mind that is your birthright. So please be reminded that you were born with the right to love and be loved. Thus, you definitely have the right to share your love. *The 7 Secrets to Peace of Mind* is therefore encouraging you not to hold back the life that is expressed in you, because it is a divine gift.

Always honor the human being you are and let each of your thoughts, emotions, and feelings become a ritual of love, because that is exactly what you are. As it is written, "God is love." Therefore you are love. All you have to do is to love yourself, love others, and show the world what a magnificent human being you are. Remember, "It is better to have loved and lost than never to have loved at all."

Please be reminded to always be yourself. In fact, you do not even have to prove who you are; the most important thing you have to do is *be*. Just take the action of valuing your life; that is what counts the most. You have the right to be yourself. You have the right to say *no* when you need to say *no* and *yes* when you need to say *yes*.

The secret way to be yourself is to do your best in everything you do. When you fail to do your best, you are denying yourself the right to be yourself. That itself can affect your present and your future. That notion reminds me of when we used to dance at the Bo Town Hall in Sierra Leone to a popular song that says, "Anything you want to do, do it well, for no one knows tomorrow . . ."

If you actually take that philosophy into serious consideration and do your best in everything you do, then your habits of misusing your words, taking everything personally, and making assumptions will be weakened. Those bad habits will occur less and less often, and they will eventually disappear. When that happens, you will effortlessly have the peace of mind you need.

Remember also that you do not have to judge yourself, punish yourself, or ever feel guilty if you just abide by the first three principles of the contract to transcend your current life. Just do your best. If you are doing your best, you will feel good even if you are still making some assumptions, even if you still sometimes react to things personally, and even if your words are not always true.

However, it is through practice and dedication that you will fully master these principles. Remember, everything you have learned in your life you have learned them through repetition. For example, you only learned to write and to speak your language or dialect because you exerted yourself. Do not be discouraged when things do not happen as planned; just do your best.

You should always do the exercises you have learned and act accordingly. That is how you will easily have peace of mind. When you start practicing these principles, it is perfectly normal not to find them very easy. However, even if you do not follow most of the principles, you should continue to do your exercises to the best of your ability.

Please do not judge yourself; do not give your inner judge the satisfaction of making a victim of yourself. If you find the exercises difficult to do one day, forget about them for that day and just start again on another day. By so doing, you will soon see how things gradually get easier with time.

What you have to do is to keep your attention focused on the present moment and live just one day at a time. As a philosopher hyperbolically said, "Little drops of water can make a mighty ocean." And as it has always been said, "Rome was not built in a day." So take your time; there is no need to rush. When you do these exercises and act accordingly, you will eventually have the peace of mind you need.

Remember also that the secrets of the ancient magi this volume is revealing to you will bring you fulfillment beyond your dreams. You can sign the following agreement at anytime by speaking this formula: "I, (your name), choose to do my best all the time and to honor the principles of the contract to transcend my life." For example, you might say, "I Emmanuel choose to do my best all the time and to honor the principles of the contract to transcend my life." By adhering to this agreement, you will be in full control of your life. All you will now need is a minimum of determination and perseverance. As a result, your efforts will be richly rewarded. Finally, you will have peace of mind, including real love and tranquility.

This new book of knowledge is also designed to reveal the secret that forms an integral part of the fabulous way of life of the ancient magi. This secret concerns principles and formulas that attract peace of mind, including true love, good health, prosperity, longevity, and inner joy. The work of these occultists hinged around their research and investigation of the spiritual world. For the ancient magi to devote their time to this task completely, they needed solid material and financial security. This is the reason why these early wise men focused first on identifying the cosmic laws that had the capacity to ensure their wealth, prosperity, and inner joy.

The purpose of this volume is to also let you know that if you want to attract the favor of providence, you need to respect certain rules that have the power to attract prosperity, wealth, and good fortune. Thus, you will learn how to implement some of these rules. And by following the outlined simple rules, you will have the knowledge to exploit the potential of the power that lies dormant within you.

THE SECRET RULES OF PROVIDENCE

- **Rule # 1:** Love prosperity to let prosperity love you
- **Rule # 2:** Have an open mind for prosperity
- **Rule # 3:** Focus your attention on prosperity
- **Rule # 4:** Allow money to circulate freely

RULE # 1: LOVE PROSPERITY TO LET PROSPERITY LOVE YOU

The first rule to attract providence is to truly love prosperity with your entire being. This statement would seem to draw your attention to the traditional thinking about the love of money, but this is the truth in the occult world. If you do not love prosperity, prosperity will evade you. I am therefore encouraging you not to make that mistake. When some people unfortunately make such a mistake, it is like rejecting the person they love and then complaining about being lonely. You should never push away the things you love or the people you love. Of course, it is simple psychology that if you continue to push them away, they will eventually avoid you too.

Therefore, seeing prosperity as a diabolical thing will inevitably distance you from providence. There is nothing wrong with wanting to be prosperous, and there is nothing wrong with living a luxurious life. The only mistake about this concept is the belief that you can be prosperous at the expense of others. That in itself is yet another totally erroneous belief that is the result of the agreements signed during your domestication process.

Therefore, you should love prosperity without any misguided sense of shame. When you do that, prosperity will love you in return. Never criticize prosperity, the power of prosperity, or its nature. Money itself is not evil but rather the perverse spirits that some people get out of it.

Rule # 2: Have an Open Mind for Prosperity

The second rule to attract providence is to have an open mind for prosperity. What this means is that, by opening up your heart and your mind to be prosperous and have inner peace, you can construct from the inside out a feeling of wealth that no one can take away from you. Tell yourself that having inner peace and *prosperity is being able to look in the mirror at any time and* see a *person of value.* Never forget that life has shined its divine light on all humanity. This is your moment.

The psychology is that *having an open mind is the key to making the best choices.* Thus, if you have the knowhow, you can reconnect with this amazing heritage of unlimited power that exists within you. This is the power that can transform the inner spiritual wealth into external material benefits. It is very true that you are here on this earth to lead a gratifying existence. This volume is therefore designed to let you acknowledge the fact that *true wealth is achieved by a change in mind-set.* This is your moment to change your mind-set for your own good.

If you only know how to do that, you will always have peace of mind, including love and prosperity, without much effort. As a result, your desires will be fulfilled. You are therefore encouraged to let prosperity always form part of the personal dream that you express most of the time. As one put it, "You get what you dream about most of the time." So, always let prosperity into your dreams.

Rule # 3: Focus Your Attention on Prosperity

The third rule for attracting providence is to focus your attention on prosperity itself. By so doing, you will be able to use your mind and your creative thoughts to promote the prosperity you need. Remember that thought is creative, just like words, which are the verbalization of thoughts. Thoughts are also impulses of cosmic energy that have the power to manifest themselves in the material world either for good or for bad.

Just because thoughts are invisible when they are in your head does not mean they do not have any impact on the material world. All the experiences you have lived through with joy and pain, achievement and failure, and wealth and poverty seem to have happened to you. But the truth is, on a very elementary level, these are the things you may have caused to happen through your own thoughts.

This is true because every thought is like a seed that will grow and then become a tree, which will bear fruits that may be sweet or bitter depending on the seed planted. So events also seem to happen to you according to whether your thoughts are positive or negative. Therefore, your destiny is contained in your thoughts and feelings. The psychology is that your awareness means you possess all things. For example, your awareness of health makes you healthy, your awareness of wealth makes you wealthy, etc.

You should therefore foster hope within your heart as the most precious of your divine gifts. This is vital because hope is the principle that will determine the outcome of your wishes. You are therefore encouraged to always hope for the best, and you will see that the result is mostly contained within your hope.

The 7 Secrets to Peace of Mind is also encouraging you to get into the habit of thinking in terms of peace, joy, love, ease, wealth, abundance, and things of the like. Most importantly, do not say, "I don't deserve it. I don't have the right. It's good for other people but not for me. Plenty of money is a bad thing, etc." These are negative phrases that will diminish your chances for prosperity. Please do not put yourself down no matter what happens. Free your mind of harmful thoughts that can only lead to failures, problems, distress, sadness, etc. Be mindful that your mental attitude is absolutely important because it has a considerable impact on your life.

When you say, for example, "I will never have enough money to do this or that," your subconscious mind records your thought, which strengthens your belief in your inability to attract wealth and prosperity. If, on the other hand, you think optimistically, for example, "I will have enough money to buy a new car or live in the house of my dreams," the energy given off by your conscious thoughts will actually and eventually create the right environment for the realization of your wish.

The secret is, as a result of your positive thoughts, like a magnet, you will attract the people, circumstances, and opportunities that will allow your wishes to come true in the material world. In other words, thanks to your thoughts and your words, you will gradually accumulate the ability to create the reality you need. This is how you will eventually become the designer of your own destiny.

THE SECRET FORMULA FOR DEVELOPING YOUR CREATIVE THOUGHTS

The question is how do you develop the power of your creative thoughts? You can learn to use the power of your creative thoughts quite simply by performing certain powerful formulas. These are formulas charged with positive energy because they reflect and articulate constructive ideas. By doing these exercises and repeating the suggested phrases, you will generate a positive energy that will automatically work for you.

Like a generator, repetition will transform your invisible mental energy into tangible energy. In other words, it will materialize the invisible universal energy into a tangible form, which is why these formulas actually have the power of creative and effective affirmations. These are the affirmations that will give you the peace of mind you need. The question however, is how do you use your creative power to your advantage? All you need to actually do is to say these creative affirmations on a daily basis or as often as possible. You can also do this in your head or you can even say them aloud, which is in fact the most effective way.

The important thing is to be fully aware of the meaning of the creative affirmations. Repeat them with all of your heart, all of your determination, all of your emotion, and all of your attention—basically with all of the forces of your conscious mind. At the same time, imagine, visualize, and feel the desired result as if it were already a reality in your life.

For instance, when my wife wanted to be reinstated into her state job, I just simply encouraged her to use the power of her creative thoughts. Without any hesitation, she did as I suggested. As a result, in seven weeks, she received the confirmation from the personnel board of the state of California that her request for reinstatement was granted.

This is just a specific example of the effectiveness and the power of your creative thoughts. Thus, this new book of knowledge will help you to start this wonderful exercise with the following formula:

"I, (your name), open myself up to the riches and benefits of the universe, and I receive them with joy." For example, you might say: *"I, Esther, open myself up to the riches and benefits of the universe, and I receive them with joy."*

Then, whenever you want to, you can use one or several of the positive formulas of your choice. The following are some of the phrases that will favor prosperity, wealth, abundance, and an influx of money into to your life:

- I have a positive mental attitude as an unlimited source of well-being, love, joy, prosperity, and wealth.
- My positive mental attitude wills all the creative forces of the universe to come into my life. These creative forces will rejuvenate me mentally, physically, and spiritually.
- My thoughts are expressed in a positive way that makes my intuition a fertile source for the rapid solution to my problems.
- A wealth of correct intuitions flow into my mind; they inspire me to be lucky at all times.
- Money is precious, and I will use it constructively for my well-being and the well-being of my loved ones.

- Unlimited wealth runs in me and through me, and I share it freely with others.
- My personal affairs are driven toward achievement, and I prosper with ease.
- Money runs freely through me, and I use it wisely, carefully, and constructively.
- My personal relationships are driven toward peace, and I am loved with ease.
- The more I give, the more I receive. Everything comes to me as if by magic. Money flows into my home in profusion.
- I have the right to have lots and lots of money. Every amount of money I spend comes back to me multiplied.
- The daily repetition of positive formulas opens doors wider and wider to joy, achievement, and peace of mind.
- By following my heart, prosperity comes into my life more quickly, and all my wishes are fulfilled in abundance.
- I learn to give benevolently because I know that the more I give, the more I receive. In the application of this sacred principle, every day brings me the opportunity to earn more money.
- I express my joy in the money that comes to me by using it for the things I love.
- My prosperity enriches others, and their prosperity enriches me.
- I agree to receive all the things I need from life.
- Wealth and prosperity become a part of my life as a result of my constructive thought.
- My skills bring me inner joy and harmony.
- Prosperity is my natural state.

You can say these phrases at any time during the day. You can say them in the morning when you wake up, while you are taking a shower, when you are going about your daily business, or in the evening before you go to sleep.

Repeat these phrases frequently, as they will charge your aura and your personal environment with positive energy. Make sure you remain focused on the meaning of the phrases you are repeating because this can prevent your mind from wandering, which might decrease the efficiency of this powerful formula.

THE SECRET FORMULA FOR PROSPERITY

You may be surprised to learn that there are powerful secret formulas that can actually create prosperity in your life. You are therefore encouraged to please pay very close attention to these formulas. These are unique secret formulas for prosperity and wealth creation that this new book of knowledge is designed to reveal to you.

They are the powerful secret formulas that were first used by the ancient magi. In fact, these formulas are known to be among the most-powerful secret formulas that are currently used by most of the elite, the super-wealthy, and some members of the members-only organizations around the world.

How to manifest your own prosperity and wealth is one of the wealth-creating secrets some members-only organizations have kept from you all these years. However, as you are commencing the new era of higher consciousness, this volume has been designed to show you the way, so please pay attention to the suggested exercises outlined herein.

THE SECRET FORMULA FOR VISUALIZING POSITIVE IDEA SEEDS

Visualizing positive idea seeds is the formula that sows positive ideas in your subconscious mind. They will allow you to develop an awareness of wealth and prosperity that will help to attract them into your life. This formula is very powerful, and it should be performed precisely as follows:

- Find yourself a quiet place where you will not be disturbed for at least seven minutes, such as your bedroom, your home office, etc. Turn off your telephone if necessary.
- Wear loose clothing so that you will not perspire, preferably in natural fabrics such as cotton, linen, wool, etc. (synthetic materials block the circulation of the cosmic universal energy).
- Settle yourself down comfortably and in a sitting position with your back straight and your hands on your thighs, legs parallel, and feet flat on the ground. Adjust your posture until you are in a position you can comfortably maintain.

- Spend a few moments relaxing. Breathe calmly, naturally, and deeply. Each time as you exhale, feel how you are becoming more deeply relaxed.

- Allow thoughts and ideas to cross your mind, and then let them dissipate of their own accord. Do not try to nourish them with any inner mental dialogue. Then, when you feel calm and receptive, close your eyes if possible.

- Imagine cosmic energy permeating everything in the universe and meeting all your needs. Allow this energy to pour into you through your breath. Let it fill you with its inspiring treasures. Remember that the universe contains all imaginable riches, and there is enough for everyone. That is the abundant mentality this new book of knowledge offers.

- Feel as if a great space is opening up in your heart to receive this abundance. Feel gentle warmth and a radiation of love and light that runs through your heart and gently dissolves all your fears, limitations, and negative thoughts.

- Now focus your attention on a virtual point located between your eyebrows, slightly below the bridge of your nose. Feel this area grow and form a sort of movie screen.

- You are now going to use your imagination and your thoughts to play a film on the screen of your closed eyelids. Concentrate hard on what you would do if you have all the money you need to be extremely prosperous.

- Allow the mental images to form freely on your inner movie screen. Visualize what you would like to see happen in your life in the greatest possible detail in terms of your finances, your wealth, your health, your prosperity, your career, your family, your inner joy, your love life, and above all, your peace of mind. For instance, if you need some money to pay off a debt, to buy something you need, to help someone you care about, or to improve your standard of living, that is the image you need to visualize. Concentrate as hard as you can on the sum of money you need.

For example:

- Imagine the sum of money you want coming into your life in the form of a check. Visualize the check itself being written out to you and the exact figures that make up the amount on it. Then see yourself depositing the check into your bank account, etc.

- Imagine what you and your loved ones will do with the large sum of money you now have.
- Visualize yourself and your love ones rejoicing, celebrating, and jubilating.

Here is another formula:

- Take a moment to imagine that you already have what you want and that your dream has already come true.
- Write down a sum of money on a sheet of paper, and focus your eyes on it for at least seven minutes. Still looking at the amount and then repeat the following formula in your head until you feel completely relaxed: "I, (your name), have the sum of (so many dollars) in my bank account" or "I, (your name), have the sum of (so many leones) in my bank account." For example, you may say, "I, Grace, have the sum of $700,000 in my bank account."

Let me give you one more example.

If you are dreaming of owning a house, visualize the house you want down to the slightest detail. Walk through the bedrooms, admire the beautiful chimneypiece in the sitting room, and wander in the big backyard, the big master bedroom, the big family rooms downstairs and upstairs, the magnificent stairways, etc.

Visualize the classic furniture you will beautifully decorate your home with, including the elegant wall units, the big screen TVs, etc. Go on to also visualize your children having fun in their new, lovely neighborhood, new, gorgeous home, new appliances, etc. Then visualize your friends and relatives saying to you, "Your house is huge, amazing, and gorgeous. Congratulations."

Here is a specific example of the power of visualization exercises. In the year 2004, I was dreaming of owning a gorgeous house in California. So I did the visualization exercise just as I have described before. You may be astonished to learn that within seven months, my dream became a reality. Thus, I was able to acquire a piece of land and hired a reputable home-building company called KB Homes to build me the house of my dream. Within seventeen months, KB Homes built me a four-thousand-square-foot, gorgeous home in Elk Grove, California.

You may also be surprised to learn that without any prior knowledge of my visualization, my wife, Mrs. Isha Charles, decorated our newly built house almost exactly as I had visualized it. Now guess what? Most of my friends and relatives who visited us at our new home said the exact words I had visualized: Day after day, week after week, and month after month, our friends and relatives who visited our brand-new home continued to say, "Congratulations, Tony, you guys' house is huge and amazing. It is gorgeous." Of course, without any doubt, our children were deeply in love with their gorgeous new home and rooms. To crown it all, the big master bedroom, the big backyard, the magnificent stairways, etc. were almost the same as I had visualized.

I could go on and on, giving you examples of incredible results of visualizations of positive idea seeds. Therefore, I encourage you to please pay attention to the visualization exercises with your entire mind because they surely work. Always remember that what others have done you can also do. Just visualize it and believe you will have it. The most important thing you have to do is to think positively about it. That is what is meant by, "If you dream it, you can do it" and "If you believe it, you will see it."

Therefore, *The 7 Secrets to Peace of Mind* has been designed to provide you with the step-by-step method of how to visualize positive idea seeds. Remember, however, that this visualization exercise should be done accordingly and persistently. Be mindful also that the true story about my house in California is a valuable independence of the manner in which fate will fulfill your own wish.

For example, the sum of money you may receive can come from different angles. It may come from a win (on the lottery or other games of chance), an unexpected inheritance, the repayment of a loan, insurance claims, compensation, a career promotion, a pay raise, etc. The psychology is that when you visualize, take action, and believe, you will surely have what you need.

Therefore, if you truly visualize your goals and take action, you will meet them without any doubt. Remember that the power of visualizing your goals and meeting them is within you. Believe me, this is a tried and true practice dating back to the teachings of Abraham. Remember the Bible story in which he was calling himself "Abraham," which means, "father of multitude," when in fact he didn't even have a child at that time.

Of course you know that according the Holy Bible, Abraham's visualization actually became reality, and indeed, he is known today as the father of multitudes. Abraham's story is just another specific example. There are thousands of such stories, right up to more-modern visualization stories like those of Starbucks's Howard Schulz, Dr. John Sandy's (as he outlined in his book *Pointers to Success*), and many similar others. The psychology is that seeing yourself in the place or situation you would like to be in is where it begins. All you have to do next is to act accordingly, believe, and be patient.

For example, when he was in high school, my son Sylvester Charles, who had never played football, came to me one day and said, "Dad, I really want to start playing football." But considering his weight at that time and the fact that with the exception of his third-grade soccer games, Sylvester has never done any sport in school, I was truly hesitant to give him my consent. That night, however, I spent a long time thinking of some powerful visualization stories. In the morning, I told my son that if he could visualize himself playing football and act accordingly, he would.

Thus I gave Sylvester my consent to play the football he was dreaming of playing. To cut a long story short, as a result of his visualization and actions, my son played football according to his dreams. And guess what? He was accepted as one of the outstanding players in the school's team. Amazingly, for both the junior varsity and varsity teams, number 75 for Franklin High was my elegant footballer, the unbeatable nose guard and defensive tackle Sylvester Charles.

Was I proud of my son for playing football? Yes! But of course, anybody's son can play football. But I was actually very proud of my son for precisely doing his visualization exercises and for taking the appropriate actions to make his dream a reality. This is your moment to do the same. When that happens, you will surely have peace of mind.

THE SECRET FORMULA FOR
WRAPPING YOUR VISUALIZATION IN LIGHT

The 7 Secrets to Peace of Mind has been designed to guide you to wrap your visualization in light by doing the following powerful exercises:

- Imagine your mental images bathing in a beautiful golden light.
- Now anchor your wish for prosperity and wealth.
- Open your hands with your palms facing upward toward the sky.
- Bring your thumb and index finger together.
- Say the following powerful phrase: "I, (your name), freely welcome all the gifts of providence." For example, you might say, "I, Cecilia, freely welcome all the gifts of providence."
- Then thank almighty God with a thought of gratitude.
- Breathe in deeply, stretch, and open your eyes.

The question now remains, what do you have to do next? The answer is "nothing." You do not have to do anything more than you have already done. It is all in the hands of God almighty now, so just have faith and believe; you will have what you wished for.

That does not mean sitting down anxiously and waiting. Once the exercises have been done, you can go calmly about your business. What these exercises mean is you should not try to resolve your problems by ordinary means; you should always request divine intervention. Therefore, you should always pray; even if you do not believe in God, you should always believe in something.

Remember also that your supra-conscious mind has already found the perfect solution for you, and it is working on making things happen in your favor. Be calm and follow with confidence all the advice it gives you, whether directly through intuitions, indirectly through your dreams, by means of various coincidences that occur in your daily life, in the form of apparent lucky events, etc.

In other words, from the moment you call on the higher power, all you need to do is to follow what comes into your mind. This will be through the intermediary of your thoughts and your creative words even if it does not seem to have anything to do with the situation. You will be sure that the higher power will start to work from that moment onward. Do not doubt the results; just be confident and allow this powerful force to work in your best interest.

Within a reasonable amount of time, you will start to see the signs that will reveal a change for the better: lucky opportunities, good news from your business ventures, sudden improvement in your lifestyle, enlightening intuitions, miraculous solutions to specific situations, etc. You should do these powerful exercises for wrapping your visualization in light at your own convenience at least once every seven weeks. When you do that, you will surely have a sustainable peace of mind.

RULE # 4: ALLOW MONEY TO CIRCULATE FREELY

The fourth rule to attract providence is to allow money to circulate freely. This is a very vital rule that you should take into serious consideration, abide by, and follow accordingly. Be mindful also that money is like blood. As such, money needs to circulate. Therefore, hoarding money and clinging on to it—whether in thought or in action—is the same as letting blood clot, with all the risks involved in that.

Money is the life-giving energy that is exchanged in return for services offered to others. Therefore, money should be used only for the satisfaction of needs. For money to continue to flow and be fruitful, it needs to keep circulating. Of course, this does not mean that saving money is a bad idea. But you must understand that there are two sides to the motivation that drives humanity to save.

First, there is a side of the motivation of saving money that is based on the negative emotion of fear. This is the motivation of saving money that tends to block the free circulation of the cosmic energy and therefore repel luck. Then there is another side of saving money that is based on the positive emotion of love. This is the motivation for saving money that favors and even amplifies the circulation of universal energy. This kind of motivation is brought under the protective wing of providence.

For some people, fear is sufficient motivation that translates into putting money aside for a "rainy day." Or as it is commonly said in Sierra Leone, putting money aside "for man can't tell." When people put money aside for "man can't tell," their savings sleep in bank accounts, in boxes, and in other secure places for "just in case." As a result, their vital energy and creativity are immobilized.

What worse thing could there be for inspiration than a life lived in continual fear of a rainy day? How harmful for the psychological and spiritual balance, and what a catastrophe for the spirit of initiative, for the entrepreneurial spirit, and for individual liberty. This is the kind of fear that is stopping most people from living in the present moment. As a result, they lose themselves in pessimistic assumptions. Their words cannot always be the honest truth. Therefore, to actually enjoy peace of mind, including love and tranquility, it is not advisable to be stingy.

Fortunately, however, for many people, saving money regularly is a means of being able to afford to treat themselves or someone else to holidays, have nice cars, plan trips, live in more comfortable homes, pay for their children's education, care for their parents who are old or sick, etc. In this case, the power of life, love, and sharing are not set against each other but rather actively promote projects and personal dreams.

Therefore, savings undertaken with a healthy mind devoted to the realization of a positive aim does not block the circulation of money or universal energy. In fact, it enhances them in a very remarkable way to ensure peace of mind and tranquility.

THE SECRET FORMULA FOR DEVELOPING YOUR OPTIMISM

The 7 Secrets to Peace of Mind is designed to make it abundantly clear that optimism is in fact the key to tranquility. Remember also that your thoughts, words, and actions of today are the seeds of your future. Thus, they will inevitably have consequences for you. Therefore please do your best to always be positive and optimistic. By so doing, your state of mind, your situation, and your lifestyle will be effortlessly improved beyond your imagination.

This new book of knowledge is therefore encouraging you to rid yourself of all morbid, sad, or anxious thoughts that might invade your mind. Please do your best to avoid any situation or anybody that might stress you out. Choose not to take part in violent arguments, disputes, or drama. When you speak, cut out the little phrases that reflect limitation, depression, criticism, or disharmony for you or others. Be mindful that phrases that reflect limitation can be true poisons.

Therefore, I am encouraging you to please continue to say your positive affirmations (not only those ones about money). Say things like:

> I will finish what I have started. I will succeed in the things I undertake. I will never be bored. I will always wake up refreshed and ready. I love myself. I love my partner. I love my family. I love my country. I will only attract positive and interesting people. I have lots of luck, etc.

Even if these phrases do not always correspond to the reality of your moment, just believe that sooner or later they surely will. Continue to repeat the same phrases until you achieve your goals. Remember also that you should not worry about finding another solution to your problem because, even if it is still an issue, it is really no more than the remains of a past that is definitely over. Always bear in mind that everything will always work out in your best interest. Therefore, you should stop thinking about your problems and definitely do not talk about them so as not to give them any strength.

All you have to do is to have faith in the power of the Almighty God and in your humanity. When you believe, things will change dramatically no matter what. Remember also that when you change your thoughts to positive ones, you can actually change anything. Thus, just remember that you are now on the threshold of the secret path to peace of mind, inner joy, tranquility, and prosperity. Due to your contact with the divine, through your devotion to the suggested exercises, you will finally access a sustainable peace of mind, inner joy, tranquility, and prosperity. You will also effortlessly secure love, unity, freedom, and justice.

The only person now who can stop you from commanding your own peace of mind is you.

It is all up to you now!

Your Peace Is Your Command!

THE 5TH SECRET

THE SECRET TO THE RULE OF LIFE

You have the power to be one with the divine and nature. You will have peace of mind when you believe . . .

Your Peace Is Your Command!

Special Introduction to "The Secret to the Rule of Life"

There are secret principles for the existence of all humanity. These principles are derived from what scholars refer to as *the rule of life*. Mankind's evolution is in essence the pathway we all follow. Therefore, we should do so with an increasingly heightened consciousness toward peace of mind, including love, liberty, unity, freedom, and justice.

Research finds that the destiny of humanity is to achieve perfection and fulfillment. This is because we are all created to live in peace with love, joy, liberty, unity, freedom, and justice. However, in order to achieve this goal, we should acquire knowledge, and we should be responsible . . . That is how we evolve as human beings. As Mao Tse Tung said, "Man must be taught to fish, not be given fish to eat."

Without any exception, all human beings stumble upon this bitter truth one day. This is the unexpected great expectation. Some people wake up to this realization and change their lives accordingly. However, some people pick themselves up without any understanding of the realization and go about their business as if it were nothing. Some others do realize it for a while but soon return to living in the same vulnerable way as before. This is because most of these people are not aware of the principles that govern life, and they have no knowledge of the causes and the effects of these universal principles.

Let us imagine, for example, a beautiful lady from a far-off village of Jimmy Bagbo was to arrive for the first time in the city of San Jose, California. Without any knowledge of the traffic rules of San Jose, she started roaming around the city by car and crashed into another car at the first stop light. Obviously, stoplights might not mean anything to this young lady other than insignificant lights amid advertising banners.

The next stoplight brings another crash. To avoid more accidents, commotions, and calamities, we should explain to this beautiful lady, without further ado, what these stop lights mean and when she must stop. Then we should let this foreigner know the rules of the roads in the city of San Jose, California. This lady might not have known when to stop because she does not know the rules of the roads in the strange city.

The same example goes for those who are living in ignorance and who realize, for example, that they are ill. "My head hurts, so I must drink medicine and the pain will disappear," the person may say. This sick person did not see the link between himself and his illness. He just simply rids himself of the signal transmitted by his body by drinking pain medicine. You will realize that the ignorant person suffering from the headache goes through exactly the same process as our stranger in the previous example. Thus, if positive steps are not immediately taken, such erroneous and diabolic process will continue until he or she starts paying attention to the rules of life that can bring a cure and peace of mind to him or her. Therefore, *The 7 Secrets to Peace of Mind* has been designed to be the panacea for all humanity.

This volume reveals the secret to the rule of life that will give you peace of mind, including love, liberty, unity, freedom, and justice.

THE SECRET PRINCIPLES OF LIFE

The secret principles of life are so vital that, in my opinion, they should have been revealed to all humanity long before now. In fact, we are the universe; just as most astronomers, parapsychologists, or physicians can tell you that we live in a cosmos and that we are also part of the cosmos. Even my ten-year-old son, Lawrence Charles, knows that we live in a cosmos. Perhaps you may say, "Yes, Tony Charles; of course every child knows that." You might be right, but do you realize what you are saying?

I encourage you to think very carefully about it . . . Cosmos is a Greek word that means order. We are living in an *order*, and we are part of the *order*. Every order is subject to principles or it would not be an order. It would be chaos, which is the Greek word for disorder. Of course you will agree with me that the direct consequence of disorder is always undesirable. However, if you know the principles of life, you can take them into account and recognize the signs and messages that life gives you and act accordingly to avoid the consequences of disorder. I therefore encourage you to please take a close look at how these rules govern humanity.

THE SECRET PRINCIPLES OF LIFE

- Causality
- Correspondence
- Resonance
- Reincarnation
- Cause and effect

THE PRINCIPLE OF CAUSALITY

The first cosmic principle of life is the principle of causality. You may have heard of the principle of causality as mentioned in spiritual stories and from many religions around the world. Or you might be familiar with the adage, "As you sow, so shall you reap" or "He who sows the wind reaps the whirlwind."

In the interest of brevity, what this principle is simply telling all humanity is, if you sow destruction in your life, you will harvest destruction. If you sow anger and hatred in your life, you will harvest anger and hatred. If you sow peace and harmony, you will harvest peace and harmony. If you sow war, you will harvest war. Please be reminded also that the care and attention invested in the seed you sow can be evident in the quality of the harvest you will have.

One of the most important concepts of the principles of life is to understand that the cosmos, just like our subconscious mind, is absolutely without prejudice. According to the cosmos, nothing is good or bad, positive or negative, black or white, valuable or worthless, etc. These judgments only have values for us as individuals. Something that is beautiful or good for you may not necessarily be so for your neighbor. As one put it, "One man's meat is another man's poison."

Let us take, for example, the poor farmers in Banta Monkeleh and Tikonko Chiefdoms in Sierra Leone, who occupy a very low level on the social scale in the nation. Few say it, but many think it. Have you ever taken time to wonder where your food would come from if all the farmers in the world were replaced with lawyers? Let us also consider the example of the Mercedes Benz driver who looks disdainfully down on the workers doing the night shift on the production line. Are these workers not the very people who manufacture those luxury cars and so make it possible for us to drive them?

You may be surprised to know also that when it comes to housework, there are some people who do not want to demean themselves by doing the unpleasant tasks in their own homes. Thus, they prefer to delegate them to paid housekeepers, maids, etc. What kind of world would we live in if nobody was prepared to clean after himself or herself? Who could deny that what is a pleasing gift for one person may not be to the taste of another person? A plant also may be a good medicine to a homeopath whereas to a gardener, it may be a weed to be destroyed immediately.

Another example is, for some people, spiders are creatures that instill fear, and they get squashed without a second thought by the same people who complain about annoying flies. Of course, the flies are around because there are no spider webs for them to be trapped in since the spiders are not there to weave the webs. My wife, Isha, and my children, Tonia, Tony, Sylvester, and Lawrence, are examples of such people. My children think of spiders as creatures that instill fear; on the other hand, my wife complains about annoying flies.

Obviously, whether we think something is good or bad, valuable or worthless, this is just a value judgment and more importantly, an expression of our subjectivity. This becomes all the more evident when we think about energy. Energy is valueless in the sense that it depends on us to make it either positive or negative. In other words, it is left with us to use energy for constructive ends or for destructive ends. Thus this new book of knowledge has been designed to let you know that as a human being, what you always do with all your mind is what life gives you. Remember also that *you are what you do most of the time.*

Creation also gave us free judgment so that with peace of mind, we could experience life in its entirety, including love, good health, inner joy, and tranquility. Remember also that life did not decree that we experience only the pleasant or beautiful things. Therefore we are absolutely free to experience what we want. Sometimes when we eventually get what we wished for, we find that it is not what we needed after all.

However, we do have the freedom to choose. Thus, *The 7 Secrets to Peace of Mind* has been designed to offer you added knowledge of how to always beware of the consequences of your choices. As the saying goes, "Be careful what you wish for; you just might get it." Be mindful also that *no man can rid himself of the spirits he has summoned.*

For example, a negative thought comes into your mind, and the more you turn it around in your head, the more you consolidate it. The consequence will be, whatever that thought is, one day it may be realized in your life. Everyone has his or her fears. For example, some people are afraid that one day they may be attacked by evildoers or that the police might arrest them when they have had one drink too many.

Or perhaps one day you might wake up with a very good idea in your head but say to yourself, "Gosh, now there's another plan that will never work." The energy generated by that thought is an order both for your subconscious and for the cosmos, and it can be taken into account. Therefore, you should be very careful of what you think about most of the time. Remember, *thinking is power* and thoughts are things.

The cosmos can also be compared to a giant computer that functions according to perfect programs. You program it with your thoughts (input), and it prints whatever is programmed into it (output). So also your subconscious mind does not know what fear is. It cannot even distinguish between positive and negative. You give it energy, an order, and it gets to work on what it has received.

Likewise, if you entertain a thought of violence with sufficient intensity for a long time, you can be a victim of an attack. Do not say to yourself afterward, "You see, I knew that was going to turn out badly." Yes, you knew it, but more accurately, you were the only one to know it. As one put it, "Each man has the right to his own thoughts and feelings." Thus you are the author of your thoughts and your feelings, and it is only you who gives them life. What you think and feel is up to you and you alone and it will sooner or later become a reality in your life. Always remember that you are responsible for your own thoughts and feelings.

THE PRINCIPLE OF CORRESPONDENCE

The second principle of life is the principle of correspondence. This powerful principle was put into effect so that humanity could realize the *great* in the *small* and the *small* in the *great*. The principle of correspondence speaks to the analogy of, "As above, so below; as below, so above." Of course you may also be familiar with the phrase, "On earth as in heaven." These phrases also qualify the fact that the same principle governs the macrocosm as well as the microcosm.

For example, science tells us that the smallest constituent element in physical matter currently known to man is an atom. An atom is made up of primarily protons, neutrons, and electrons. Protons and neutrons together form the nucleus of the atom. Please be informed also that it is the incredible speed at which electrons gravitate around the nucleus that creates the envelope of an atom. As such, the whole is maintained by an electromagnetic force. Remember also that atoms differ depending on the number of electrons and protons they contain.

It is also important to know that the human magnetic field turning on itself is identical in aspect to that of our galaxy turning on itself. This bio-magnetic field is like a bubble of energy enveloping the body. The very high vibratory frequency of this bubble of energy makes it invisible to the naked eye except for those who have the gift of clairvoyance, for whom it appears in the form of a colored cloud that parapsychologists refer to as the *aura*.

This new book of knowledge is also designed to let you know that everything is constructed according to a perfect system that is not necessarily recognizable at first sight but that emerges when you look more closely. Life itself, just like the microcosm and the macrocosm, is governed by perfect principles. These principles are to be found everywhere in our solar system, in the blood cells, in electricity, and in magnetism. And since matter is maintained and determined by electromagnetic forces, we human beings are also matter. Thus, we are also subject to principles, such as the law of attraction, the law of gravitation, the law of repulsion, etc.

The principle of the analogy, "as above, so below," can only work if we are prepared to acknowledge the fact that the universe is a cosmos and a system. Therefore, there is no place for chance occurrences. Chance in the form of an event that could not have been predicted and not in line with the principle could transform all the cosmos, or order, into chaos, or disorder.

For example, when an engineer builds a computer, what he constructs actually represents a little cosmos. The computer is built according to principles, and its functioning depends on the application of those principles. Thus, if you were to deliberately weld onto the computer's connections a series of transistors, capacitors, or resistors that played no part in its circuit, which was designed according to a specific principle, those elements, which represent chance, would force the entire system to descend into chaos. When that happens, the computer can no longer function as it should.

The same principle is true of our world, which would cease to exist upon the occurrence of the first event that arose by chance. For instance, if Mr. Siaka Stephens drops a stone from a certain height, it is not by chance that it falls downward; it is obeying the law of gravitation. If, as the stone drops, it happens to fall on the head of Mr. Sorie Fornah or Mr. Francis Minah or Mr. Bambay Kamara, this also is not the result of chance but rather of a law that the stone will strike any of those powerful individuals. Nothing is down to chance—neither the fact that Mr. Bambay Kamara, or Mr. Francis Minah, or Mr. Sorie Fornah gets hit by the stone nor the time when it happens.

To get a very clear understanding of this principle, please think very carefully about the following questions: Have you ever wondered why a star never leaves its orbit, why a blood cell never circulates against the direction of the bloodstream, or how a spring flower never blossoms by chance in winter? Have you ever heard of an electron leaving by chance the orbit it spins around the nucleus of the atom? The fact is every matter is made up of basic elements that in turn are formed of atoms, protons, and electrons, whose movements are absolutely perfect and rhythmic.

Therefore, after taking the previous questions into consideration, now ask yourself this question: Why could human beings be the only ones to be exposed to chance while everything else in us and around us is subject to a regular rhythm? This new book of knowledge has therefore been designed to tell you frankly that there is no such thing as chance. Everything that happens is governed by a principle. Of course, that principle may not be obvious to you at first, but that does not mean you can deny its existence. In fact, remember that stones were falling way before you knew about the law of gravity.

The psychology here is to remind you that anything that happens to you happens because that is how it has been designed by the *higher power*. The secret is if you think very carefully, you will find out that anything that happens to anyone in this world, happens to him or her for his or her own good. For instance, the coffee that spills on your white shirt just when you are about to leave home for work is not by chance. Powerful forces may be delaying you at home so you can avoid an accident on your way to work at that time. There are many such examples to let you know that nothing happens by chance.

Thus, this new book of knowledge is encouraging you to always do what needs to be done and then relax with faith that everything is in order. Therefore, blaming other people for the things that happen to you can only generate further problems. As a human being, you should take responsibility of your own actions and obey the principles of life. Always remember, however, that *whatever happens to you in this world happens to you for your own good.*

THE PRINCIPLE OF RESONANCE

The third principle of life is the principle of resonance. Humanity is subject to the principle of resonance in the same way as a tuning fork or a radio receiver is. A receiver set to short-wave frequency cannot pick up anything on medium-wave frequency or long-wave frequency. The same is true for human kind. Someone who is full of hate or jealousy is not receptive to peace of mind. Always remember that each of us is capable of receiving all aspects of reality with which we are in resonance. Psychology tells us also that as human beings, each of us sees only what we want to see.

For example, you are reading this book now. Seven months later you read it again and discover something quite different from the first time you read it. Why? It is because you have evolved. Your horizons, your way of thinking, and your way of seeing things have changed. You have a different paradigm now. The education procured from reading this new book of knowledge the first time around may have created a paradigm shift for you. As a result, you will never see things the same way again.

It is also common for us human beings to feel the need to seek out those who are similar to us. Thus we say, "Birds of a feather flock together." You will notice that if you are in a bad mood, you will take the way you are feeling out on those around you. Let us take, for example, someone who is always complaining. You will find out that if that person did not change his or her attitude, he or she would never be short of good reasons to complain. Life, on the other hand, always brings good people together with those who are happy to be alive.

Another example is a person who always manages to find fault in others, saying, "That guy is an idiot. He is a failure, and everything he does is wrong." As such, if this critic sees everything negatively, he will see this written in his negative eyes and in his grim demeanor. No one will ever say that such a person is a kind human being. As such, there is hardly any pleasure in his company. As a result, friendly people will avoid him like the plague. He will, however, find people who think as he does who may back him up in his beliefs because: "Birds of a feather flock together."

Responsible people, on the other hand, know how to enjoy themselves. Wherever they are, they create a good atmosphere. They know how to smile and how to share. Such people will be surrounded by fun and pleasant people and will often be invited out by good people because they know how to give and how to receive.

Remember: "Birds of a feather flock together." There is no value judgment in this phrase. There is no good, and there is no bad. The complainer and the jovial person simply get back what they give out. This may take both of them far, each on a different path. The complainer, caught in a vicious circle, will see his situation worsen. On the other hand, all will go smoothly for the happy person who will become ever more fulfilled.

The true, unaffected goodness that pervades happy people attracts people like themselves, reinforcing the goodwill they are capable of sharing. And if it happens that one day something happens that takes their smile from them, their friends will soften their anguish and pass them a little of the joy they have so often given out.

However, as for the complainers, their future does not look quite so bright. They will end up blaming others for the difficult life they lead. They will never see that, in fact, they cause their own sadness. That is one of the reasons why some people are always complaining about their jobs while others are always happy with what they do, regardless of what it is.

For example, my brother, Mr. Sylvester Charles, served in the Sierra Leone Police Force for over forty years. But because he loved his job, every day of those many years was an exciting day for him at work. As such, he was always a pleasant team player on duty. This diligent police officer, number 774 Charles, happily retired with dignity as a senior police officer after his many years of devoted service to his nation.

Therefore, this new book of knowledge is designed to let you know that the era of slavery is over. Every human being is free to be where he or she wants to be and with whom he or she wants to be. In fact, my wife Isha and I have been happily together for decades, and we are still counting. Some people, on the other hand, are always complaining about their spouses. But the truth is, nobody is making them stay with their spouses when all they do is to argue with them, lead a hellish life, etc. With currently seven billion people on this planet, those who are not happy with their spouses have every freedom to find someone else who can make them happy and have the love and the peace of mind they deserve.

The fact is if the complainers really want to live in harmony with their spouses, they will make every effort to understand the root cause of their problems and do what they need to do accordingly. In fact, from the very moment complainers change themselves inside, the environment they live in will change itself accordingly and effortlessly. The truth is *if you really want to live in peace with your spouse, you need to look in the mirror and then change yourself inside.* This is the secret.

Always remember that *the people in your life are a reflection of the way you are.* That is what is meant when people say your friends often give back what you give out. If you lie, you will be lied to. If you cheat, you will be cheated on. If you are afraid, you will have to confront your fears. If you are aggressive, you will always get mixed up in disputes. If you are full of love, you will attract love. If you live your life with joy, you will always find a reason to rejoice. As my sister in-law Janet would put it, "One life to live, my dear." Therefore, *if you change the way you see things, those around you will reflect it like a mirror.*

Be mindful also that excessively watching violent films, horror movies, and bad news on the TV can have a severe negative impact on your life. Think about this: For many years, the violence of our actions and the destructive power of our thoughts due to the violence of the actions we see have released enormous amounts of energy that still continue to reach us. Some people are so attracted by the negative suggestions they get that they make their own violent films.

Please be reminded that it is not the major political events that mostly cause violence in your circumstances, but rather the little omissions of peace and love in your daily lives. The quality of what you read, what you watch, what you say, and what you do depends on the quality of your life and what you make of it. The principle of resonance functions with perfect symmetry. Remember the adage, "As above, so below." Remember also that: "As you make your bed, so you will lie down on it."

One thing you should never forget however is that your body is the reflection of your soul. Therefore, if disharmony reigns deep within you, it will eventually show in your body. If you are irritated, your body will feel it and express it to you in the form of illness. If you are not centered, this will be visible externally. If you lack drive, it will come through in your handshakes, and so on.

Of course, *it is common among human beings to blame others for everything*. That is, for everything that does not suit you, you lay the blame at the feet of a wide range of culprits. You may blame members of your family, the government, the weather, etc. You even sometimes cite circumstances, society, sects, drug abuse, the devil, etc. You waste your precious time accusing external forces for being the cause of all your ills because you make them responsible for your own destiny.

The good news, however, is that this allocation of blame to external sources will cease to be a possibility from the moment you accept the cosmic and spiritual principles this new book of knowledge is revealing to you. These principles reveal that everything that exists and the way in which it exists is nothing but the manifestation of causes that are of mankind's own making.

It does not matter whether you are talking about an internal or external state, an illness, an accident, the massive destruction by the tsunami in Japan, the rebel war in Sierra Leone, the great oil spill that was discovered on the Gulf Coast in the United States of America on June 20, 2010, the state of our earth with reference to the global warming, etc. It is we, the human beings, who are the cause of most of our situations, and we have to answer for that. Maybe that is what it means when John F. Kennedy said, "Our problems are manmade, and they will be solved by man." some of you may respond, "But how does this concern me? I have only been in this world for less than fifty years."

For example, during my preparation to write this new book of knowledge, one OBA member who told me not to mention his name asked me these questions: "How come I was severely 'drilled,' or hazed, several times in the Bo Government Secondary School when I was a 'greener,' or when I was a freshman? What did I do for that to happen to me? How did I deserve it?" What I told that honorable Bo School boy was that part of the answer lay in his questions.

According to the principle of cause and effect, he deserved whatever happened to him in the Bo School. He himself contributed to what he called his "bad luck." In other words, it was he who, one day, originated that *cause* that he no longer remembers. This cause might date back to his early childhood when maybe he himself was a bully, his prenatal stage, or his previous life. This volume is therefore reminding everyone that just because you do not have proof of your previous lives does not mean you have not had them.

For instance, the earth was already round long before anyone had proof of it. Before that time, there were scientists and specialists who said the earth was flat, and those who thought differently were even punished for their beliefs. The difficulty lies in the fact that most of us do not remember our previous lives, in which we were responsible for actions the effects of which we may now be going through. Not knowing about your past acts, however, does not protect you from their consequences, whatever they may be. When you read this aphorism and let it resonate, you will surely think back about each year of your life and make the effort to make the necessary changes . . .

THE PRINCIPLE OF REINCARNATION

The forth principle of life is the principle of reincarnation. Some scholars may raise the objection that reincarnation does not exist. They may be right, because the doctrine of reincarnation is no longer featured in most sacred literature. This is how the first Christians came to be deprived of the most important basis of their religion.

However, Christians were given by way of compensation the doctrine of the resurrection of the flesh on the last day. This was not necessarily a very good deal, and it is still a mystery to humanity. However, many scholars will continue with the research, and some of us will also be in touch with powerful spiritual advisers: Rev. Ross, Rev. Turay, Rev. Kainwo, Rev. Gbudema, Rev. Dumbuya, and the many others who may help us with our studies in search of the truth that will eventually enlighten all humanity.

Let us actually take a close look at the subject of reincarnation. As it has already been said, we live in a world of matter, and matter is subject to the

179

principle of polarity. The rhythm and oscillation that are the basis of all life are born out of constant exchange between two poles, such as the positive pole and the negative pole. Please remember that the terms positive and negative do not have any implicit value judgment. They simply reflect what happens at atomic level, with the nucleus being charged positively (+) and the electrons being charged negatively (-).

Of course science tells us that nothing stands still. Thus, everything is in vibration, and everything is moving. For example, the needle of a pendulum that swings to the left will oscillate at the same amplitude to the right. In fact, this rhythm is to be found everywhere. For example, your "breathing in" inevitably gives way to your "breathing out." Your waking state is succeeded by your sleeping state; summer is followed by winter; the rainy season is followed by dry season; day is followed by night; light is followed by darkness; etc.

There are two poles in electricity and magnetism, just as there are two energies in human beings—the feminine and the masculine, the yin and the yang. In the same way, death follows life. So it is crystal clear that this rhythm is everywhere in life. However, some people who have faith only in religion or others who believe only in science still refuse to accept that these principles apply to life. Do you see the contradiction? I really hope you do. I am sure one does not have to be a graduate of Christ the King College to understand this biblical concept.

Thus, you will no doubt agree with Rev. Fr. Jerry Lambe and the many other scholars with in-depth knowledge on this topic that the rhythmic change of the soul through life can be referred to as the transmigration of the soul, simply known as reincarnation. However, you are free to disbelieve that "life" in matter is subject to polarity. "Life" itself is divided into two worlds: this world and the other world. We die in this world, and we are born in the other world, which we experience as reality. Then we die in that other world, and we are reborn into this world. He who can break away from the subjectivity of appearances will realize that birth and death, this world and the other world, are ultimately no more than two sides of the same coin.

The same thing happens in sleep when the soul leaves the physical body. During what we refer to as dreams, we experience another reality that has its own pain and sadness, its own joys. Some people can remember their dreams in detail, while others insist they never dream. Their memories of their dreams may be absent, but they have indeed dreamed. We are happy to wake up, just as we are happy to go to sleep because we know that after a good sleep, we will awake refreshed.

The 7 Secrets to Peace of Mind is designed to let you know that there is no way of describing waking and sleeping as being positive or negative. This is because they cannot be ascribed to any system of values. Thus, if we apply that same notion to life and death, it means that all fear of death is superfluous because the same thing happens as with sleep. It is just that the lapse of time is too great for us to be able to imagine.

Of course, without any doubt, humanity has always been afraid of death. However, the truth is, no one gets out of here alive. Death then is the culmination of life. We can rest after death before plunging once again into the adventure of life in a physical body. However, if you cannot recall a memory, ask some people who have gone through a near-death experience (NDE) or clinical death and let them tell you about their view of death. You will be astonished to know that more than 90 percent of those individuals had a positive (pleasant) experience that freed them of all fear because this personal experience gave them the opportunity to know what most of us are afraid to know.

The development of our soul is a long process of learning and progress for which innumerable bodies are required. The immortal part of the spiritual being—the soul—could be described as dressing itself in a bodily envelope for each incarnation. Our true self is not the physical body but rather our soul, called our "energetic body" or our "body of light." This is the body that holds all our memories and that is imperishable. It is this energetic body, which is also known as the "aura" that most clairvoyants see and use as a source of information.

This learning process is designed to ensure that we experience life in all its forms because life is a long journey, with many mistakes and changes along the way. The successive incarnations could be compared to grade levels in school, each with its homework, problems, tests, difficulties, and achievements. These times of study are followed by holidays, during which we sometimes have to work on gaps in our knowledge and correct our mistakes before passing into the next grade level. Our level of skill will determine the class in which we find ourselves. If we have learned nothing, we have to stay in the same class. If we have learned our lessons, we will go up to the next class, where further and more difficult tests await us.

Unlike school, however, "life" has infinite patience with us. Souls always have opportunities to learn what they do not yet know. In response to the question on why things happen to you—for example, why you were born into a poor family, why the rebels attacked your people, why you were victimized, why you did not win the election, etc.—this new book of knowledge lets you know that *to live is to learn.* This is a fact whether you accept it or not. Life, according to the guiding principles, ensures with absolute fairness that each one of us learns exactly what we are willing to accept or what we oppose. Therefore, we might perhaps question the meaning of life without the underlying concept of reincarnation.

You will agree with me that we clearly do not all start out with the same advantages in life. This is not always the fault of society. In fact, whether you are religious or an atheist, it is difficult to explain to someone precisely why some people were born poor, deaf, paralyzed, crippled, or weak without mentioning reincarnation.

Just saying "God works in a mysterious way" does not help; for example, consider a crippled person who is trying to make sense of his life. And man cannot live his life without giving it some meaning. Giving your life meaning is a fundamental need to have peace of mind. That is in fact one of the reasons for writing this new book of knowledge to be my humble way of service to all who may want to change their lives for the better. As Abraham Lincoln rightly put it, "In the end, it is not the years in your life that count. It is the life in your years."

THE PRINCIPLE OF CAUSE AND EFFECT

The fifth principle of life is the principle of cause and effect. To make things even easier to understand, parapsychology has introduced two new concepts known as "karma" and "dharma." The principle of karma (in Sanskrit, "the deed or the action") is the principle of cause and effect that ensures that human beings are confronted with their problems until they resolve them. Therefore, every thought, every feeling, and every action is immortal. In order words, they can later come back to you like a boomerang. You may have heard the phrase "what goes around, comes around."

According to karma, humanity takes full responsibility for its destiny. Obviously, there are some people who still refuse to accept this fact. However, the denial of reincarnation is entirely understandable. Of course, some scholars have introduced and disseminated theories that appear perfect. However, most of these theories rest on science, and they only make references to university studies.

The problem is such theories deprive mankind of self-responsibility and place most of the blame on external sources such as politics, religion, the system, and society in general. According to the law of cause and effect, you get back what you have caused to happen. Someone who uses violence can be on the receiving end of violence in that very lifetime or in a subsequent lifetime. People like Adolf Hitler, Foday Sankoh, and many others exhaust their karma just like any other person.

Buddhism, on the other hand, describes dharma as all the enjoyable, constructive experiences accumulated over the course of numerous previous lives, which counterbalances karma. Dharma is the skill or the talent we are born with for living our lives. Dharma is always a little bigger than karma to allow us to pay off our karmic debts. From this angle, some people may think suicide is an escape from the task they have chosen to perform in this life before being reincarnated.

In my opinion, however, that may not be a good idea, and it should not be encouraged. In fact, if you do that, you may unfortunately rediscover this same task in another life. Nobody can escape this process. Each and every one of us has to accept the consequences of our actions—no more and no less. This new book of knowledge is therefore designed to offer you the opportunity to know how to *be very careful with what you do or say at all times, even when no one is watching you.* As one put it, "Whatever you are doing, do it as if the whole world is watching you." Or as a popular song goes, "Anything you want to do, do it well, for no one knows tomorrow." When you earnestly do that, you will surely have the peace of mind you deserve.

Some parapsychologists or psychics who can sometimes see *aura*, which is the luminous body that surrounds the physical body, can also sometimes see a person's karma and dharma. However, they may not necessarily see the future. What they do is they look at the current status of the person and the actions that correspond to that status. The psychology is, according to the person's current status and his actions, a powerful parapsychologist or psychic can predict the consequences that may result if the person did not make serious changes or sacrifices. Sometimes, psychics can even suggest some sacrifices the person should offer and some changes he should make in his current life to alter his destiny. It is therefore apparent that one can actually alter his or her destiny if the appropriate actions are taken in a timely manner.

It is also possible for the relationship between karma and dharma to change if you act in a constructive way toward greater love for yourself, for others, for animals, and for nature as a whole. To achieve this goal, you should always remember the philosophy that anything you do, you should do it for *peace, hope,* and *love*. This is the *PHL* philosophy that will save you from the iniquities of your previous lifetime.

Just take a moment and imagine, for example, somebody who was a killer during the rebel wars in Sierra Leone and Liberia. Or imagine someone who took part in the 9/11 terrorist attack on the United States of America in 2001. Or imagine someone who worked in a concentration camp in a previous life where, through ideology, he mercilessly killed thousands of people, including even the handicapped. Such actions can surely have impact on that person's karma. Let us suppose that the soul of that person now inhabits a new body in another country in a different lifetime. Then one day he goes to see a clairvoyant who sees the deeds he was responsible for in his previous lifetime and predicts a difficult future for him. This is what he risks happening to him if he continues to live as before.

But then, in full awareness, to make amends for what he has done in his past life, he agrees to work in a home for the disabled. This is a wise decision to change his life, to do good things without seeking anything in return. This decision, to change his life and selflessly do good things, will help him and of course, will also help the handicapped people he may be serving. Or again, he may decide, in full awareness, to fundamentally change the way he thinks and acts. Or he can live his life according to the *PHL* philosophy. If the person honestly makes these new decisions, his destiny will be modified accordingly.

The principle of reincarnation tells us that we are reborn in a series of bodies that are every time perfectly suited to us. Each of these bodies is learning to overcome the specific tests that correspond to us. We may be reincarnated one time male, another time female; one time black, another time white; one time tall, another time short; etc. We could be reborn into a rich or poor family, into a Muslim or Christian family, in the body of a man or a woman, etc. This is how we can live every experience life has to offer.

It is therefore completely nonsensical to judge people on the basis of the color of their skin, their tribes, their beliefs, their cultural background or origins. It is nonsensical, because each of us will pass at least once through all these different experiences. Thus, according to the doctrine of reincarnation, passing wrong judgment on others, hating others, or starting wars indicates absolute weakness. And it is wrong.

Therefore, the principle of reincarnation is absolutely fair. It is a powerful principle that is perfectly logical and just. As it has always been said, "A boomerang comes back with the same force with which it was thrown." For example, if you scream in a forest, you hear the echo of your scream at exactly the same level. If you are guilty of brutality, then you may one day suffer brutality. If you are greedy and taking advantage of the generosity of others while selfishly keeping what you have to yourself, you can experience a life of hardship.

Without any exceptions, human beings will be given every opportunity to experience what they have inflicted on others and with equal intensity. This noble principle of cause and effect can be observed everywhere in nature: in physics, in chemistry, in our environment, and in our bodies. If, for example, you inject strong chemicals into your system in the form of drugs, your system will react accordingly, and you alone will pay the price for making it ingest those chemicals. If, on the other hand, you lead a constructive life, acknowledging that love and goodwill are superior principles, you will be rewarded accordingly.

Now take some time and think very carefully about your own belief system. Are your values, your religious beliefs, and your reality the results of your personal experiences? Or are you just regurgitating the opinions of others or what is popular at the time? Have you ever had an experience that had a decisive impact on you? Have you ever seen a vision, heard voices, dreamed what was going to happen to you, or had a near-death experience or an astral journey? Have you ever had a premonition, been spontaneously cured, or communicated by telepathy?

If the answer is yes to any of those questions, you will have good reason to consider it in everything you do. Most people have never had any such experience personally, but neither do they make any particular effort to find out if what they believe is true or if continuing with the same beliefs is a good idea. Dr. Martin Luther King's statement, "The time is always right to do what is right," is very appropriate here. However, one thing I know very clearly is that knowing about these past lives is not the important thing now.

What is important now is for you to live every moment of your life in truth and justice. Then apply the *PHL* philosophy and do anything you have to do only for *peace, hope,* and *love.* This *PHL* philosophy is the best way to compensate for any ills you may have caused in your past lives. If you have already purified the greater part of your karma and you are living in a constructive manner, you should take care not to be drawn in another direction. By making the best use of your virtues, you will be able to accelerate the process that will free you for eternity.

Honestly, as you already know, it is not always advisable to know your past. It is actually the *here* and the *next* that matter, whatever they may be. The way we can evolve now is by applying the great and well-known principle of selfless love, living in truth, being a fair person, and maintaining a balance between reason and emotion. For most people, however, this may be a confusing prospect, and they may ask themselves how they can go about it. A very fitting answer is to be found in an ancestral saying, "Do as you would be done by." This is the well known golden rule.

THE POWER OF THE GOLDEN RULE

The golden rule is one of the most powerful rules in modern philosophy. This new book of knowledge has therefore been designed to encourage all humanity to obey this powerful golden rule in order to have a sustainable peace of mind. The well-known golden rule, "Do as you would be done by," is a universal principle that is found in many religions around the world. Here are just a few examples:

In Christianity: Do unto others as you would like them to do unto you.

In Islam: None of you truly believes until he wishes for his brother what he wishes for himself.

In Hinduism: Do not do to others what would cause pain if done to you.

In Buddhism: Treat others with the same patience, compassion, and loving kindness with which you would like them to treat you.

In Confucianism: Do not do unto others what you do not want them to do to you.

In Taoism: Regard your neighbor's gain as your own gain and your neighbor's loss as your own loss.

In Judaism: What is hateful to you, do not do it to your fellow man.

In accordance to the above golden rule, this new book of knowledge offers the opportunity to reflect on the following questions: Would you like someone to lie to you, steal from you, or insult you? Of course you would not want any of those to happen to you. Therefore, in the interest of a sustainable peace of mind, you should avoid behaving in those ways towards others, no matter who they may be.

If you feel happy when someone gives you a gift or when someone seeks out your company, start by behaving toward others in the same way. When you do that, you will see how gradually and effortlessly you will have the peace of mind you need. If you lack courage at first, visualize yourself in the process of carrying out these actions. As a result, many things will be changed for the better in your life almost effortlessly.

Whether you are a Christian, a Muslim, an atheist, etc., it is possible to live in love and always remember that *Selfless love does not judge*. In fact, it is not associated with any organization, church, mosque, synagogue, race, nationality, political party, etc. Selfless love is within everyone's reach, and it is free. Of course, it is not always easy, but you should make every effort to express selfless love seven days a week.

Therefore, by playing your part in the cosmic order, you will finally comprehend true love and have the peace of mind you deserve. Please be informed that true love is the kind of love that cannot be measured by any instrument. *True love is the kind of love that cannot even be proven, but it is real all the same and all the time.* In fact, it would be ridiculous to say that love does not exist just because you cannot prove it. Those who know true love know it exists and have no need for proof. Always remember that *love is the ultimate power.*

I love the way Mother Teresa put it when she stated, "If we want a love message to be heard, it has got to be sent out. To keep a lamp burning, we have to keep putting the appropriate oil in it."

Thus, from now onward, love, truth, and divine light will enlighten your path.

Your Peace Is Your Command!

THE 6TH SECRET

THE SECRETS TO LONGEVITY AND WELL-BEING

You have the power to be whole in mind, body, and spirit. You will have peace of mind when you believe . . .

Your Peace Is Your Command!

Special Introduction to "The Secret to Longevity and Well-Being"

The 6th Secret to peace of mind is the secret to longevity and well-being. Of course, it is abundantly clear that your longevity and your well-being are the most important matters to you and to your loved ones. This new book of knowledge is therefore designed to reveal the three major secrets to longevity and well-being:

The first secret to longevity and well-being is *concentration.* The second secret to longevity and well-being is *balance.* The third secret to longevity and well-being is *positive attitude.* These three secrets will be used to create good effect at any moment of your daily life. The power and the effectiveness of these three secrets will be considerably increased if you regularly put them into practice.

Concentration Is the First Secret to Longevity and Well-Being

You may no doubt be astonished to know that the number one secret to longevity and well-being is *concentration.* However, most of the time, you are barely conscious of what you are actually doing. This is mainly because there are so many projects, memories, words, and images rapidly chasing each other through your head, overlapping and interlacing in a totally free and chaotic manner.

Please be reminded also that you are not alone. Unfortunately, in the current fast-moving society, there are not many people who can devote their attention exclusively to one thing and then keep their thoughts on track without getting distracted. The problem is, most people disperse and dissipate their mental energy all the time. Sometimes, however, it is possible for such individuals to concentrate hard in the heat of the moment, perhaps when influenced by a powerful emotion or during an urgent necessity. But even then, they are just submitting to the situation rather than controlling it.

Obviously, this is not the deliberate, calm, and active kind of concentration *The 7 Secrets to Peace of Mind* is drawing your attention to. This new book of knowledge is about the kind of concentration that will open the doors that lead to your well-being and longevity. Due to the knowledge of this secret, there are people who in just seven days can produce work that their comrades would find difficult to accomplish in three weeks. There are people who, when presented with a problem to solve, will give it just seven minutes of thought and then come up with a perfect solution.

There are lawyers who can even start to study some case files for only about seven hours before attending a hearing. For example, I once met a Sierra Leonean lawyer who studied my cousin's case with the great state of California for just about seven hours and went on to make a very successful representation in court.

There are also some medical doctors who are content with examining a patient for a very short period of time before successfully carrying out an operation. They are also capable, during the course of that operation, of successfully modifying their techniques each time a new factor comes to light. There are some Sierra Leonean doctors who are such diligent, gifted, and talented people in modern society.

The truth is most of these people perform well because they know the secret. They know how to focus their mind effectively. How do they manage to do that? That is the secret of concentration this new book of knowledge has been designed to reveal to you. This is your moment!

THE SECRET POWER OF MAXIMUM CONCENTRATION

Maximum concentration is the power to focus all your mental forces on a single issue and not allow yourself to be distracted. Science tells us that if you get the sun's rays to shine through a magnifying glass and direct the focused light onto a piece of paper, it can burst into flames. Likewise, if you really concentrate on a single issue as hard as you can without getting distracted, you will no doubt experience a flash of enlightenment.

By properly using this secret formula, problems that creep into your mind will be easily resolved after a few minutes of concentration. Remember also that concentration is the faculty that makes great people. When you really want to do something worthwhile, you should channel your attention and focus your power on it. Many individuals with great well-being are people who are capable of concentrating their minds on well-being.

However, to actually acquire greater comprehension of the mechanism involved in concentration, you should consider two main aspects:

1. There is a type of concentration that involves regular practice sessions, using specific places, times, and body postures. Those exercises are also possibly accompanied by certain breathing techniques.
2. The other type of concentration is brought to bear on life itself as it happens. It goes with its obvious repetition but with all its variation and surprises as well.

Although these aspects of concentration can be exercised independently, nonetheless, an esoteric principle known as the principle of complementarities links these two types of concentration. This is because the practices support and reinforce each other. The philosophy of understanding and observing this phenomenon of complementarities is one of the main keys to well-being and peace of mind.

THE SECRET PRINCIPLE OF RECIPROCATION

The principle of reciprocation is an important phenomenon in the concentration process for your well-being. This principle simply means that if you make use of your powers of concentration regularly, you will eventually possess a permanent high level of concentration in your everyday life.

The ability to concentrate in this way will automatically make you more discerning. Not only will you be able to recognize when luck is smiling at you personally, but most importantly, you will be capable of keeping your objectives firmly in your mind. As such, you will always stay on track. In other words, you will remain focused at all times. As a result, you will take maximum advantage of the opportunities that the universe sends you. You will then be able to turn those God-given opportunities into concrete victories. Some of those victories could be material victories, emotional victories, economic victories, relationship victories, social victories, political victories, spiritual victories, etc.

This principle is a reciprocal process that will let you remain focused when dealing with everyday situations. In fact, it will make your regular concentration exercises even more profitable. In turn, the quality of your overall concentration will be tremendously enhanced.

When that happens, you will eventually quit the vicious circle of the same old problems that occur when you dissipate your mental energy. With that, you will finally enter into a virtuous circle of efficiency and harmonious relationships. Fortunately, this will result in your peace of mind, including your well-being and longevity.

THE APPROPRIATE TIME FOR MAXIMUM CONCENTRATION

As is written in the holy book, "There is a time for everything." Therefore, it is a wise idea to have an appropriate time for your concentration exercises. If you want to achieve a good level of concentration, you should make the effort to train yourself regularly, at a certain time, and in a step-by-step manner. By so doing, you will learn to use your mind and your mental power like a tool that is wholly reliable and available when needed.

However, any time of the day is favorable for concentration as long as you are sure that you will not be disturbed for at least seven minutes. If possible, you should not be disturbed by any noise, visitors, or even phone calls. It is also important to choose the time of the day when you really feel fresh and alert. This might be in the morning, in the afternoon, in the evening, or in the night, depending on your temperament. Once you have chosen your time, stick to the same time for at least seven days.

Eventually you will condition yourself in a very positive way, and you will look forward with excitement to the same time each day when you will be alone to just concentrate. In fact, it will seem like you are giving yourself a treat—some space and time that will be all yours for recharging your batteries. You may regard this routine as a discipline if you want to, but it is one that nevertheless offers the pleasure of perpetual favorable discoveries.

To achieve this goal, is a matter of getting into a habit just like a musician practicing the piano every day, a gardener watering her vegetable patch, or washing your face every morning. Once this habit has become ingrained through practice and has become part of you, it will get easier and easier for you to concentrate. Thus, the energy you need to concentrate will come to you automatically, and concentration will be just as natural and spontaneous a thing as a flower exhaling its perfume.

THE IDEAL VENUE FOR MAXIMUM CONCENTRATION

You can actually do your concentration exercises anywhere as long as you can do them without being disturbed. However, it would be more ideal to have a special place reserved especially for your concentration activities. If you do not yet have one, you can even use a corner of your bedroom. It is also preferable to position yourself so that you are facing a blank wall or a bare surface so that your eyes cannot be drawn toward a mass of objects. If it is at night time, you can do your concentration exercise with a dimmer light or with the flame of a candle, for example.

If you prefer doing your concentration exercise outdoors, for example, under the shelter of a tree, against the backdrop of a garden, a lake, or a mountain, it is okay. These kinds of places can also give very good results as long as you are not bothered by heavy wind, hot sun, insects, etc. However, for a beginner, you cannot beat the peaceful and neutral surroundings of a room at home where you can feel perfectly at ease.

POWERFUL POSTURES FOR MAXIMUM CONCENTRATION

There are good body postures that are very powerful for maximum concentration. Therefore, to quickly achieve your goal, you are encouraged to be prepared for some successful and powerful body postures for concentration as suggested in this new book of knowledge. These appropriate postures will help you to concentrate quickly and efficiently. They are postures that were developed by powerful gurus who were in possession of esoteric secrets from the Far East. Those were the gurus who had profound knowledge of how energy circulates around the human body.

However, although *The 7 Secrets to Peace of Mind* is designed to suggest good body postures, nevertheless, it is left to you to choose the posture that seems to suit you better. Be mindful also that the position you adopt should be steady and comfortable for you. Steady does not mean stiff or heavy. Comfortable does not mean soft or languid. You need to be straight without being rigid and firm without being tense. You also need to be relaxed without being floppy.

If you do not need to use a cushion, simply sit down on a folded blanket or on a mat. It is not advisable to wear tight clothes during this exercise. Your concentration will be more effective if you wear clothes that are loose and are good energy conductors like linen, cotton, silk, wool, etc.

To help you find your center of balance in a sitting position, it might be useful to rock your upper body backward and forward a few times. Then sway around in circles from the waist, slowly and attentively, first in one direction and then the other. Take the greatest care as you settle into the right posture because achieving perfect concentration depends mostly on your posture.

The three most powerful and successful postures for maximum concentration are *the European posture, the Asian posture, and the African posture.*

THE EUROPEAN POSTURE FOR MAXIMUM CONCENTRATION

One of the best postures for maximum concentration is the European posture. Should this be the choice for your concentration exercise, the following simple exercises can help you:

Sit down and then bend your left leg and hold your left heel pressed against your perineum, which is situated between the anus and the genital organs. This is important because it stimulates energy. Then draw your right leg toward you and insert your toes between the thigh and the calf of your left leg.

Depending on how supple you are, your right knee may not actually be resting on the ground. You can solve this problem by sliding some form of padding, such as cushion, folded blanket, etc., under your bottom so that it raises your pelvis. Then both your knees will be touching the ground and providing proper support for your spinal column, which will remain straight and make it easier to breathe freely. You can also do it any other way that suits you better.

After a bit of experimentation, you will soon sense that you are in the correct position to concentrate. You can then do your concentration exercise for at least seven minutes every day until your goal is procured.

THE ASIAN POSTURE FOR MAXIMUM CONCENTRATION

The Asian posture is a powerful posture for maximum concentration. Should you prefer this posture, the following exercises are what you have to do:

Kneel on the ground and keep your knees tightly together. The whole section of your legs from the knees to the toes should be touching the ground. Spread your heels, but keep your big toes in contact. In this way, when you sit back on your legs behind you, your bottom will come to rest in the basket formed by your feet.

If you notice that your ankles or your knees are too stiff, you may be finding this rather difficult at first but please do not give up. If it is your ankles, place some padding like a cushion or blanket between the ground and your ankle joints. If your knees are the concern, place a similar pad between your thighs and your calves. On the other hand, if you are very supple, place your bottom directly on the ground between your opened-out heels with the inside of your calves touching the outside of your thighs. This firm and agreeable posture is good for concentration and even for digestion if you do it for at least seven minutes every day.

When you hold this position for too long, you might feel like you have pins and needles in your legs when you move. And if you get up too quickly, you might feel as though your legs are going to give way under you. If this happens, give your blood time to start flowing normally again through your legs because they have been constricted. You can quickly get the circulation going freely again by massaging, rubbing, and wiggling your toes.

THE AFRICAN POSTURE FOR MAXIMUM CONCENTRATION

One of the most powerful postures for maximum concentration is the African posture. Should you adopt this posture, simply do the following exercises:

Find yourself a wooden box, bench, stool, or an armchair with a straight back. Sit in the chair and have your back resting firmly against the back. Place a little cushion on your back if necessary. Your thighs should be horizontal, your calves should be vertical, and your feet should be flat on the ground with a gap about the width of your pelvis between them. Then do your best to comfortably stay in that position for at least seven minutes every day.

For example, an African warrior and ruler, Bai Bureh of Sierra Leone (February 15, 1840–August 24, 1908), was one of the most powerful adopters of the African posture for maximum concentration. That fearless, great, and wonderful strategic war planner was an iconic user of the wooden box method during his daily concentration exercises.

In each of the three postures (the European posture, the Asian posture, or the African posture), you can either rest your palms flat on your thighs or turn them over so they are open toward the sky. Whichever posture you adopt, your arms and shoulders should remain perfectly relaxed, and you should not press your elbows against your thighs.

During your concentration exercises, make the effort to keep your head straight, without tilting it to one side or the other or forward and backward. You should aim for the feeling that your spine is being held by a thread from the sky, and this more or less passive verticality will be maintained all down the spinal column. Imagine this entire axis to be like a glowing, empty tube with energy rising and descending inside.

Always do your best to prevent your neck from getting very stiff. If necessary, loosen it up with a few different movements. For example, raise and lower your chin a few times. Then turn it toward one shoulder and then the other. Nod your head and describe some complete circles first in one direction and then in the other direction.

The Secret to Successful Concentration

There are some powerful secret concentration practices that will enhance your well-being and longevity:

1. Whatever kind of temperament you may have, always approach these concentration exercises in calm and confident manner.
2. Do not be too eager for results.
3. Keep your everyday concerns at bay as far as you can.

The following are some formulas that will be particularly useful for developing your ability to successfully concentrate. These formulas have been tried, carefully selected, and they work. You can experiment with them and then choose the one or ones that suit you best and correspond most with your needs. They are the *visual* concentration, the *touching* concentration, and the *breathing* concentration formulas.

Visual Concentration

Obviously, visual concentration is done by sight. It is a powerful concentration exercise during which you should do the following:

Start by being settled down, perfectly still, and quiet in the body posture of your choice. Fix your eyes on a specific point. This point can be a small object like a colored spot stuck onto a wall, the flame of a candle that is high enough to be at eye-level, or perhaps a small picture of a geometric or symbolic figure. For example, you can fix your eyes on a square, a circle, a cross, a star, a triangle, etc. Or you could even choose an object like a flower, a shell, or a crystal. If you are new to concentration techniques, it may be easier to direct your eyes toward the ground and gaze at a specific point or object situated about a meter in front of you at an angle of about forty-five degrees with the ground.

One of the advantages of this type of concentration with your eyes open is that it prevents you from falling asleep during your concentration period. The psychology is you should remain acutely alert, vigilant, and lucid, without allowing yourself to think about the object you are contemplating. Just look at it. Do not allow your attention to be diluted by an inner discourse. Reasoning and analysis have no place here. This should just be pure contemplation.

In general terms, you should initially practice your concentration exercises for at least seven minutes. Then as you get better at it, you can gradually increase the duration. In the early stages of your practices, it is normal to have some trouble keeping your mind riveted on the object in question. In fact, you should not worry about that because, no matter how much effort you make in the beginning, you can be distracted in spite of yourself by some intruding reverie or reflection.

Above all, do not judge yourself, do not reprimand yourself, and do not get discouraged. This is to be expected and is even part of the exercise. It may seem a bit paradoxical, but when you become aware that you have allowed your attention to slip, you become aware at the same time of what it really means to hold your concentration. This mechanism obeys the law of opposites. The psychology is that it is impossible to comprehend the notion of heat if you have never experienced cold, or poverty if you have never experienced wealth, or light if you are unaware of what it is like to be in the dark, etc.

Every time you find that your mental energy is tending to disperse, you should methodically drag your attention back to your object. Then gradually you will develop your absolute power of concentration that will eventually give you the peace of mind you need.

Be mindful also of the possibility that if you stare at something fixedly for a long time, your vision may become cloudy, or you might start blinking uncontrollably or you may even experience an unpleasant prickling sensation. However, if you experience any of these, do not worry; this is just another normal step in your apprenticeship.

If this happens to you, at the end of the exercise or whenever your eyes feel tired, vigorously rub the palms of your hands together until they get warm and then cup them over your closed eyes. Experience the darkness, and allow your eyes to absorb the warmth. Once they are completely relaxed, move your palms down over your cheeks, and using your fingertips, gently touch, press, and massage your closed eyelids and all around the sockets.

TOUCHING CONCENTRATION

The touching concentration is a powerful concentration exercise that should be done with your eyes closed and your eyelids, jaws, and neck relaxed. This type of concentration should also be done in the body posture of your choice. In this case, you will concentrate by touching an area of your body on which to anchor your attention.

For example, you can concentrate by touching the heart region in the center of your chest. Focus your attention on this specific point, to the exclusion of all other parts of your body. You can help yourself with imagination, visualizing a beautiful, rosy or golden light radiating from your chest. Or you can help yourself by concentrating on your heartbeats.

This powerful concentration exercise is very beneficial for your well-being and longevity. It is also both soothing and harmonizing because it balances the vital centers of your abdominal region and the intellectual centers of your brain.

BREATHING CONCENTRATION

The breathing concentration is one of the most powerful concentration exercises. To concentrate successfully during this exercise, you should be able to hold your body posture easily and comfortably throughout the exercise. If this is not properly done, little tensions may accumulate, and they can disturb your respiration. As a result, your breathing can be irregular, and this may prevent you from focusing your mind properly.

A successful way to remedy this potential concern is to base your concentration exercise on your breathing itself to keep it regular. With the help of this special type of concentration, any physical or mental tension will be effortlessly dissolved. Remember also that a large percentage of your body is oxygen. Thus, it is crystal clear that breathing properly is vital to your longevity and well-being.

The 7 Secrets to Peace of Mind is therefore designed to give you a support guide in your training. Thus, this new book of knowledge is revealing a tried and tested technique called the "so ham" mantra:

- As you inhale, say the syllable "so."
- As you exhale, say the syllable "ham."
- Allow yourself to be carried by the powerful rhythm of these inner sounds.
- Repeat them for as long as you can until the music of the "so ham" mantra really penetrates your being and becomes an intimate part of your breathing.

There is nothing wrong with doing this exercise the other way around (i.e., saying "ham" as you inhale and "so" as you exhale). In any case, these variations sometimes occur all by themselves.

Once you have mastered this exercise, the next step is to imagine that a point of light is descending to your navel as you breathe in and rising back up to either your heart or your throat, depending on what you feel as you breathe out.

Another variation of this exercise is to observe your breath as it comes and goes (i.e., as it flows spontaneously). You do not have to say the mantra anymore. In this exercise, you do not intervene at all; you just allow the breathing process to do its own thing, whatever that might be. If it is rapid, it is rapid; if it is irregular, it's irregular; if it is slow, it is slow. Just let go and let it be. All you have to do is be aware of the air flowing through your nostrils, your throat, and your lungs down into your abdomen. Feel the air, and be conscious of your chest and abdomen rising regularly with the passage of your breath.

This exercise in which you concentrate on your breathing can be done with your eyes open or closed, whichever way you prefer. They can even be combined with the visual concentration exercise if you want to. That is, you can repeat the "so ham" mantra to yourself while you gaze at an object.

Whenever you decide to terminate a concentration exercise, make sure you do not wrench yourself out of your stillness too abruptly. You should instead move your body gradually. For example, move your shoulders, your hands, your neck, your feet, etc., until they become supple. Massage them lightly until you feel the warmth of your blood flowing through. Keep still for about seven minutes, and then get up slowly.

VALUABLE TIPS FOR SUCCESSFUL CONCENTRATION

If you are a beginner at concentration techniques and practices, you may encounter various obstacles during your concentration period, especially during your first few exercises. For example, you might have an itch, you might have indigestion, you might feel sleepy, etc. This is often due to a certain physical fatigue that becomes apparent when you start to concentrate. Or perhaps your ankles, your knees, your back, etc. might start complaining because the postures may not be easy at first.

Just in case you encounter any of those obstacles, do not leap to the wrong conclusion that you are not good at concentration exercises or that they are not worth all the time you are putting into them. However, if you are overcome by a wave of discouragement, just let it pass and accept it. Get up and turn your attention to something else. But always remember to do your concentration exercises again when you can.

This type of experience is also part and parcel of your apprenticeship in concentration techniques. Always remember that concentration is an undertaking that demands a certain amount of enthusiasm, perseverance, and humor. You need to be able to laugh at yourself rather than imagining you are being persecuted by adverse forces as soon as an obstacle arises. You should also be on your guard against one very powerful type of obstacle that you may encounter during the course of your exercises. That obstacle is *the enemy within*. That is the part of you that persuades you that all this is a waste of time.

In short, *the enemy within* wants you to live in stagnation or in just the same stressful way you have been living. This enemy does not want you to have peace of mind, including well-being and longevity. So always be mindful of *the enemy within*. However, if you refuse to give in, you will soon understand that *the enemy within* is wrong or has a short memory. By continuing to do your exercises, you will remind *the enemy within* that in fact, it is precisely because you are fed up with living a stressful life that you have decided to do these exercises with the hope of having peace of mind.

Remember that you are doing these exercises to sense the force that is deep inside you that is willing to help you and to guide you. You are also doing these exercises to submit to a discipline that will have a good effect on your personality. When you diligently apply yourself to these exercises, you will naturally be immune to distraction, perplexity, doubt, etc. You will also acquire a sharp attention and a presence of mind. You will be able to bring to bear on all of life's activities. You will also be able to perform any job effectively and precisely. Above all, you will have the longevity, the well-being, and the peace of mind you deserve.

As you continue to do your step-by-step exercises, you will develop your concentration level so much that it will become almost automatic for you to concentrate. Eventually your level of concentration will be so high that you will be completely absorbed in your tasks and always focusing on your peace of mind, including your well-being and longevity. As a result, nothing can distract you or stop you from going forward. This is your moment!

BALANCE IS THE SECOND SECRET
TO LONGEVITY AND WELL-BEING

The 7 Secrets to Peace of Mind is designed to remind you that being *balanced* or *level headed* is a very important issue for your longevity and well-being. Be mindful also that your balance has a tremendous influence on your peace of mind. Therefore, to achieve good results in the things you do, you should first master your emotions. Thus, you should be level-headed, which also means you should be balanced. Emotions like fear, anxiety, envy, jealousy, anger, etc., should not disturb your serenity. You should not allow them to affect your actions at all.

If you are an adult, you may remember that during your school days, your teachers had the task of developing your intelligence and your memory. That is great. And no doubt your parents also tried to educate you on your will power. That is even better. But neither of them will have taken it upon themselves to school you in the art of controlling your emotionalism.

One thing you should never forget is that, however unbridled, emotionalism can be a source of serious problems and worries for you and for the people around you. It allows obstacles to emerge in your path and block your movement. Emotionalism can allow extraneous forces to push you this way and that way. Therefore, if you are not very careful, emotionalism can even force you off the road into a ditch.

Due to emotionalism, many situations and events in life have a strong impact on human personalities. In fact, emotionalism sometimes provokes exaggerated reactions, such as elation, anger, envy, greed, infatuation, jealousy, worry, anxiety, impatience, despair, etc. Remember that all these emotions are parasites. They are parasites that can come from nowhere, regardless of your strategies and plans. These parasites can suck out all your energy and divert you from the path of peace of mind and tranquility. Thus, if you did not make a quick turnaround in your life, you will unfortunately find yourself on your way to inferno.

THE SECRET FORMULA FOR TAMING YOUR EMOTIONS

There is surely a secret formula that has the power to tame or control your emotions. But what does controlling your emotions mean? This new book of knowledge is designed to let you know that mastering your emotions does not mean suppressing them. Most people who say they are free from emotional problems, who claim to have mastered their emotions, are deluding themselves. The truth is what those individuals are actually doing is suppressing their feelings. They are in fact denying their emotional problems because they are afraid of being overwhelmed by them. You should never allow your emotions to drag you off course, and do not give them full rein so that you are totally at their mercy.

With the help of *The 7 Secrets to Peace of Mind* and your willingness to do the appropriate exercises as outlined, you will actually tame your emotionalism at anytime. In a society where it is seen as cool and macho to be strong and insensitive, people stifle their emotions so much that even when they do surface, they are no longer conscious of them. One of the things this new book of knowledge will let you learn is to be aware of your emotions by recognizing their patterns or the way in which they manifest themselves.

Therefore, please take the courage to ask yourself the following questions about your emotions and honestly answer them to yourself for your own benefit:

1. When you are affected by your emotions, where do you feel it in your body? (Just think of all the popular expressions like fear gives you a knot in the stomach, love warms the cockles of your heart, anxiety gives you a lump in your throat, shyness brings a blush to your face, etc.)
2. How does your emotion influence your behavior?
3. Why do you suppress your emotions? If you do, how do you suppress them?
4. Conversely, why do you allow your emotions to run away with you?
5. Are you capable of choosing what emotion you feel?

When you reflect deeply and answer these questions honestly, and in various circumstances, they will help you to become more aware of yourself in a very remarkable way.

Once you are familiar with your emotional patterns and are capable of recognizing them quickly, you can pass on to the second stage. This is the stage that consists of detaching yourself from your emotions and merely observing them. When that happens, you will be on your way to the peace of mind that will eventually lead you to nirvana.

This new book of knowledge is designed to let you understand that *you* and *your emotions* are two separate entities. The fact is that you have just simply assumed these emotions. Unfortunately, most people have a tendency to become identified with their emotions. Psychology tells us that in reality, no emotion is a fixed personal trait. Thus, if you are constantly displaying one emotion, you may simply be repeating scenarios that fill you with the same emotional energy.

Let us consider the following example: One day you got angry with a certain situation. Ever since then, as soon as that situation arises again, you fly into a towering rage. The fact is you enter into this angry state because you are not sufficiently aware of your emotions. After this, people say that you are an angry person, and you unconsciously do everything you can to confirm their assumption and their paradigm.

That is a mistake you should avoid. My advice to you is this: just because a situation repeats itself, that does not mean you have to react in the same way. To avoid doing that, however, you need to be fully aware of your emotions, which is not always easy. In other words, if you are half asleep and not really conscious of your emotions, they will rule you and wickedly manipulate you.

However, this will not happen to you anymore because *The 7 Secrets to Peace of Mind* is designed to show you how to stand back and take a fresh look at your emotional reactions. Once you are conscious of your emotions and start to observe them and detach yourself from them, it will be easy for you to accomplish the third step, which consists of transforming your negative emotions into positive ones.

You should also remember that every emotion has two types of energy. One type is a negative energy, and the other is a positive energy. Now let us go back to the previous example. If you allow yourself to lose your temper, you might be blinded by your anger. When that happens, there is a danger that you can do or say things that are different from what you intended to do or say.

In other words, you will have experienced the negative side of anger. This negative side is the one that drains all your energy, deprives you of your free will, and makes you regret your actions later. In fact, one negative emotion may lead to another. For example, you may go from guilt to remorse, then to shame, and then to sadness. If you are not very careful, this may take you around and around in a vicious circle of negativity.

However, if you do not allow these angry feelings to become part of you but merely observe them, you then become capable of tracing your anger back to its source or origin. By so doing, you can use its inherent energy positively and constructively. Thus, rather than blowing your top, which gets you nowhere and may even be detrimental to your future and to those around you, you will henceforth use this energy to find solutions to any problem.

In the end, by using your power of concentration, by accepting your emotions instead of forcing them back into your subconscious, and by observing them and detaching yourself from them rather than unleashing them, you will convert these emotions into positive forces. These are the forces that will eventually bring you peace of mind, including your well-being and longevity.

The psychology is this: when you are fully aware of your emotions, you can manipulate them consciously instead of them manipulating you wickedly or being ruled by them unwisely. By so doing, you will manage to master your emotional reactions, which will cease to pollute you physically, mentally, or morally. Then you will have the peace of mind you deserve. This is the secret. Your peace is your command!

SECRET FACTS ABOUT EMOTIONS

1. Your emotions can help you to know yourself better because they reflect each of your terrestrial experiences, and whether these are ugly or pleasant they can help you to evolve.
2. Your emotions can form a rich palette, which brings color to your experiences.
3. Your emotions are not you; they are just simply flowing through you. Allow them to pass without you getting caught up with them. Just simply act as a witness to them.

4. Accept your emotions, recognize them, and be a spectator. Then you will be able to transform them to your advantage.

One very important philosophy you should always remember is that to successfully maintain your balance and your emotions, you should cultivate a quality of level-headedness. Level-headedness can help you to overcome many objects. When level-headedness is reinforced by concentration, it helps you to always remain a detached observer of your emotions.

For example, if your mind were a car, then your emotions would be the speedometer and the brakes on your four wheels. By applying your brakes, you can steer clear of obstacles and negotiate dangerous bends and crossings. Using your speedometer, you can establish a good, steady speed that does not put your life at risk or put a strain on your car.

The other side of the coin is the hothead who thrashes his car, hits bends at top speed and risks losing control, overturning his vehicle, or smashing into obstacles. These kinds of individuals with no brakes or speedometers are better described as barbarous because they are uncivilized and hypersensitive.

This new book of knowledge is therefore encouraging you to always be level-headed. Thus, you will have more controlled reactions and balanced temperament. As a result, you will effortlessly get along with others. Then your peace of mind will be assured.

The Secret Formula for Being a Very Important Person (a VIP)

Do you really want to be a significant individual? Do you want to be a very important person (a VIP)? If your answer is yes, well, I have good news for you. *If you really want to be a very important person, then just be yourself.* To actually tell you the truth, *never try to be anybody else because everyone else is either already taken or dead.* So, my good friend; just be yourself.

As my son Tony Charles would simply put it, "I don't follow people, and I don't copy anyone. I am myself; period." I actually commend my son, and I am proud of him for his noble attitude of self-respect. In fact, this new book of knowledge has been designed to let everyone know that confidence and self-respect are the keys to any sane and solid foray into the realm of importance. Without them, one can easily flounder and fall prey to the jackals at every turn. So do not ever allow yourself to be thrown off course; no matter what the circumstances may be.

Life can also be compared to a river. Imagine two boatmen going down the river. One has oars and a rudder, but the other has lost his equipment. The first one steers his boat well and safely reaches the mouth of the river as planned. Unfortunately however, the second boatman makes no progress due to the effect of the current, which sends him zigzagging here and there.

Therefore, to share the fortune of the competent boatman who safely reached his destination, you need to find yourself a pair of oars and a rudder. You also need to know how to use them. For example, you need concentration and level-headedness to keep yourself under control so that you are not pushed and pulled all over the place by external propositions or unnecessary current events.

One thing you should always remember is that people who are balanced expend energy in an even and steady manner. They are hardly subjected to sudden ups and downs. They are not full of high spirits and optimism one moment and then dejected and defeated the next moment. The secret is that their level-headedness protects them from temperamental fluctuations.

Remember also that those who are level-headed are always themselves. They can face up to any adverse circumstances or situations calmly, confidently, and peacefully. Level-headedness implies calmness, self-possession, self-confidence, self-respect, and self-control. The level-headed person is not dominated by his entourage; on the contrary, he governs and influences it. An example of one of those kinds of noble people who I know is my father, Chief Moses Congofoh Charles, who I also know as a very remarkable and personable gentleman. (I will always love you, Papa. You are indeed an honorable man and a person of value.)

The 7 Secrets to Peace of Mind is therefore designed to encourage all humanity to be level-headed. One of the most powerful formulas for level-headedness is to repeat the following phrases silently or loudly at least seven minutes a day:

> I have a single aim in my life. My aim is to have peace of mind, improve myself in everything I do, including intellectually, socially, physically, spiritually, politically, emotionally, financially, and morally.

These phrases can also serve as the foundation on which you should build your destiny. Therefore, you should recite them as often as you can. In fact, if you so desire, you can use such a powerful phrase as a mantra or as part of your concentration exercises. By doing that, you will effortlessly absorb the positive energy this powerful formula offers.

The psychology is that you cannot be well-balanced if you are torn between two different aims. The aim of improving yourself encompasses all your interests. These phrases will also bring you the calmness that will always help you to remain poised. Subsequently, you will have the longevity, the well-being, and the peace of mind you surely deserve.

To easily achieve this goal, you should get into the habit of putting positive thoughts into all your actions. Whenever you decide to do something, think about it very carefully before going ahead. One good method is to write down on paper the actions you want to take and save the paper until the following day. Then, when you wake up in the morning, read the paper again three more times. If you think you still want to take the same actions, then you may go ahead, but please do so consciously. One of my spiritual advisers, Hajah Fanta Kakay-Sesay, is a strong advocate of this fundamental formula, which is in fact the mother of peace to all humanity.

The psychology is that when you get into the habit of establishing a good plan before taking any action, you will not easily get bogged down with unforeseen tasks. And if the unexpected happens anyway, you will be able to cope with it without losing sight of your initial plan. Again, you can do this by using your concentration power. The secret is you should never allow yourself to get ruffled in the slightest. Always do your best to remain calm and indifferent to the things that happen to annoy you and to the reasons they happened. If something bad happens, or if a vexing situation arises, just say the following phrases to yourself:

Everything will be fine, everything will settle down, and everything will eventually work out. All is well.

You should never allow panic to get the upper hand when you are attacked by adversaries who are stronger than you. Just stay calm and keep smiling when your opponents are expecting to see you looking dejected and defeated. Your first victory over them will be when you are able to say to yourself, "My turn will come."

However, do not set out to wreak vengeance after a defeat. Do your best to avoid this type of negative emotion because it is very debilitating. If you are ever faced with such temptation, what you should do is to just bounce back as quickly and strongly as you can. Believe me, you will find this easier than you think if you only focus on it with your entire mind and with all your heart.

Should you have to beat a retreat, you should do so coolly and sedately. Then you will score at least one point. As a result, although they might not admit it, your adversaries will admire your calmness, your intelligence, and your strength. They will understand that your intentions are upright and honest. Believe me—they will respect you for your level-headedness even though they may pretend otherwise. I am telling you this because I have been there.

This new book of knowledge encourages you also to constantly inspire yourself with the following positive affirmations:

- In any trying situation, I will make the best of everything to bring about a peaceful outcome.
- I will remain cool. I will exert every influence to develop my inner calmness and mental equilibrium.
- I am in complete control of myself.

Always remember that your subconscious mind acts on what you believe, so believe in your affirmations and let your subconscious work on your behalf. Eventually you will be more measured in your thoughts, feelings, words, and actions. As a result, you will have the peace of mind you need, including your well-being and longevity.

POSITIVE ATTITUDE IS THE THIRD SECRET TO LONGEVITY AND WELL-BEING

The phrase "attitude is everything" plays a very important role in everyone's life. Thus, the third secret to longevity and well-being is positive attitude. This means that your attitude has a great effect on your entire life. Therefore, to enhance your well-being and longevity through a positive attitude, you should acquire a personality that is both strong and flexible. It needs to be strong so that you can pursue your aim in life without losing heart and flexible so that you can easily adapt to circumstances. Thus, you should learn to have positive attitude in some circumstances and accepting attitude in other circumstances.

Let me explain this very clearly. Every time you summon your energies to resist an obstacle, you should be active and positive. Every time you find yourself faced with circumstances beyond your control, you should be both passive and accepting. Therefore, you should regard every event as an opportunity to build your character and your self-image.

Always remember the following prayer when you need the courage to move on:

Oh, God, give me the courage and wisdom to change the circumstances within my control. And give me the courage and wisdom to accept the circumstances beyond my control.

Thus, to be a positive individual, you should always have faith in God and confidence in your humanity. To easily do this, you have to be yourself in all circumstances. Never try to be like anyone else. You have your own personal identity. In fact, every time you try to imitate someone, you are nobody, because as I mentioned before, everyone else is already taken or dead. Remember also that any attempt to be someone else is an insult to the force that animates your inner being—the divine entity that resides in you.

The best you should do instead is to allow the divine force to operate within you until you know yourself better. This divine force can uncover all your possibilities and guide you accordingly. So never be ashamed or be afraid to express your true self. The universe needs you just as you are, with all your good qualities and your faults. Love yourself, respect yourself, and be genuine. When you do that, you will surely be in harmony with yourself and with all humanity. If you honestly show yourself as you are, others will trust you more readily and they in turn will be more honest with you.

Most importantly, when you are yourself, you increase your ability to concentrate better and master your emotions better. This is because when you are yourself, you are intuitively linked to your inner force, which is that divine part of you that is full of love and wisdom. That inner force knows what is good for you and communicates it to you through your tiny inner voice, which you should always listen to. This is just as if you were offering your hand to a child—your inner child, who is the being in you, that has remained pure and genuine, with all its freshness and spontaneity, with all its love and creativity. Give it your love, and it will protect you at all times, wherever you may be and in all circumstances.

Remember that if you sometimes find it difficult to stay in a positive frame of mind, do not hesitate to resort to using the positive affirmations that have been devised for you in this volume. By using these powerful formulas, you will reprogram your subconscious, which is a prodigious store of untapped energy that serves your interests. Proceed as indicated, and adopt the body posture you normally use during your concentration exercises. After you make sure that you will not be disturbed, breathe deeply, calmly, and naturally, without forcing it. Simply be aware of your breath like a column of warm air flowing in through your nostrils and then down through your throat and chest to your abdomen.

You should also pay attention to the rhythm of your inhalations and exhalations. As soon as you feel calmed and focused, with your eyes closed, direct your attention to your chest, which is rising and falling regularly as you breathe. Then say the following affirmations out loud (this is very important) while really feeling them in your heart, Express all the love that you have for yourself:

- I love myself, and I accept myself as I am.
- I have found the fountain of love in me.
- I have found security inside myself, and I am developing my own values.
- I am opening myself up to change, and I am concentrating on the goals I want to achieve.
- I am developing endless confidence in myself and in my intuitive, inspired, and creative potential.

After that affirmation, allow your love to flow freely and to nourish you with its energy. Then repeat the same affirmations three more times silently in your head. When you have finished, breathe deeply, open your eyes, and thank the almighty God by expressing your gratitude for this affirmation and meditation. Eventual, you will feel peaceful, calm, and confident. Your mind will be clear and focused.

With practice, you will be capable of performing this affirmation effectively in any circumstance. You do not have to be in a specific physical position or location to do this practice. Eventually you will condition yourself in a positive way and give yourself a firm footing that you will be able to exploit. All you will need to do is to concentrate on your breathing for at least seven minutes, fixing your attention on your heart, and then say your personal affirmation to yourself to feel instantly recharged with positive energy.

Therefore, to free yourself from any kind of limitation, make every effort to always remain in a positive frame of mind. Have confidence in your human abilities and faith in the divine power. Be mindful also that the positive nature of any powerful healer is due to his faith in his own powers.

For example, it is the faith of the lion-tamer that forces the lion to crouch in the corner of its cage. The tamer does not actually have any special magnetic power. Even though the fierce animal may have no doubts about its own physical strength, it thinks twice about pouncing on an enemy or seizing a prey that seems to be displaying a great positive attitude and confidence. This is also a good illustration of the fact that *mental power is superior to physical power.* That is why I always believe that "the pen is mightier than the sword."

Therefore, it is possible that your destiny can be determined by your mental power, which can also result from your character. Remember also that your character can be the result of your habits and your habits can be the consequences of the things you repeatedly do. Those things themselves are the products of suggestions, so if you want to shape your destiny, you should get into the appropriate habits.

These habits are formed through your subconscious because it is in your subconscious that your habits exist in a latent state. Remember, your subconscious builds your character, so you need to work on it constantly and determinedly. If you want to elevate your life, you need to use your conscious mind to work on your subconscious mind, and it is your subconscious mind that will form your character, which will subsequently create your destiny.

THE SECRET FORMULA FOR INFLUENCING YOUR SUBCONSCIOUS

There are secret formulas that have the power to command concrete effects on your subconscious to influence it. Allow me first of all to digress a little. There is a powerful energy called cosmic energy. Every human being is a channel through which the force of cosmic energy strives to find a creative outlet. Therefore, when you want to influence your subconscious, you should be a channel that is always open to this powerful energy. Each and every one of us is a focal point of this divine energy, a bit like a light bulb is the focal point of the electric current.

This cosmic energy flows harmoniously, peacefully, rhythmically, and joyfully. When you allow it to operate constructively within you, then you are in harmonious agreement with the divine power. Thus, you will display harmony, good health, love, well-being, peace of mind, tranquility, and all the riches of the infinite power. On the other hand, when you allow yourself to indulge in remorse, resentment, hatred, jealousy, selfishness, self-condemnation, or any other form of negative thinking, this divine energy is trapped and then you are affected by all kinds of disorders. That is why it is so important to always maintain a positive attitude and to have control of your emotions.

The 7 Secrets to Peace of Mind is designed to show you a powerful way of freeing this cosmic energy inside you, through prayers. Please remember also that your thoughts are prayers. Praying is thinking in accordance with universal principles and eternal truths, just like an engineer thinks and works on the basis of mathematical principles or a chemist works on the basis of the laws governing the mixing of chemicals. In essence, prayer is the act of thinking constructively. It does not really matter what church, mosque, synagogue, temple, or faith you belong to. All this new book of knowledge is suggesting is to *please believe in something and always pray. Prayer is the art of talking and listening to God. Prayer is powerful.*

The laws of cosmic energy encompass everyone; there are absolutely no favorites. Therefore, the good thing about praying is that the cosmic energy in you becomes what you want. Your constructive thoughts harmonize with the cosmic energy, and it responds according to the nature of your thoughts. Therefore, your prayer should show a firm, positive, constructive frame of mind and total conviction. Thus, when you submit your desire to your subconscious mind, a positive response will manifest itself.

Here is a suggested prayer. However, you can make up one of your own using your own words to express your personal desires. But if it is okay with you, you can pray as follows:

> I forgive myself for having entertained negative thoughts about myself or about anybody else, and I am determined to refrain from doing so again. I radiate love and goodwill toward all beings in the world. I affirm that the love, light, harmony, truth, beauty, abundance, and security of God are earned, freely and joyously, and I know that I am blessed and enriched beyond my wildest dreams. Amen.

If possible, you should repeat this prayer aloud every morning and every evening. The psychology is that as your thoughts dwell on these truths, your ears hear them too, and so you will have two faculties working for your benefit. These truths will penetrate your subconscious. So as you concentrate regularly on the prayer, which reflects your thoughts and sincerely expresses your desires, you are creating a healthy habit. This will have an effect on your subconscious and eventually on your destiny.

You should therefore train your subconscious by constantly using what we call "auto-suggestion." Here are a few suggestions to think about: In order to have peace of mind, you should be in good health, have good intentions, develop a strong will, train yourself to be disciplined, be orderly, be methodical, and improve your temperament in appropriate ways.

The 7 Secrets to Peace of Mind is therefore encouraging you to implement a program. You might, for example, decide to get into the habit of rising early in the morning to pray, or you might decide to do some physical exercises every morning. You also might train yourself to think positively at all times, to concentrate, to meditate, and to consume fewer substances that are damaging to your health.

Basically, you will behave in all circumstances like a person who is a positive and disciplined individual. As a result, you will be able to make a conscious decision to gain more control over your emotions. The simplest method is to just choose one emotion to begin with—let us say impatience, for example. Perhaps you decide you need to curb your impatience. When you spend all day looking forward to the time when you can relax, do this patiently. As soon as the slightest thing happens to make your patience wear thin, say to yourself, "I will remain patient, and I will take advantage of my impatience to observe its pattern in detail so that I can detach myself from it."

When you continue to do that, by the time evening comes, you will realize that instead of showing your impatience several times during that day, you may have only shown it a few times. With your conscious mind in charge in this way, you will gradually manage to check and master each of your emotions, and you will finally reach the point where you are no longer impatient. After about seven weeks of diligent practice, you will be calm and even better. Subconsciously, you will have acquired the habit of being patient, calm, and peaceful. Thus, the people around you will not only benefit from your behavior, but will also have your respect.

Once you have gotten a grip on the first emotion, you can then teach yourself another new habit, like spending more quality time with your loved ones or reading more. If you continue like this for at least seven weeks, you will gradually form a number of good habits that no longer require any effort. You will be kinder to people, you will be less tired, and you will be more peaceful. In other words, your well-being, your health, your career, and your longevity will all benefit from the favorable effects of this step-by-step, positive evolution.

When that happens, you will eventually acquire a calm and patient temperament created consciously to begin with and then displayed automatically after a while. This is the way to mend your faults and acquire the good habits and the qualities that will let you have a sustainable peace of mind. You are therefore encouraged to precisely do the appropriate exercises for your own good. Please remember also that *when it is all said and done, more will be done than said.*

As a philosopher once put it, "Better a heart with no words than words with no heart."

Your Peace Is Your Command!

THE 7TH SECRET

THE SECRET TO BELIEVING IN YOUR HUMANITY AND DIVINITY

You have the power to be awakened to the divine within. You will have peace of mind when you believe . . .

Your Peace Is Your Command!

SPECIAL INTRODUCTION TO THE SECRET TO BELIEVING IN DIVINITY AND IN YOUR HUMANITY

The 7 Secrets to Peace of Mind has been designed to remind you to always believe in Divinity and in your humanity. This is actually based on the noble philosophy of believing in God and also, believing in yourself. Of course there is no doubt that you truly believe in God. However, even if the world seems to be changing too quickly or even if events in your personal life seem daunting or confusing, this new book of knowledge is encouraging you to keep on believing in God and in yourself. Please remember to always turn to God for help whenever you need it; you will never be deceived.

Please do not ever forget that the divine power is the only power that has never changed and will never change. In your moments of prayers, divine power is the power that guides you to make the right decisions. As a result, you will be empowered to take the right actions when necessary. God is your source of wisdom, knowledge, and understanding. Remember also that God is the ever-lasting love that leads you to form meaningful relationships and take purposeful actions at all times. When you believe in God and in your humanity, you are assured that harmony will always transcend temporarily troubling appearances.

As you connect with the divine power through prayers, you will truly know that all things are possible. This volume is therefore encouraging you to believe in God, believe in yourself, and always face the world with courage and confidence. If you find yourself in challenging circumstances, always remember to check your perception of the situation. Remember that your faith does not lie in the trouble that surrounds you; your faith lies in God. In fact, when you are in difficult situations, your faith gets stronger as you seek connection with the divine.

The 7 Secrets to Peace of Mind is also encouraging you to foster your faith by thinking solely of God's power and protection. By so doing, you will eventually feel the divine power within, and you will have a different perspective of any seeming difficult situation. As a result, your anxiety will gradually evaporate and you will go through your apparent challenges with dignity and calmness. Remember that you are always enfolded in God's peaceful and loving presence. Therefore, whenever you feel you have been pushed to the wall, just allow God's magnificence to flow through you.

Remember these phrases: "Believe in God and you shall never perish"; "Let go and let God." The psychology is, when you cling to what you may perceive to be a problem, your mind races to try to fix it. And when you are in that mode, you will be dealing with the problem instead of allowing the solution in. However, when you release your grip, divine wisdom will flow through you and easily solve your problem.

Let me make it abundantly clear, however, that the idea of letting go and letting God is not about giving up; it is about handing your situations over to the divine power while you are still playing your own part. Therefore, instead of casting your hands up in despair, you should open your heart, open your mind, and pray to the almighty God to come to your aid at all times. Thus, in the silence, the answers you may have been chasing will easily and miraculously rise to the surface. So please do not be troubled; be still and believe.

Believing in God and believing in yourself will always free you from troubles. If ever you find yourself in negative circumstances again, do not lose hope in finding a solution. In fact, that should be your chance to face the problem spiritually by turning to God. You should always pause and redirect your attention away from the situation itself and think positively about what God can do for you. This is how you will be connected with the divine power within. As a result, you will consciously let go of any anxious thoughts. When that happens, you will actually feel the grip of negativity loosing. Do your best to always pray for knowledge, wisdom, and understanding to find the way forward.

Please allow me to make it known that during my decades of professional service around the world, I have been privileged to meet with a variety of individuals from all walks of life. Over those years, I discovered powerful formulas that, when applied to a person's thinking, can actually encourage him or her to believe in himself or herself.

Therefore, in order to quench my thirst for helping all humanity, I have included most of those powerful formulas for you in this new book of knowledge. Please read them very carefully and perform the appropriate exercises accordingly. Eventually you will start down the pathway that will change your life in a profound way for good. As a result, the things you want most in your life will be effortlessly drawn to you. Thus, all that will be needed of you is to believe in God and believe in yourself. Then take the right action and be patient.

Over the years I have seen people having peace of mind against all odds, and I have also known others who seemed to have everything going for them, yet they looked miserable. It may be true, however, that some of these individuals had very good luck and the others had very bad luck, but more often, it is not fate that spells the difference. Generally people look peaceful or miserable more because of their attitudes about themselves. Therefore, rather than it being a case of happenstance, their actions decide whether they should have peace of mind or whether they should be in distress.

Through my experiences religiously, professionally, academically, socially, etc., I have come to realize that *people who believe in God, who believe in themselves, who take action, and who believe in their power to think positively, regularly have peace of mind.* Those who do not believe in God, who do not believe in themselves, who do not take action, and who constantly mope and complain generally become distressed, and sometimes depressed. However, this new book of knowledge is designed to show you the right way.

So if you do not yet know this, please be informed that believing in God and believing in your humanity are more significant than believing in your talents. Remember also that attitude is more important than talent. Sure, you can get farther faster if you have bucket-loads of talent and a good attitude. But time, fortitude, and determination often trump talent. That is in fact why winners always strive to win. Even if you may not be currently thinking of yourself as a winner, it is time for you to change your attitude, and you will be transformed accordingly.

You can also change your attitude by changing your inner dialogue with yourself. With the exception of some artists, mathematicians, and others who may on occasion think in nonverbal, abstract ways, most of us actually carry on conversations with ourselves inside our heads using words. This means that in order to process information and go about our daily lives, we as human beings must carry on an inner dialogue of some sort. Otherwise we will not be thinking in any meaningful way or be able to reason complex problems.

Be mindful, however, that your inner dialogue can be helpful or harmful to your chances for achievement. For example, if a person's inner dialogue becomes negative, he or she is apt to have stress in the things he or she does. People in this mind-set think or perhaps even say to themselves and those around them things like, "This won't work," "I will never amount to anything," or "I'm such a loser." Of course, those negative individuals think this way because they do not believe in the power of God, and they do not believe in the power of their humanity.

Subsequently, these negative thoughts often become self-fulfilling prophecies to the unconscious mind. In effect, such negative thoughts tell some people that they will be miserable and reinforce to them that they should give up. Unfortunately therefore, most people give up before reaching any point of achievement. These kinds of individuals will be miserable because their inner dialogue tells them so. As a result, they will unconsciously sabotage their own efforts. They will be in distress because they have been telling themselves that distress will come their way.

Fortunately, *The 7 Secrets to Peace of Mind* is designed to let you know that these negative inner dialogues will be overcome when you replace them with more-positive statements. Once that is done, achievement and peace of mind will be at your command. Therefore, you should always listen to your thoughts and then challenge all dialogues that are negative. When you get a negative thought, counter it with a positive thought. For example, if you think, this won't work, add at first—but if I keep working at it diligently, it will surely work.

Eventually when you continue to monitor your thoughts, you will make the effort to tell yourself, for example: "This problem is big, but if I continue to work at it, there is every possibility that I will solve it." You definitely do not minimize the problem by just saying these words, but the psychology is that you do not make it larger than it really is in your mind.

Furthermore, you give yourself credit for being capable of working hard and solving problems if you believe in yourself. You should therefore challenge and argue with all your negative thoughts. Strive to first modify them, and then replace them with positive thoughts about yourself. Eventually this will have a dramatic effect that will greatly improve both your daily life and your attitude. Gradually your good attitude will have a positive effect on your family, friends, relatives, and most of the people around you. The truth is that nobody likes to be around a negative person.

I am also encouraging you to push yourself toward thinking fewer negative thoughts about other people. Although it is true that there are some real nuisances that you may cross paths with in life, nevertheless, just remember that most people try to do the right thing most of the time. Always give people the benefit of the doubt when necessary, and encourage them to think in positive ways. Do not be shy about giving compliments when they are justified, and always share credit for any achievement.

As you continue with your transformation from negative to positive, and gradually believing in God, and in your humanity, you will find people around you who will help you to achieve your goals. By monitoring and changing your inner thoughts about yourself and others, you will motivate yourself toward greater achievement and peace of mind. You will then enjoy each achievement, and you will not be discouraged by the occasional setbacks you may experience on your journey to your peace of mind. This is the secret.

Your Peace Is Your Command!

The Secret to Believing
in the Fulfillment of Your Goals

Setting goals and believing in the fulfillment of your goals are the fundamental ideas of this new book of knowledge. Of course it is common knowledge that most people go through life without knowing what they really want. Thus, instead of making things happen, they always let things happen to them. They stumble through life and act as if this existence is only a rehearsal for the real thing. Unfortunately, it is not. The life you are living as a human being is the only one you have now. You should therefore take good care of it and make the most out of it.

Do not make the mistake of just letting things happen to you without your consent. Always seize the reins of your existence and take charge of what is going on in your life. You should figure out what your dreams are and then decide how you will realize them by setting short-term and/or long-term goals. For example, you should decide where you want to be seven hours from now, seven days from now, seven weeks from now, seven months from now, or even seven years from now.

Notice I did not say set realistic goals or practical dreams. That is because I have seen people achieve the impossible simply because they believed in God, they believed in their humanity, and they had goals that they strived to achieve. As a result, they got the peace of mind they needed against all odds.

This does not mean that you should just daydream or that you can possibly walk from Freetown to New York City. But what I mean is that, if it is humanly possible to achieve anything, you should never rule it out as something you, too, can do. It may take you some time and determination, but if you set your mind on anything, work diligently to achieve it, and believe in yourself, you will eventually achieve it.

However, there are people who wander aimlessly through life without any goals, and they often become old before their time, bitter, and resentful. Their dreams—which they never worked to achieve—never materialized. Sometimes it is not their fault that things ended on a sour note, but however, that does not make it less tragic. Often those individuals only reacted to events. Thus, their dreams were never likely to come to life. This new book of knowledge is therefore encouraging you to *always believe in yourself, even when no one else does.* Above all, *always strive to make things happen instead of allowing things to happen to you.* This kind of offensive mentality is the philosophy that will eventually make you transcend any level.

Remember also that those who do not believe in themselves and those who do not take action are the people who eat life's potluck meals of beans and corn bread or roasted cassava and bonga fish soup when in fact, with a little effort, they would have had the steak they actually deserved. With the help of *The 7 Secrets to Peace of Mind,* you will never be like those kinds of people. Thus, you are encouraged to please decide what you really want out of life and then take the right action to make it happen.

Therefore, before you read any further, please do the following exercises for your own good:

Sit down quietly and create a rough map of the future you need. Get a pen and paper, and list what you need to achieve, what you need for your family, where you want live, etc. Decide what kind of car you will drive, what kind of home you will live in, where you want to go on vacation, etc. Think very hard, and write down all your dreams. Do not rule out anything just because it seems too fantastic and you think you might not achieve it. Chances are you will get a sudden burst of enlightenment from powerful forces. Or it may even be within your grasp. Write down each and every thing you desire. Go into detail if possible. Use several pages if you need to:

_____

_____

_____

_____

_____

_____

_____

_____

When you are finished making your list, save it and continue reading the rest of this new book of knowledge. After you finished reading, continue to do the appropriate exercises and then get back to your list and do what is necessary to be done.

THE SECRET TO CAREFULLY PLOTTING YOUR COURSE

It is a remarkable idea to always take your time to carefully plot your course prior to taking any constructive action. As a human being, you have the God-given power to chart your own course according to your choices. The secret is if you really want to realize your dreams and have peace of mind, you should not allow things to just happen to you. You should consciously choose the path to take with a clear knowledge of where you want to go.

However, this does not mean that everything will be handed to you on a platter. So be forewarned that at times, you may hit roadblocks or you may have to take detours in life. But the secret is, never lose track of your dreams, and always believe that God will see you through. Believe in yourself, and know where you should be headed to have the peace of mind you need. Always ask God in prayers if the course you are embarking on will lead you or show you the way to the destination you desire.

Do your best to never again be a victim of circumstances; always be in charge of your own life. Once you have the list of your goals and dreams on paper, the next question is how do you go about realizing them to have the peace of mind you need? First, think of your task as a journey. For example, when you get ready to go on a vacation, you might simply drive in the general direction of your destination and with a little luck, eventually arrive where you want to go.

Sometimes this works, especially if your journey is a very short one. However, the more complex the journey and the farther away the destination, the less successful this tactic becomes. You waste time on dead ends and find yourself going down dirt roads when a two-lane road would have been available had you known about it by carefully plotting your course. The secret is, you can get to anywhere you want to go much faster if you are using the modern global positioning system (GPS) or if, before you start your trip, you first get a map, study it, and then carefully and wisely plot your course. When you do that, you can easily and quickly get to your destination without wasting time on the road.

The same is true with realizing your dreams in the arduous and complicated journey of life. When you wisely plot your course, you will get to where you want to be a lot faster and with a minimum of backtracking. Therefore, once you have your list of what you want in life, your next task is to spend some time meditating or praying for how to achieve your goals. This may take time, but believe me, *every minute you spend praying will save you days, months, or even years of going astray.* This is the secret.

THE SECRET TO DEVOTEDLY PRIORITIZING YOUR GOALS

Always take the initiative to devotedly prioritize your goals so you can easily gain the peace of mind you need. While doing so, you should also prioritize your list of dreams in the way that you can first concentrate on achieving the things that will best enable you to realize your other dreams.

For example, if two of your dreams are to have a nice vacation home on the beautiful beaches of Lumley in Sierra Leone and also to have a well-paying job, then getting the cash first by procuring a well-paying job before building your dream vacation home would be the logical way to prioritize your goals. This plan will most likely give you the opportunity to realize both dreams faster.

It is therefore a good idea to always give some thought to the logical steps you need to take to arrive at your destinations easily and quickly. After you prioritize your list of goals, spend some time considering what steps to take to achieve each of your dreams accordingly. However, do not be astonished to learn that some goals might require further adjustments, such as further education, relocation, reduction, motivation, inspiration, application, etc. In any case, do not be discouraged by what you need to do in order to achieve your goals. Instead, just write down the logical steps that will get you there. Then start with that first step and keep going through the rest of the steps one by one until you eventually get to where you want to be.

One powerful method of prioritizing your goals is by transforming each step you need to fulfill your dream into a goal in itself. For example, if you want to be a medical doctor, then you will need to add the steps of obtaining a high school certificate or a GED, procuring a university education, and then pursuing the medical profession you want.

The psychology of making these steps into individual goals is that you can mentally congratulate yourself for achieving each of your dreams. As such, each step will become an important and a separate achievement of its own. The secret is that this method will promote a more positive attitude because instead of taking a very long time to achieve one big goal, you will be enjoying many contributory achievements and celebrations along the way.

Although that may seem like an odd way of viewing things, psychology tells us that as a human being, every time you tell yourself, "Good job—I did it," you are a little more positive in your outlook and thus more likely to push yourself a bit harder with the next step you tackle. In fact, in this example, you can even break things down further into smaller goals. For example, each year of school can be one of your dreams you can mentally cross off and congratulate yourself for doing. Therefore, it is always a good idea to divide and achieve your goals step by step and then turn each step into a victory.

The secret is you should never minimize your achievements. So please keep on believing in God and in yourself. Always take some time to note any progress you make, no matter how small it may be. Remember also to review your past achievements from time to time. All these things will help you obtain and maintain a positive outlook about yourself, and you will become all the more peaceful and powerful in your undertakings. Just continue to do these things, and little by little, you will get closer to your goals and eventually realizing your dreams. Remember to always believe in God, believe in yourself, know where you want to go, and know what steps you need to take to get there. This is your moment!

THE SECRET TO FAITHFULLY DEALING WITH SETBACKS

It was Nelson Mandela who said, "The greatest glory in living does not lie in never falling but in rising every time we fall." I strongly agree with this powerful visionary, and I hope you do too. Thus, this new book of knowledge is encouraging you to always learn to faithfully deal with setbacks so you can smoothly have a sustainable peace of mind. One important notion you should remember is that to get to where you want to go, you should not give up on your journey at the sight of the first detour sign. As such, you should never allow any unexpected expectation to spell the end of your journey; instead, they should only be part of the process. What you need to do, therefore, is to deal with them faithfully and smoothly as they come your way. Then gracefully move on.

Please allow me to tell you a lamentable story about a young music student who was learning to play the French horn. This little girl was frustrated every time she made a mistake in practice. Once the girl became flustered by that first mistake, she made more and more errors, all the time getting more and more discouraged. This created a terrible downward spiral in her practices. As a result, the poor little girl never made much progress and was always choking at critical moments in performances.

The problem was, the poor girl had programmed herself to expect perfection, and whenever she made even a minor blunder, it set off a chain reaction that ended in disaster for her. Despite her music teacher's efforts to help her not to see her mistakes as calamities, the poor little girl never changed her outlook and thus never blossomed to be the amazing French horn player she wanted to be.

Therefore I say to you, *never allow your mistakes to put you down*. Remember that it is common among the living to make mistakes. In fact as one put it, "To err is human." In life, some people learn from their mistakes and do not let those mistakes hold them back. Others worry over their mistakes and get upset, and in the process, they even make more mistakes or retreat, never to realize their dreams. Thus, they deprive themselves from enjoying the prosperity and peace of mind they deserve.

The truth is, in order to be progressive in life; you should expect mistakes, unexpected expectations, and setbacks. However, that should not cause you to give up and stop striving. As the German philosopher Friedrich Nietzsche, said: "That which does not kill us makes us stronger." Therefore I tell you, *if you really want to have peace of mind, you should learn to embrace your shortcomings. You should take your faults in stride as you press forward until you finally achieve your goals.*

During my professional tenure in the area of social services, while doing the research for my counseling psychology program, and in preparation to write this new book of knowledge, I met with many people who failed in life just because they gave up quickly and prematurely. Their common problem was that the moment they get one or two setbacks, they quickly throw in the towel or surrender. Lamentably, all their battles were lost; as a result, their dreams were never realized.

Fortunately, with the help of *The 7 Secrets to Peace of Mind*, you will not be like those kinds of people. This new book of knowledge has been designed to encourage you to learn to see your setbacks as only temporary. Please be courageous enough to learn from your mistakes, hone your skills, and always view failures as stepping-stones that can lead you toward your destination. This volume is therefore encouraging you to *always keep on keeping on until you achieve your goals.*

One more open secret you should know is that everyone has failures and setbacks. However, the sad part is if you let failures stop you, you can hardly enjoy personal victory. The people who know this secret never let hard times detail their dreams. You now know the secret, so you, too, should learn to do likewise. Always persist and take away troubles in your stride. When you do this, eventually you will achieve your goals and have the peace of mind you need.

THE SECRET TO ALWAYS FOCUSING ON POSSIBILITIES

You can always focus on possibilities by learning to see possibilities in everything you do to develop yourself. One powerful strategy for seeing possibilities in your dreams is by examining everything you experience on a daily basis. The secret is that you should always focus on possibilities with an eye toward determining whether what you are experiencing might help you reach your goals. You should therefore treat everything in your life as a potential stepping-stone toward reaching your goals.

For example, when you meet someone, ask yourself if he or she might help you realize any of your goals. Maybe he or she knows someone who can give you a break or has a skill or information that you can use to achieve your goals. Therefore, in everything you do, whether you are reading the newspaper, watching TV, reading a book, listening to public speakers, or surfing the Internet, do so with an eye toward discovering information that might help you to reach your goals or realize your dreams.

Most of the time, your everyday life offers tools and opportunities that can be exploited if you are alert enough to notice them. If you are sleepwalking through life, you may miss many golden opportunities. *The 7 Secrets to Peace of Mind* is therefore encouraging you to please wake up, ignore all the distractions in life, and become fully aware of what is happening around you. Examine and consider how anything might be transformed into an opportunity for you to promote yourself.

Remember, when you hear a speech or read an article, it may contain important tips or pieces of information that can carry you toward your dreams. Therefore, be always alert for anything that might be of use in achieving your goals. Look at everything you see, and everything you encounter, as a potential tool. Weigh it against what you need in life, and see if it can be of help in promoting peace in your life. If it does not offer any help, do not waste any time on it. Drop it and move on because *anything that does not serve your purpose serves no purpose.*

This new book of knowledge is drawing your attention to the following helpful ideas:

Always pay special attention to anything that might help you have peace of mind. Do not kill time. Always use your time very wisely. Your entertainment should never be things that just kill time. Instead, the things you do in your free time should lead you toward your life's goals. Even when you are stuck in a traffic jam or sitting in a dental office, be alert to a chance event, a magazine article, or anything that might give you a bit of knowledge or an opportunity that can help you realize your dreams.

The 7 Secrets to Peace of Mind is therefore encouraging you to make every effort to always learn to expect opportunities at any time. Learn to view each person you meet, each event you attend to, and anything that happens to you as a potential opportunity. Weigh everything in your life to determine how it can present an opportunity for you to get closer to your goal. This is the secret, and your moment has come!

NEVER DO ANYTHING HALFWAY

It is a good piece of advice to never do anything halfheartedly. Thus, you should learn to always give your best shot to anything you do. Whether you are taking a small step toward a goal or you are engaged in a make-or-break effort to realize a longtime dream, never do anything halfway. No matter how big or small the task may be, give it your best shot. Not only will this philosophy improve your chances for a sustainable peace of mind, but it will also help you develop the self-discipline that is found in people who are perceived as diligent, hopeful, perseverant, and patient.

Never be meek in your endeavors. Live your life with gusto. Do your best, and never dwell on your mistakes or setbacks. Keep doing your best, and little by little, you will achieve whatever goals you set for yourself. Just do your best each day and you will get closer to the mark. Always remember that everything you do, if you do it well, will move you closer to the realization of your goals. So keep going forward and never look back.

When you adhere to these fundamental and powerful principles, you will always be as peaceful as you make up your mind to be. Remember also that *positive attitude and a mount look are added edges that can help you achieve whatever you desire.* The problem, however, is that many people underestimate their own powers and overestimate the obstacles that block their way. As such, they quickly give up for no good reason. As a result, they always miss the opportunities to gain the peace of mind they deserve.

The sad thing about quickly giving up is that some people often do so without any concrete reason other than their unfounded fears. Most of the time those kinds of individuals do not even ask for the honest advice they need. They fear that if they ask for advice, someone might laugh at them or think they are ignorant. In fact, some people are reluctant to even go to the bank and ask for the loans they need because they are afraid that the banker might reject their applications. Please do not be like those kinds of people. *Always remember that the opposite of fear is knowledge.* Now you have the power.

If you are actually bold enough and you have the intention to achieve your goal, the only thing that is generally risked is a very small, momentary discomfort. Unfortunately, just to avoid that small risk, most people too often fail to take that next step toward obtaining their desires, and so their dreams are never realized. However, with the help of *The 7 Secrets to Peace of Mind*, you will never make such mistakes again. Always be bold and risk having people say no; you will find they often say yes instead.

Never hesitate to ask for help or for advice when you need it. And whenever you need someone's help to achieve your goal, you should not give up; persist until you get what you want. The Bible tells us that persistence and patience will always pay off. Failure often comes from giving up when you might have met your goal had you only waited a little longer or attempted one more time.

When one person rejects your request, simply ask someone else. When one route fails, take another. When one door is closed, open another. When all the doors are closed, open the window. When there is a roadblock, go around it, go over it, or go under it, but do not quickly wave the white flag and simply give up. Never give up just because someone said no to you. Always remember this: "Persistence pays off 99 percent of the time, while giving up leads to failure 100 percent of the time." Remember also that most of your limitations are just in your head but not actually in the situations you face.

This new book of knowledge is therefore reminding you to never be tempted to do anything half way; always give everything your best shot to achieve your goals. If you did not meet your target the first time around, do not give up. Just pick yourself up, dust yourself off, move on gracefully, and be hopeful. As it is commonly said in Sierra Leone, "The downfall of a man is not the end of his life." You are therefore advised to always do it again wisely and never give up. Let me therefore remind you of the powerful words of Winston Churchill when he laconically said: "Never give in—never, never, never, never, in nothing great or small, large or petty, never give in except to convictions of honor and good sense."

The Secret to Conquering the Fear of Failure

Henry Ford was the wise and diligent fellow who stated, "Failure is simply the opportunity to begin again, this time more intelligently." This concept should therefore lead you to the realization that failing to succeed in something does not always mean you are a failure. This new book of knowledge is therefore designed to remind you that, actually, there is never a sense of failure. The fact is, most of the time, what you perceive as failure is just another life lesson. Unfortunately, however, the fear of failure is one of the greatest maladies of modern society. The truth is if you really want to promote yourself, you should not be afraid to fail. Part of the tendency for some people to give up too quickly comes from their conditioning by family members, schools, friends, communities, professions, etc.

For example, most children too often are told that they are likely to fail at almost everything they do. Thus, this fearful idea causes them to live like little mice that fear calling attention to themselves, lacking self-respect and getting little respect from others. Later in their lives, those mice-like children can eventually become overly cautious adults. These are the people who never take chances because they are afraid they might fail. Their fear of failure keeps them from ever achieving anything great, and it keeps them from ever overcoming the barriers that are holding them back.

Fortunately, with the help of *The 7 Secrets to Peace of Mind*, you will not be like those kinds of people. You will always strive to be an honorable individual of dignity. You will not be like those human mice. You will learn to risk failure cautiously. Eventually you will discover that worthwhile people will respect you more, even if you sometimes fail.

Just think about the following comparison for a moment: Who is more heroic—the guy who gives his best shot and fights all the odds but unfortunately loses, or the guy who meekly goes through life never doing anything special, never venturing anything new, and just acting like an anonymous cog in the machine? Of course you will agree with me that people admire the underdog who takes a chance. They admire him even if he fails. There is truth to the old saying, "It doesn't matter if you win or lose; it is how you play the game that matters." Therefore, you should always do your best and always play all out. In the end, people will admire you for doing your best, even if you lose.

Remember also that even if you fail sometimes, you will always win on a more important level. In fact, most people admire the guy who comes in last in the race if they think he has given his best shot. Trust me; I was a long distance runner, and I know that many runners have finished last to the applause of a crowd that knows they have done their best and have overcome whatever handicaps they may have had.

The 7 Secrets to Peace of Mind is therefore designed to remind you that you do not have to be in the first place to be a winner in the game of life. All you really need to do is to always give your best shot. Often this will be enough not only to make people admire you for attempting but for also doing your best. When you give it your best shot, you cannot always lose. In fact, you will not only gain admiration, but will also gain the courage to pursue your goals again.

In short, you cannot miss by bucking the odds, even on those occasions when you may technically fail. In fact, you can even learn from your mistakes if only you pay attention. Furthermore, please think about the following suggestions very seriously:

Never ever fear failure. Never play the part of the coward. Dare to take chances and strive for progress and peace of mind. Always seize the day and live your life with honor; because you are the honorable one.

Be mindful, however, that there are always a few people in your social environment who may laugh at your failure. You know who . . . However, when you are a target of anybody's scorn, such unscrupulous individuals will only have the power to make you miserable if you let them. Please do your best to always ignore them (because you have done your best). Sooner or later, you will know that they have no power over you.

Eventually they will make themselves look bad for laughing at you. Thus, although you may have suffered temporary disappointment, you will still be an honorable person of dignity. Eleanor Roosevelt said it best when she stated, "No one can make you feel inferior without your consent." This volume is therefore encouraging you to please do your best and to not give anyone the upper hand to put or pull you down.

In fact, when the scornful fail to have an effect on you, the good people in your social environment who see or hear them will recognize them for what they really are—unscrupulous. Such wicked individuals will soon see their contempt turned back against them. Therefore, always ignore these unfair critics and villains; do not give them any power over you. Bear in mind also that most times, what appears to be an insurmountable problem often melts into nothing with a heroic assault. Remember therefore that all setbacks and misfortunes are permanent only if you allow them to be. So this new book of knowledge is encouraging you to *never fear failure, and never stay down. Always get up cautiously and move on.*

The psychology is, if you are determined and if you get back onto your feet with wisdom after being knocked on your butt, you will always find a better route to achieve your goals. In most cases, once you rise to continue your striving, you will find that the obstacles were in fact only temporary or mental. You will even find that others may admire your efforts and come to your aid.

The 7 Secrets to Peace of Mind is therefore encouraging you to learn that it is significant to always move forward and stay positive. If you ever experience any disappointment, just remind yourself that this occurrence will make you stronger and more resilient and may eventually lead you to something greater. In fact, when you actually take a moment to reflect on your so-called failures, you will later learn that most of your misfortunes of yesterday led to your fortunes of today. This volume is therefore encouraging you to accept every misadventure as a critical step toward achieving your goals. After all, great achievements are more appreciated when earned after overcoming life's difficult challenges.

Please be reminded, however, that these good things mostly happen when you keep on doing your best and taking the necessary actions. It is also advantageous to always learn from your failures before doing your best again. This is the way you can easily find the door that finally opens through which you will get to the dreams you have been working so hard to attain. Remember also that during your heroic struggles, you should always be positive, knowing you will eventually reach your goals if you continue to do your best. By so doing, with the proper attitude and mind-set, you will always be as powerful as you choose to be. Therefore, your peace is your command!

YOUR LOVELY SMILE IS THE MASTER KEY TO EVERYTHING

Your lovely smile is the metaphorical master key to everything you do or say to achieve your goals. Psychology tells us that anybody can have peace of mind by sincerely smiling from the heart. This is true because life is all about feeling good. Therefore, to assure your peace of mind, just simply smile from your heart and keep on smiling. As a result, the people of the world will smile to you.

Remember also that positive attitude can always play a powerful role in gaining the peace of mind you need. Another effective method of obtaining this positive attitude is by smiling at anybody you meet. If there is no one in your proximity, every chance you get, look at your reflection in a mirror and just smile. After all, let me reiterate, life is all about smiling and feeling good. So please keep on smiling in order to keep on feeling good.

However, before you begin to think about this smiling exercise as a crazy notion, it is important to understand what this little formula can actually do for you. Psychology has discovered that when a sad person forces a smile, he or she will immediately feel good. In other words, putting on a happy face will eventually make you feel happier. Psychology tells us also that smiling at yourself in the mirror creates an amazing mental feedback system that will cheer you up. And that smiling at yourself can also cause you to feel better about yourself. Therefore, instead of seeing yourself in the mirror and thinking, My God, look at that face, you will actually look forward to the pleasure of seeing the smile you will flash at yourself.

While you are doing your smiling exercises, you should also learn to look at yourself in the eyes. Please be reminded that many people judge your sincerity by whether you look at them in their eyes. Therefore, regardless of your culture, the idea of looking at people in their eyes will actually enable you to make a good first impression. Beyond that, when you look at people in their eyes, they also tend to look at you in your eyes, thereby concentrating less on your other features. They will then break eye contact by looking away if you continue to maintain eye contact with them. The psychology is, when you do that you will give people a positive impression of you without allowing them to register any downside to your appearance.

The 7 Secrets to Peace of Mind is also encouraging you to always remember that the ideas of smiling at people and looking at them in their eyes are very valuable habits that can effortlessly open doors. In fact, psychology tells us that the lasting impression most people make of someone occurs during the first thirty seconds they meet the person. Just think very carefully about that and see how significant it is. Therefore, if you let people notice your friendly smile and if you make eye contact with them, they will picture you as a personable and friendly person with piercing eyes that seem intelligent and thoughtful. They may not notice any of your flaws; but rather, they will only notice your good points and your amicable smiles.

Remember also that during the initial thirty seconds you meet with someone, a lasting picture of you is created in that person's brain. That picture does not change much even with the passage of a long time thereafter. In other words, those who have met you will remember you by what they noticed about you most during those first thirty seconds. They will not remember you by the features they might note later on after your initial meeting with them.

One more advantage of always having a friendly smile is that seeing a person smile causes others to also smile back. That again sets up a feedback loop in their brain that makes them happier as well. So remember that your smile will not only cheer you up, but those who see it and then smile back will be cheered as well. That is why you should always smile and let the people of the world smile back to you. By so doing, you will be known as a person who lights up a room by just entering. As a result, you will always have the peace of mind you deserve.

So *please keep on smiling and let the people of the world smile at you.*

Your Peace Is Your Command!

EPILOGUE

Your peace of mind is a ship, and you are the captain.

Your Peace Is Your Command!

Colin Powell, one of the most admired and heroic figures in modern society put it best when he said: "It is not where you start in life that matters; it is where you end up and what you did along the way." And I strongly agree with the honorable man.

Thus, in a nutshell, *The 7 Secrets to Peace of Mind* assures you that when all is done as said; your peace will finally be at your own command. You now know the insider secrets that will help you to realize your dreams and promote your chances of having the peace of mind you always needed. You can easily do this by first figuring out exactly what you need in your life and then carefully plotting the course that will let you procure all that you need. You can also achieve this goal by adopting a positive attitude, refusing to give up, always smiling, and carefully tackling any problem life sends your way with ease.

Those are some of the qualities that will transform you into a heroic figure that people will admire or even root for. Eventually you will not only increase your chances of being peaceful, but you will also make the world a better place for all humanity. You now know the secrets to achieving the things you might have thought impossible. I am therefore encouraging you to please apply the suggestions outlined in this new book of knowledge. Be sure also to make a regular update of the list of things you want to achieve in life. Remember however that your list is not set in concrete, so do not hesitate to add new goals as they come to mind.

Be mindful that you can easily succeed in having the peace of mind you need when you precisely do the appropriate exercises. Of course, simply knowing the secrets that have been revealed to you by this new book of knowledge will help you, but applying the knowledge you have procured will help you even more. In fact, it is by diligently applying this secret knowledge to your life that you will quickly realize your full potential.

You are encouraged to please put the secret formulas you now know into practice; then make perseverance and smiling part of your daily life. This is the time for you to roll up your sleeves and get to work. Now is the moment for honing your skills so that you can realize your dreams and multiply your chances of having the peace of mind you need.

Thus, I would love to relay an unforgettable message I once received from my uncle, Honorable Joseph Thomas Ngomba, who was a very powerful Member of Parliament of the government of Sierra Leone. He was later appointed to the position of the government representative to the Sierra Rutile and Sierronco mines, in Sierra Leone. In addition to his distinguished political affiliation, Hon. J. T. Ngomba held many ranking membership positions in the most powerful members-only organizations in Africa. That powerful leader was also a great philosopher and a remarkable teacher. When I was awarded a scholarship to further my airlines education in Amman, Jordan, my honorable uncle and guru gave me a powerful message at the time of my departure. The great sage told me never to forget this life-changing message:

> Believe in yourself; your presence is a present to this world. You are a unique individual. Your life can be what you want it to be. Take your days just one day at a time.

> Count your blessings, not your troubles. You will make it through whatever comes along. Within you are so many answers. Understand, have courage, and be strong.

> Do not put limits on yourself. So many dreams are waiting to be realized. Decisions are too important to leave to chance. Reach for your peak, your goal, and your prize.

Nothing wastes more energy than worrying. The longer one carries a problem, the heavier it gets. Do not take things too personally. Live a life of serenity, not a life of regrets.

Remember that a little love goes a long way. Remember that a lot . . . goes forever. Remember that friendship is a wise investment. Life's treasure is people together.

Realize that it is never too late. Do ordinary things in extraordinary ways. Have health; and hope; and joy; and faith; and love. Take the time to wish upon a star.

Above all, do not ever forget . . . for even a moment . . . how very special you are.

To my greatest astonishment, and although he did not mention the origin, nonetheless, that great master later told me that this powerful message has been around the world for ages and is still circulating among a select few groups of individuals and members-only organizations. Anyway, to cut a long story short, I promised my uncle that I would surely relay this life-changing message to all humanity. Thus, this is your moment! This message is for you. Please pass it on to your loved ones and to all humanity. So it was written; so I have relayed it; and so you shall pass it on. As the Bible said, "Nor does anyone light a lamp and put it under a basket, but on the lampstand, and it gives light to all who are in the house." You can also help to spread this good news by giving someone a copy of *The 7 Secrets to Peace of Mind*.

This new book of knowledge is also waking up all humanity to the conscious awareness that all of the seven billion people on this planet are firmly interconnected. We are all interconnected in this universe that has being continuously expanding for 13.7 billion years and still going. Therefore, because we are indispensably interconnected, *The 7 Secrets to Peace of Mind* is encouraging you to please live in peace and harmony with all humanity. *When we live in peace and harmony, we can contagiously stimulate joy to the world and peace on earth.* In fact, Mother Teresa put it best when she said, "If we have no peace, it is because we have forgotten that we belong to each other."

Remember also that *the ultimate meaning of life is people in harmony*. Therefore, this new book of knowledge is reminding you to always pay keen attention to the people in your life. Thus, I am please to share with you a magnum opus about the people in our lives that my uncle, Paramount Chief Tommy Jombra the Seventh, gave me during my good-bye meeting with him prior to my departure to the United States of America. Paramount Chief Tommy Jombra the Seventh of Banta Monkeleh chiefdom in Sierra Leone is a descendant of powerful rulers and great sages. As a powerful philosopher and master, my uncle Paramount Chief Jombra the Seventh adequately addressed the emotional subject of "paying attention to the people in our lives" as he gave me the following powerful and emotive message that has been revolving in a select few circles around the world for years:

> Sometimes people come into your life and you know right away that they were meant to be there, to serve some sort of purpose—to teach you a lesson; or to help you figure out who you really are or who you need to become. You never know who these people may be. It could be your roommate; it could be your neighbor, or your teacher, your long lost friend, or your lover, or even a complete stranger. But when you lock eyes with them, you know that at any moment they will affect your life in some profound way.
>
> And sometimes things happen to you that may seem horrible, painful, and unfair at first; but in reflection, you find that without overcoming those obstacles you would have never realized your potential, your strength, your willpower, or your heart. Everything happens for a reason. Nothing happens by chance or by means of good luck or ill luck. Illness, injury, love, lost moments of true greatness, and sheer stupidity . . . etc. All these occur to test the limits of your soul.
>
> Without these small tests, whatever they may be, life would be like a smoothly paved, straight, flat road to nowhere. It would be safe, and comfortable, but it would be dull, and utterly pointless.

The people you meet who affect your life, and the success and downfalls you experience, help to create who you are and who you become. Even the bad experiences can be learned from. In fact, they are probably the most poignant but important ones. If someone hurts you, betrays you, or breaks your heart, forgive him or her, for they have helped you learn about trust and the importance of being cautious when you open your heart.

If people love you, love them back unconditionally. You should love them not only because they love you, but because they are also teaching you to love and how to open your heart and eyes to things. Make every day count. Appreciate every moment and take from these moments everything that you possibly can; because you may never be able to experience it again. Talk to people that you have never talked to before, and always listen. Allow yourself to fall in love, break free, and set your sights high. Hold your head up because you have every right to.

Tell yourself what a great individual you are and let the world know that you are a person of value. Believe in yourself; for if you do, it will be easier for others to believe in you. You can make of your life anything you wish. Create your own life and then live it with absolutely no regrets. Most importantly, if you love someone tell her or him; for you never know what tomorrow may have in store.

Learn a lesson in life each day that you live. Today is the tomorrow you were worried about yesterday. Was it worth it?

My answer to that that question was a resounding *no* because *I am never afraid of the unknown.*

What is your answer to that question and why?

_____

_____

_____

_____

However, since we are all interconnected, please take a moment to contemplate on this great philosophy, and then share it with the people in your life and with all humanity. This is a way of shining your light on others who could do ditto. As author Marianne Williamson wisely put it: "As we let our own light shine, we unconsciously give other people permission to do the same." Thus, I am encouraging you to please help spread this message around the world . . .

The 7 Secrets to Peace of Mind also draws your attention to these noble qualities and values that should be exhibited in everything you do or say:

> *Honesty, thoughtfulness, peacefulness, gratefulness, honorableness, loyalty, piety, faithfulness, helpfulness, diligence, friendliness, positive attitude, cooperativeness, patience, trustworthiness, understanding, integrity, good character, love, forgiveness, dependability, enthusiasm, reliability, generosity, flexibility, a sense of humor, and respectfulness.*

The above are some of the qualities and values that will eventually make you who you become.

Now please honestly answer the following questions to yourself and make some adjustments if necessary: Do people use some of the above-mentioned qualities and values when they talk about you? Do any of those qualities and values ring true when you think about yourself in your quiet moments?

_____

_____

_____

_____

If you say yes to any of the above questions, then clap your hands and rejoice because your peace of mind is on the way. However, if you say no to any of those questions, please do not be troubled; *The 7 Secrets to Peace of Mind* is here to help you. Thus, by making the necessary adjustments, you will surely generate peace of mind for yourself and for the people around you. As a result, you will feel good about yourself, and you will be in harmony with your true nature. Eventually you will find out that, regardless of any situation you may be in, life is always about feeling good.

Furthermore, *The 7 Secrets to Peace of Mind* is designed to remind you of the fundamental forces of peace, joy, and love. These are the most powerful forces endowed to you by the divine. Be reminded also that the greatest of these three forces is love. It is love, because love is power. Therefore, you should always claim the power of love to obtain a sustainable peace of mind. In the world, there are many forms of power. However, regardless of outward appearance of wealth, strength, authority, etc., *the power of love is greater than any power on planet Earth.*

Thus, this new book of knowledge is encouraging you to turn your attention to the power of love that moves in and through you. You are also encouraged to give up any fear so you can realize the fullness of love. With faith, you can love even those who seem to be your adversaries, and you will not be tempted to judge anyone. Even when people do not recognize your love, you should love them anyway. Even when people do not appreciate your love, you should love them anyway. Even when people do not return your love, you should love them anyway. As Mother Teresa truthfully put it, "If you judge people, you have no time to love them." Remember also that it was Bob Manley who said, "Truth is, everybody is going to hurt you; you just gotta find the ones worth suffering for."

Please be reminded that love is the harmonizer that unifies people one to another and soul to soul. With true love, you can clearly see the nothingness of petty jealousies and petty differences. Thus, you can clearly see the power of cooperation and unity. This new book of knowledge is therefore encouraging you to always give expression to the overflowing power of love within you and please love everyone unconditionally, even those who hate you. In fact, in Luke 6:27 it is written, "I say to you that listen, Love your enemies."

The 7 Secrets to Peace of Mind is based on the philosophy of peace, hope, and love. Let me further remind you that the greatest of these three is love. Thus, I strongly agree with Daphne Rose Kingma's creative poem titled "Love":

> It is love that fashions us into the fullness of our being—not our looks, not our work, not our wants, not our achievements, not our parents, not our status, not our dreams. These are all the fodder and the filler, the navigating fuels of our lives, but it is love—who we love, how we love, why we love and that we love—which ultimately shapes us.
>
> It is love, before all and after all, in the beginning and in the end, that creates us. Today, remembering this, let yourself acknowledge and remember the moments, events, and people who bring you, even momentarily, into a true experience of love, and allow the rest, the inescapable mundane of life, like a cloud, to very quietly drift away.

Thus, in order to maintain a sustainable peace of mind, you should always remember that unconditional love is the answer. As Mohandas Gandhi put it, "Where there is love, there is life." Let me remind you also that "God is love." Therefore, *with love, all things are possible.*

Please do not forget also that positive attitude is always a vital component of a sustainable peace of mind. *Positive attitude can help to reinforce the core values that will inspire you to action.* Regardless of your past or your fear of the unknown, what is important now is how you choose to respond to anything. You are therefore encouraged to pay attention to the following words of wisdom from great thinkers of ancient and modern times:

> "A person who never made a mistake never tried anything new."
>
> —Albert Einstein

> "Knowledge is power, but practiced knowledge of vital secrets is even more powerful."
>
> —Moses Congofoh Charles

"You have to expect things of yourself before you can do them."

—Michael Jordan

"You'll see it when you believe it."

—Dr. Wayne Dyer

"Desire is the starting point of all achievement, not a hope, not a wish, but a keen pulsating desire which transcends everything."

—Napoleon Hill

"Set your course by the stars, not by the lights of every passing ship."

—General Omar N. Bradley

"Even if you're on the right track, you'll get run over if you just sit there."

—Will Rogers

"The best thing to give to your enemy is forgiveness; to an opponent, tolerance; to a friend, your heart; to your child, a good example; to a father, deference; to your mother, conduct that will make her proud of you; to yourself, respect; to all men, charity."

—Benjamin Franklin

Remember also that *it is your birthright to have peace of mind.*

From the above powerful words of wisdom and with the help of *The 7 Secrets to Peace of Mind,* you will surely find strength, inspiration, and motivation; as a result of which, you will never be the same again. Keep in mind also that when a door of opportunity begins to open, it is still your choice whether to go through it or not.

Finally, *The 7 Secrets to Peace of Mind* is leaving you with the following words of piety and inspiration that will always give you the peace of mind you need: *believe, be blessed,* and *be inspired.* Remember also that you are now free of fear and apprehension. Remember that the divine power is within you, and you are never alone. No entity, person, or situation has the power to negate the goodness of God in you. Remember to always live your life with certainty and enthusiasm.

You now know the secrets and this is your moment. Congratulations!

Your Peace Is Your Command!

A Message for All Humanity

Always remember that, whoever you may be, your way is not the only way.

Remember also that without any doubt, you will surely wake up to the realization at a certain time in your life that, "It is not what you have that matters; it is who you become."

"When you were born, you cried, and the world rejoiced. Live your life in such a manner that when you die, the world cries and you rejoice."

Thus anything you do, honestly do it for peace, hope, or love.

Your Peace Is Your Command!

A Message for the Top 1 Percent

When you are good, better, or the best, please help some of the rest . . . Until *we* are good or better, or *we* are better or best.

Something to ponder: *Who are we?*

Answer: *"We are the 99 percent."*

Your Peace Is Your Command!

ACKNOWLEDGMENTS

Gratitude, acknowledgment, and thankfulness are the most important keys to a peaceful life.

Your Peace Is Your Command!

"If I have seen further, it is by standing on the shoulders of giants."

—Sir Isaac Newton

With that in mind, I am first and foremost, sincerely thankful to God almighty for giving me this opportunity, including but not limited to the inspiration, wisdom, knowledge, understanding, courage, and strength to do what I needed to do to write *The 7 Secrets to Peace of Mind*. It has always been my dream to serve all humanity, and I needed help from all and sundry to fulfill my goal. Thus, this new book of knowledge is a collection of dynamic and life-changing information that is birthed from God's blessing and also from the help of diligent support groups, organizations, individuals and an extensive network.

To mention a few: I am sincerely grateful to my brother, Mr. Sylvester Musa Charles and the rest of my family members whose support and prayers contributed to making me who I am. My mother, Hajah Isata Charles; my father, Chief Moses Congofoh Charles; my brothers, Chief Joe Amadu Charles, Chief Tommy Brima Charles, Chief Foday Korgbai Charles, and Imam Amara Tondoma Charles; and my sister, Hajah Jebeh Charles-Kallon. Also to Hon. Joseph Thomas Ngomba; Mrs. Maligba Ngomba; Mrs. Agnes Charles; Mrs. Kardy Charles; Mr. James Fineboy; Mr. Peter Fineboy, Pastor Kainwo; Pa. Gibrila; Pa. Kamanda; Pa. Deemoh; Pa. A. J. Momoh; Pa. Gbondo; Chief Abdulai Yorpoi; Chief Korgbai; Chief Jombra; Chief Charles—Gbanya; Chief Margai; Maa Sita; Mee Kaymar; Mee Soko; Chief Betty; Mr. Anthony Gbondo Smith; Mrs.

Fatmata Gbondo; Mr. Joe Kaiyengay; Ngor Njarmy; Ngor Kardy; Ngor Njabu Sulaiman; Yae Kula Lebbie; Madam Akiatu Kamara; Mr. Victor Charles; Mr. Johnny Mansalay; Mr. Sylvester Charles (Junior); Miss Isata Mansalay; Mr. Prince Charles; Miss Sylvia Ngande Charles; Mr. Denise Charles; Miss Diana Isata Charles; and many others.

I am also thankful to my dream team. This powerful team, led by my wife, Mrs. Isha Charles, is the force that kept me focused on the big picture. This team fueled me up with encouragement and support that kept me going. As one put it, "It takes teamwork to make the dream work." Thank you, my wife, for your leadership of this amazing team of powerful academics and interlocutors.

Individually, I am grateful to the leader of my dream team, Mrs. Isha Charles. Thank you so much, honey, for a job well done. I commend you also for typing the greater fraction of my handwritten words that have eventually metamorphosed into this new book of knowledge. Thank you also for your comfort and words of encouragement that kept me stable and tranquil even in the midst of the inescapable writer's turmoil and blocks. Thank you so much, darling, for making my noble dream to serve all humanity a reality.

Let me extend my individual gratitude to you, my children. You are the dedicated members of the dream team who worked diligently with great sense of duty and determination to make this project a success. Thank you, my dear lady and gentlemen, for a job well done.

Thanks to the financial adviser of my dream team, Miss Tonia Isata Charles. Thank you for your wise financial decisions. Thank you also for your vision and all your support. May God almighty continue to guide and bless you abundantly wherever you may be, my daughter.

I am grateful to the computer expert of my dream team, Mr. Anthony Brima Charles. Your brilliant and versatile computer knowledge was extremely instrumental in making this project far less arduous. Thank you for your indispensable expertise. May almighty God continue to guide and bless you in all your undertakings, my son.

I now extend my gratitude to the lexicographer of my dream team, Mr. Sylvester Foday Charles. Thank you for your majestic role as the coeditor extraordinaire for this unique project. Thank you for co-leading the instinct team, for taking care of my syntax, and for refocusing me when I was sometimes out on a limb. May the grace of the almighty be with you, and may you be guided and blessed at all times, my son.

Furthermore, I am thankful to the graphics designer of my dream team, Mr. Lawrence Amara Charles. Thanks for your help in choosing and designing the cover for *The 7 Secrets to Peace of Mind*. With the help of your brother, Sylvester, you took my vision and turned it into a picture for the world to see. The power of God will continue to bless, guide, and protect you in everything you do, my son.

In a nutshell, I am very glad to tell the world that the writing of *The 7 Secrets to Peace of Mind* as a panacea to help all humanity has been our joyful family project. My wife and my children understand my desire and determination to write this new inspirational book of knowledge with the hope of serving human kind. Therefore, the relentless support I continue to receive from my family is a clear manifestation of the fact that we are one in heart and mind. We have been walking this walk of faith as a faithful family for many years, and we are still moving forward. God will continue to bless us and guide us as we keep on keeping on.

My sincere gratitude now goes to the pillar of my dream team, my cousin in-law, Madam Janet Mahoi. Your wisdom and inspiration firmly held my dream team in place during times of distress and temptations. Thank you so much for your constant provision of the delicious dishes of jackeytomboy and jolabaytay. Thank you so very much for your support and your words of encouragement that kept the dream team going against all odds. May God almighty bless you, guide you, protect you, and grant you all your good wishes.

I would now love to extend my gratitude to my longtime friends: Dr. John Sandy, author of "Pointers to Success"; Mr. Joe Kapia, author of "West African Journal"; Dr. Sheik Ahamed Bangura, professor, Mr. Ibrahim Koroma, CPA; Mr. David Momoh, entrepreneur; Mr. Idris Amara, entrepreneur; Mr. Amadu Turay, entrepreneur; Mr. Emmanuel Jigba, entrepreneur; Mr. Mohamed Koroma (Okoro), entrepreneur; and Mr. Mohamed Bangura, entrepreneur. You are my brothers who constantly called me when I was sometimes swamped and delved into reading, researching, and writing. Your friendly conversations helped greatly when I was sometimes in writer's block. Thank you, my dear brothers. God will continue to bless our decades of friendship.

The same gratitude now goes to some of my cousins, nieces, nephews, in-laws, friends, etc., who consciously or unconsciously contributed. My heart goes to you: Mr. Prince Kobba, Mrs. Grace Kobba, Mr. Joe Freeman-Wai, Mrs. Edna Freeman-Wai, Mr. Emanuel Gbondo, Mrs. Nancy Gbondo, Madam Denise Johnson, Mr. Edward Mammy, Mrs. Janet Mammy, Mr. Osman Sanneh, Mrs. Kardy Sanneh, Mr. Mustapha Turay, Mrs. Esther Turay, Mr. Ibrahim Sesay, Mrs. Cecilia Sesay, Mr. Joseph Bondo, Mrs. Rosemond Yah Bondo, Dr. Mamoud Hassan, Mrs. Regina Hassan, Mr. John Moody, Mrs. Joan Moody, Madam Marion Alie, Madam Frances Alie, Madam Vickie Alie, Mr. George Sannoh, Mr. Abu-Barkarr Kamara, Mrs. Doris Kamara, Mr. Joshua Sulaiman, Mrs. Ann-Marie Mallah, Mrs. Theresa Jigba, Mr. Junisa Lebbie, Mrs. Mabel Lebbie, Mr. Cecil Sulaiman, Mrs. Fatmata Sulaiman, Mr. Momoh Lahai, Mrs. Amy Lahai, Mr. Edrisa Bassey, Mrs. Henrietta Bassey, Mr. Larick Karvon, Mrs. Doreen Karvon, Mr. Prince Sulaiman, Mrs. Komeh Sulaiman, Mr. Woody Bangura, Mr. Foday Labbie, Mr. Munda Amara, Mrs. Hajah Amara, Mr. Augustine Koppoi, Mrs. Olive Koppoi, Mr. Aiah Bangura, Mr. Esequie Bangura, Mr. Fengai Moiwa, Mr. Momodu Sorie, Mrs. Eku Sorie, Mr. Sahr Maturie, Mrs. Henrietta Maturie, Mr. Yusuf Mansaray, Mr. Milton Kamara, Mrs. Maxine Kamara, Mr. Patrick Bockari, Mrs. Deborah Bockari, Mrs. Mary Turay, Mr. Sahr Mbawa, Mrs. Rachel Mbawa, Mr. Umaru Lamin, Mrs. Jeneba Lamin, Mr. Abu Bonapha, Mrs. Angela Bonapha, Mr. Joseph Musa, Mrs. Esther Musa, Mr. Augustine Fallay, Mrs. Zainab Fallay, Dr. Mohamed Berete, Mr. Mohamed Lamin, Mrs. Musu Lamin, Mr. Sylvester Johnny, Mr. Joe Mustapha, Mrs. Janet Mustapha, Mr. Mohamed Conteh, Mrs. Iye Conteh, Mr. Aluie Iscandari, Mrs. Kiptiatu Iscandari, Mr. Saidu Kamara, Mr. Sahr Bangah, Mrs. Grace Bangah, Mr. Henry Kamara, Mrs. Mariatu Kamara, Mr. Tamba Demby, Mrs. Catherine Demby, Madam Nelly Amas, Madam Tida Turay, Madam Sally Karvon, Madam Rose Momoh, Madam Eunice Jackson, Madam Lillian Koker, Madam Amy Kamara, Madam Olive Yamba, Madam

Regina Abu, Madam Cecilia Momoh, Madam Glory Udoffia, Madam Lola Davis, Mrs. Anne Sesay, Madam Kadie Mattia, Madam Fatima Turay, Madam Isatu Jalloh, Madam Juliana Brainard, Madam Rose A. Madam Donna Mahwie, Madam Jayne Hunter, Madam Carolyne Wolokolie, Mr. Archie Smith, Mrs. Sallyann Smith, Mr. Sam Smith, Mrs. Alberta Smith, Mr. Samuel Mahoi, Mrs. Isha Mahoi, Mrs. Roselyn Momoh, Mr. Idris Amara, Mrs. Martha Amara, Mr. Mendekia Morsay, Mrs. Kenie Morsay, Mrs. Admire Sillah, Mr. Vamba Freeman, Mrs. Melisa Freeman, Mr. Sahr Fania, Mrs. Neneh Fania, Mr. Amadu Barrie, Mrs. Fanta Barrie, Mr. Michaele Cole, Mrs. Nassah Cole, Mr. Tamba Mbawa, Mr. Harold Fofanah, Mr. Alan Papa Kamara, Mr. Abdul Hassan Barrie, Mr. David Kamara, Mr. Usuf Kabbia, Mrs. Aminata Kabbia, Mr. M. S. Kabba, Mrs. Ramatu Kabba, Mr. Amara Kamara, Mrs. Ramatu Kamara, Mr. Junior Kabba, Madam Khady Blaq, Mr. Foday Kamara, Mr. Ibrahim Koroma, Mrs. Mytee Koroma, Dr. Don Taylor, Mrs. Esther Taylor, Mr. Bismarck Maddy, Mrs. Marrie Maddy, Mr. Raymond Strasser-King, Mrs. Mabel Strasser-King, Mr. Raymond Koker, Mrs. Nepoh Koker, Mr. Abu-Barkarr Barrie, Mr. Momoh Mallah, Mrs. Martha Mallah, Mr. Abdulai Jalloh, Mr. John Mustapha, Mrs. Fati Mustapha, Hon. Dr. Lansana Nyalay, Hon. Dr. Matthew Timbo, Hon. Erick Jumu, Dr. Abu-Barkarr Karim, and many others. Any unintentional omission, however, is regretted. Thank you all, and may almighty God bless you abundantly.

I am also thankful to my spiritual advisers, prayer partners, gurus, masters, organizations, business partners, and support services partners. To mention a few: Mualaymu Vandi Konneh, Hajah Fanta Sesay, Rev. Kevin Ross, Rev. Jim Lee, Rev. Mary, Rev. Fr. Alfredo Tamayo, Rev. Fr. Leon Juchniewicz, Rev. Fr. Francis Stevenson, Pastor Moses Kainwo, Pastor Peter Kainwo, Pastors Ansu and Stella Turay, Pastor Daniel Gbudema, Pastor Jehu Gyimah, Pastor Moses Dumbuya, Pastor Sam Babatuunde, Pastors Gbenga and Lola Talabi, Pastor Sulay, and the many others.

In addition, I am thankful to the following: Tegloma; COBBA; The Global Information Network, including Mark Hamilton and Kevin Trudeau; World Ventures, including Helen, Dwight, David, Tom, Dale, and Byron; 5linx, including Doris Campbell and Raymond Komba; Amway Global, including David Stone and Tim Grady; Mr. Mohamed Ali-George, CPA; Dr. Yanzhi Zhu; Dr. Ruben Shahbazian; Dr. Fu; Mr.

Kester Oudney; Mr. Ravi Kumar; Mr. Larry Tompkins; Madam Magdalina Blanco; Madam Nahren Shahbazian; and the many others who gave me their blessings, support services, expertise, and wisdom. Thank you all for your motivational and inspirational partnership. Almighty God will bless you all.

My sincere thanks go to our family friend, Mr. Javier Gonzalez and his family. Thank you so much for your benevolence and your support. May God continue to bless you and your family, and may you have good health, peace of mind, and long life.

Furthermore, I am thankful to my friend, a professional barber, Mr. Christopher Harris for driving all the way from his barber shop biweekly to give my family haircuts in the comfort of our home. Thank you so much, Chris, for saving me more time to work on this life-changing book.

Finally, I am very thankful to iUniverse and their diligent staff members, including Mr. George Nedeff, who made my vision available to all humanity. Thank you all for a job well done.

Once again and above all, I thank the almighty God for giving me the courage to take part in the movement of courageous and authentic writers who are diligently writing to extricate all humanity . . .

Thank you all and may God bless you all, everyone!

Your Peace Is Your Command!

THE AUTHOR

Tony Charles is a psychologist specializing in counseling psychology.

The distinguished counseling psychologist, has also earned diplomas in behavioral psychology, clinical psychology, and family psychology from the American Psychological Association. He is a renowned motivational and inspirational speaker. Furthermore, Tony Charles is a former ranking member of very powerful members-only organizations around the world, including but not limited to the Society of Human Resource Management (SHRM),The Global Information Network (GIN),and The NeoThink Society (NT).

He has served extensively for decades as a professional in the areas of health and human services, social services, and managing human resources in the United States of America. Tony Charles also served in the airline industry for Sierra Leone Airlines (SLA), British Caledonian Airways (BCal), and the Royal Jordanian Airlines (Alia) in Africa, Europe, and Asia. His responsibilities also included but were not limited to representing West African airlines to the International Air Transport Association (IATA).

Tony Charles is the Distinguished Founding Fellow of the Community Information Services; cofounder/executive director of Community Development Initiatives; former chairman of the Board of Directors of UJIMA for Africa; former chairman of the Board of Directors for the Tegloma Organization of Northern California; former CEO of Sierra Financial Services; former managing director of Sierra Enterprises; former manger of Sierra Leone Stars; ex-president of Sierra Leone Social Organizations; and former financial secretary/vice president of Sierra Leone Students Association in the United States of America. Mr. Charles has also served as a reputable leader in an array of other leadership positions worldwide, including his services in the Bo United Nations Students Association (BUNSA).

Thus, in appreciation of his competent leadership and dedication to community development, Tony Charles has been a recipient of prestigious development and leadership awards including but not limited to community leadership awards, outstanding community performance awards, noteworthy contributions to community services awards, remarkable volunteer services awards, devoted leadership awards, and valuable organizational leadership awards.

Tony Charles lives in Elk Grove, California, with his family.